ENCOUNTERING JESUS

a debate on Christology

STEPHEN T. DAVIS, editor

JOHN B. COBB, JR.

JOHN HICK

REBECCA D. PENTZ

JAMES M. ROBINSON

JOHN K. ROTH

MICHAEL WYSCHOGROD

John Knox Press
ATLANTA

Library of Congress Cataloging-in-Publication Data

Encountering Jesus : a debate on Christology / Stephen T. Davis, editor . . . [et al.].
         p.   cm.
    Bibliography: p.
    Includes index.
    ISBN 0-8042-0537-X
    1. Jesus Christ—Person and offices. I. Davis, Stephen T., 1940-

BT202.E48 1988   87-18950
232—dc19   CIP

© copyright John Knox Press 1988
10 9 8 7 6 5 4 3 2 1
Printed in the United States of America
John Knox Press
Atlanta, Georgia 30365

Contents

Introduction

This is a book about Christology. Christology is a branch of Christian theology, perhaps its chief branch. As the word suggests, it concerns Christ. Christology deals with Jesus Christ, the founder and central figure of the Christian religion. Christology can be defined simply as systematic theological thinking about Christ. It asks questions about the life and teachings of Jesus (what he said and did), about the person of Jesus Christ (who he was), about the work of Jesus Christ (what he accomplished), and about his significance (what he means to us).

Christianity has always centered on and indeed been obsessed with Jesus. The Christian faith depends on Jesus—without him there would be no Christian church or Christian faith. Naturally, therefore, Christians have always wondered about Jesus: who is he? what did he say? what did he do? how is he related to God? how is he related to us? The mere fact that such a thing as Christology exists is itself significant—in many other religions there is no comparable discipline centering on the founder.

Even in the New Testament, Jesus was a puzzling enigma who was understood in a variety of ways. The earliest of the Gospels, that of Mark, is shot through with christological questions:

Who is this who teaches with authority? (1:27)
Who is this who forgives sins? (2:7)
Who then is this, that even wind and sea obey him? (4:41)
Who do men say that I am? (8:27)
But who do you say that I am? (8:29)
Are you the Christ, the Son of the Blessed? (14:61)

Christology has always been the focus of Christian theological thinking, but the great age of Christology was the fourth and fifth centuries. At the Councils of Nicea (A.D. 325) and Chalcedon (A.D. 451) a christological consensus emerged that, with a few exceptions, dominated Christian thinking about Christ till the nineteenth century. Interestingly, that basic Christology was not in dispute and survived throughout the two great schisms of the Christian church—that between the East and the West in the eleventh century and that between Catholics and

Protestants in the sixteenth.

But perhaps our era, the second half of the twentieth century, will someday be seen as another great age of christological ferment. The old orthodox formulations seem to have lost their hold on theologians, and many competing interpretations of Jesus are available today. A number of the most able Christian theologians and biblical scholars have in recent years devoted themselves to Christology—people such as Raymond Brown, Martin Hengel, Hans Küng, Jurgen Moltmann, C. F. D. Moule, Wolfhart Pannenberg, Karl Rahner, Rosemary Reuther, J. A. T. Robinson, Edward Schillebeeckx, Piet Schoonenberg, as well as the contributors to *The Myth of God Incarnate* and the books that appeared in response to it. Almost everyone seems to hold that new answers must be given to christological questions, but what those answers are to be is very much in dispute.

A distinction—in part terminological and in part theological—is often made in Christology between "the Jesus of history" and "the Christ of faith." Not everyone observes the distinction; some claim to see unacceptable implications in it. Nevertheless, nearly everyone who writes about this topic wants to be clear that at times in Christology we speak merely of the man Jesus who lived in first-century Palestine. At other times, theologians also want to speak of this Jesus as Christ (or Messiah) and as the incarnation of the Logos (or Second Person of the Trinity). The name "Jesus" is usually reserved by theologians for talk of "the Jesus of history" and the titles "Christ" or "Jesus Christ" for talk of "the Christ of faith" that the church has traditionally believed him to be.

Recently another illuminating distinction has been made and widely accepted—this one between two types of Christology or ways of doing it. Theologians who practice *Christology from above* begin with doctrinal affirmations about Christ's person and ontological status and later move to consideration of the life and teachings of Jesus of Nazareth. That is, they start with the doctrines of the incarnation and the Trinity and then ask exactly how the Logos, or Second Person of the Trinity, took on human form. More popular today is *Christology from below*, an approach that begins with the Jesus who actually lived and taught in first-century Palestine and moves later to ontic christological affirmations.

This book about Christology was written by a group of biblical scholars, theologians, and philosophers of religion who teach, or have taught, at the Claremont Colleges in Claremont, California. It follows the format of a 1981 book by the same editor and publisher entitled *Encountering Evil: Live Options in Theodicy*. Each of the five main chapters in the book revolves around the Christology of one of the book's contributors. Each chapter consists of three sections. The first and longest section, the contributor's Christology, represents his or her latest thinking about Jesus Christ. The second section consists of the other four contributors' critical responses to that Christology. The third section consists of the contributor's attempt to defend her or his Christology against the criticisms of the others.

Our method in writing the book was as follows: the Christologies were written first and during the same period. They were then collected and distributed to the five contributors, at which point the critiques were written. These too were then collected and distributed, and the final responses were written. In general, and with the exception of the editor, no one saw anyone else's work till everyone did.

Let me introduce the five main contributors. John B. Cobb, Jr. is Ingraham Memorial Professor of Theology at the School of Theology at Claremont and Avery Professor of Religion at Claremont Graduate School. Cobb is well known as one of the world's foremost process theologians. Stephen T. Davis, the editor of the book, is a professor of philosophy and religion at Claremont McKenna College. He is an analytic philosopher of religion with fairly conservative and Reformed theological leanings. John Hick is Danforth Professor of the Philosophy of Religion at Claremont Graduate School. One of the most eminent philosophical theologians in the world today, Hick is a Christian who is also involved in interfaith dialogue. Rebecca Pentz, a young Ph.D. in philosophy of religion who is also interested in theology, was till recently a lecturer in philosophy at Scripps College. The rest of us were saddened when a move to another state interrupted a promising Claremont career. James M. Robinson is Arthur Letts Jr. Professor of Religion at Claremont Graduate School and director of the Institute for Antiquity and Christianity. A world-renowned biblical scholar, Robinson is a former president of the Society of Biblical Literature.

For two reasons, I believe readers will find this book fascinating and helpful. First, a great variety of approaches is represented here—those of biblical scholars, theologians, and philosophers, whose viewpoints are as diverse as process thought, conservative evangelicalism, global theology, feminist theology, and theology with an existential slant. The contributors differ markedly in thinking about the life of Jesus, about the authority and reliability of the Christian Scriptures, about the continuing relevance of Chalcedonic orthodoxy, about what is believable by and helpful to modern people, and above all, about who Christ is and what he means to us today. There are even striking below-the-surface differences about what Christian theology is and how to go about doing it.

Second, the give-and-take format of *Encountering Evil*, which was widely commented on, is repeated here. This book is not, then, an ordinary anthology containing a series of collected articles on some subject. All the essays were written especially for this volume, and each contributor has subjected the other Christologies to searching criticism and has been forced to defend his or her own. Readers will find this a lively and argumentative book in the best senses of those words. The various viewpoints represented here and the energetic debate should be taken as revealing how important Christology is to the Christian faith and how seriously the contributors to this book take it. Furthermore, the differences among the contributors are not artificial or contrived; for better or worse, they reflect some of the real differences on Christology in the Christian community. Our hope is that the book will greatly enhance the reader's understanding of the problems of Christology and of the christological options available today. Perhaps the book will even help some readers decide for themselves who Jesus is and what he means or ought to mean to us today.

Christology is a theological discipline that has typically been internal to Christianity. (This is perhaps not true of all topics dealt with by Christian theologians—e.g., theological anthropology, theological ethics, theodicy.) That is, Christology is a discipline that has been carried on by Christians and has mainly been of interest only to Christians. But perhaps this is no longer true. Perhaps the christological stakes are now so high and the relations among the religions so intricately woven that non-Christians too want to listen in and even comment on christological discussions.

As a symbol of our recognition of this reality, we have invited Michael Wyschogrod, professor of philosophy at Baruch College of The City University of New York, to contribute a Jewish postscript to our volume. Though recognized throughout the world as an expert in Jewish-Christian dialogue, most of the other contributors to this book first met Wyschogrod through his participation in a recent theological conference in Claremont on "The Jewishness of Jesus." Wyschogrod is Director of the Institute for Jewish-Christian Relations of the American Jewish Congress. He is also the author of four books and some sixty articles, many of which are relevant to the concerns of this book.

A Christian postscript, written from the point of view of a Presbyterian layperson, is provided by John K. Roth. Roth is a Russell K. Pitzer professor of philosophy at Claremont McKenna College. An expert on American philosophy and the philosophy of religion, Roth has in recent years become interested in the philosophical and theological issues raised by the Holocaust of World War II.

As readers will discover, the focus in the main part of the book is not an attempt to reach consensus on Christology. What we have instead tried to do is explore various christological options, exposing both their strengths and vulnerabilities. Nevertheless, in his concluding essay, Roth notes certain impressive points of agreement among the main contributors to the book.

Let me pose these questions for the authors and the readers of this book: who is Jesus? what was his significance? what ought he mean to us today? Or as a man named Saul (later the Apostle Paul) plaintively asked on the road to Damascus: "Who are you, Lord?" (Acts 9:5).

1 An Inspiration Christology for a Religiously Plural World
JOHN HICK

Where should we begin? With the man Jesus of Nazareth, who lived in Palestine nineteen centuries ago and who became the founder of the Christian religion—though, paradoxically, without intending to do so since he apparently expected the end of the age within a few years? Or with the Christ figure of developed Christian theology and faith, the eternal Second Person of a divine Trinity, who once lived a human life and now reigns as Lord of all?

There is a dilemma here. On the one hand it would seem that an incarnational faith, rooted in history, must go back to the historical Jesus; yet the modern study of the New Testament documents has shown how relatively little certain knowledge we have of him. The idealized Christ, on the other hand, is unaffected by the defects of historical evidence, so that we can glorify him without limit. The result is an absolute figure who is the one and only way, truth, and life for the whole human race and whose totalitarian claim thus clashes with our contemporary awareness of God's saving grace within other streams of religious life.

I shall return later to the relation between Jesus and the non-Christian majority of human beings. In the meantime I propose to resolve the methodological dilemma by beginning with the historical Jesus. Although our assured information about him is very limited, the New Testament obviously reflects the existence of a real person, who was critically important to many who encountered him and whose existence has been of ultimate significance for hundreds of millions since. On the basis of this we can at least try to imagine ourselves as first-century persons encountering Jesus of Nazareth. *Imagine* is the right word, even though it must be imagination under the broad control of historical evidence. This evidence is drawn from the New Testament, from other documents of the same period, and from wider information concerning the ancient world. Because we are trying to imagine a distinctively religious personality we shall, in interpreting the evidence, also use our knowledge of other religiously impressive people of whom we have read or whom we have encountered.

For those of us who are Christians, the figure of Jesus has profoundly affected us by meeting our own spiritual needs, so that the pattern of those needs has inevitably influenced our perception of him. Accordingly, imaginative reconstructions of the historical Jesus are bound to differ because we use partially different ranges and selections of historical information and also because we bring to that information different experiences of religiously impressive humanity and our own varying spiritual needs. Indeed because of this last element our respective pictures of Jesus will say something about us as well as something, hopefully something that is historically well-founded, about the Jesus who was a part of public human history.

Before exposing my own imaginative reconstruction, let me note a possible objection. It might be said that for Christian faith, Jesus was not a "religiously impressive man" but was God incarnate and as such absolutely unique, not comparable—even remotely—with great religious figures such as the founders of other religious traditions or with such religiously impressive persons as we ourselves may have had the good fortune to encounter.

From a Christian point of view this would, I think, be a mistaken objection. The traditional doctrine of the incarnation affirms that Jesus was true man as well as true God. As man he belonged to our earthly history and is to be accepted as an authentic human being. And if he was a man, who preached a religious message, influencing his hearers so powerfully that many became his disciples and that through them a new world religion came into being, it seems safe to say that he must have been a religiously very impressive person. If so, we can, in forming our imaginative pictures of him, appropriately draw not only upon our all too scanty historical information but also upon our knowledge of other religiously impressive persons.

I see Jesus as dominated, at least in the most important moments of his life, by his awareness of the overwhelmingly evident reality and presence of God—the God of whom he had learned from his Jewish tradition. He was aware of God as both limitlessly gracious and limitlessly demanding—both as the loving Heavenly *Abba* who welcomes home the prodigal son (Luke 15:11–24) and also as the holy and righteous one who makes a total and absolute claim upon human beings. So powerful was Jesus' awareness of the Heavenly Father in comparison with the awareness of those around him, including the official religious leaders of his time, that he must have been aware of an unique calling and responsibility to communicate the reality of God by proclaiming the imminent coming of the divine kingdom and the insistent divine claim upon each man, woman, and child. He must thus have been conscious of a special role in God's dealings with the people of Israel in those last days before the kingdom came in power and glory. Inevitably he would, as God's voice to his contemporaries, have had a central position, in his own mind and in the minds of those who responded to him, within the crisis of the end time in which he and they believed themselves to be living.

When we seek to imagine ourselves as Jesus' contemporaries, we must of course remember that we would not be the same persons that we now are: we would be first-century Palestinian Jews. As far as our individual relationship to God is concerned we can perhaps assume that we might nevertheless be at heart essentially the same persons. Although in that society we could never have doubted, intellectually, the existence of God, we would not necessarily on that account be living consciously in God's presence either more or less than we are today. There would therefore be an immense contrast between Jesus' powerful and pervasive sense of the divine Thou, with his consequent absolute certainty of God's reality, and our own feeble and intermittent God-consciousness. We may know from our own experience something of what it is to encounter a person who is much more powerfully aware of the divine presence than we are ourselves and the shape of whose life embodies a response to the claims of the divine reality.To encounter such a person is to be profoundly challenged. For the very existence and presence of an authentic saint focuses the liberating divine claim in turn upon others. And if that claim should be specifically articulated and directed to oneself, the impact must be all the greater. I envisage a first-century encounter with Jesus as having this deeply challenging and disturbing quality, demanding a radical reordering of one's existence: "The time is fulfilled, and the kingdom of God is at hand; repent, and believe in the gospel" (Mark 1:14); "Unless you turn and become like children, you will never enter the kingdom of heaven" (Matt. 18:3); "Another of the disciples said to him, 'Lord, let me first go and bury my father.' But Jesus said to him, 'Follow me, and leave the dead to bury their own dead' " (Matt. 8:21–22); "He who finds his life will lose it, and he who loses his life for my sake will find it" (Matt. 10:39); "If any man would come after me, let him deny himself and take up his cross and follow me. For whoever would save his life will lose it, and whoever loses his life for my sake will find it" (Matt. 16:24–25); "One thing you still lack. Sell all that you have and distribute to the poor, and you will have treasure in heaven; and come, follow me" (Luke 18:22); "You have heard that it was said, 'You shall love your neighbor and hate your enemy.' But I say to you, Love your enemies and pray for those who persecute you, so that you may be sons of your Father who is in heaven" (Matt. 5:43–45); "You cannot serve God and mammon. Therefore I tell you, do not be anxious about your life, what you shall eat or what you shall drink, nor about your body, what you shall put on" (Matt. 6:24–25). All these may well not be Jesus' *ipsissima verba*, but nevertheless they clearly reflect something of the impact of his challenging demands upon his hearers.

Such challenges are also moments of judgment in which we turn toward or away from God. If we turned to God, as God's claim was mediated to us through Jesus' words, our lives would begin to be reordered around a new center; and the divine love would shine in our hearts, creating a joyful trust and releasing a new love of our neighbors.

But the historical Jesus whom we are imagining ourselves as encountering was not only a preacher of God's love and claim but also a healer, expressing the divine love in action. It seems that when a human being is sufficiently attuned to the life of God, divinely established psychic laws can come into operation to produce "miraculous" healings and providential coincidences. This was strikingly evident in the life of Jesus. Because he was so open and responsive to God's presence, the divine creativity flowed through his hands in bodily healing and was present in his personal impact upon people, with challenging and re-creating power.

I conceive, then, that a close encounter with Jesus in first-century Palestine would be a conversion experience. It would perhaps begin by our witnessing or hearing of one of his healing "miracles." It would continue as a deeply challenging call, a claim threatening to revolutionize our life, shattering our self-centered world of meaning, and plunging us into the vast unknown universe of God's meaning. And it would grow into a profound sense of the sovereign goodness and love of God, relieving us of anxiety for ourselves and empowering us to love and serve others, gladly bearing witness to the divine power that had thus changed us.

This or something like this would, as I see it, be Jesus' "existential" impact upon us. And this impact would be bound up with a body of ideas that we would accept on Jesus' authority and assimilate with a greater or lesser degree of comprehension.

Perhaps the most important such idea would be the one already mentioned—the apocalyptic conviction of living in the last days of the age. The end was about to come in catastrophic judgment, to be followed by a new age, the kingdom of God on earth, in which all things would be made new. This seems to have been a powerful theme in the teaching of Jesus (Mark 9:1; 13:30; Matt. 10:23; 16:28, 23:36; Luke 9:27) and consequently in the outlook of the early Christian community (1 Peter 4:7; 2 Peter 3:3–10; James 5:8–9; Heb. 10:25; John 21:22; 1 John 2:28; 1 Thess. 2:19; 3:13; 4:15; 5:23; 1 Cor. 4:5; 7:29; 11:26; 15:51; Rom.13:11–12).[1] But looking back across nineteen centuries and knowing that the Christian expectation gradually faded as the end failed to arrive, we may suppose that Jesus was so intensely conscious of God's surrounding presence and power that he expected this to become publicly manifest in the immediate future. His sense of the kingdom knocking on the door of the present moment reflected, I am suggesting, his own vivid sense of God's immanent presence.

Immanence, we could say, was expressed as imminence.

Jewish tradition in Jesus' time offered at least two images of the one who was to fulfill the role of the last prophet, the herald of the end that also was to be God's great beginning. One was that of the Messiah, who was to be of the royal line of David and to reign as king in the new age in which Jerusalem would be the center of the world and in which God's will would be done on earth. The other was that of the Son of man in the Danielic prophecy:

> "and behold, with the clouds of heaven
>   there came one like a son of man,
> and he came to the Ancient of Days
>   and was presented before him.
> And to him was given dominion
>   and glory and kingdom,
> that all peoples, nations, and languages
>   should serve him;
> his kingdom is an everlasting dominion,
>   which shall not pass away,
> and his kingdom one
>   that shall not be destroyed." (Dan. 7:13–14)

Both these images were used by the early church, though they were probably adopted initially in different places, perhaps the Messiah image in Jerusalem and the Son of man image elsewhere in Palestine or Syria.[2] It is clear that Jesus used the term *Son of man*, though possibly not as a title but simply as an accepted way in which a man could refer to himself. It also seems that others sought to thrust the title Messiah upon him, though it does not seem that he himself accepted it. We know that his powerful sense of the divine presence and his experience of the divine power working in his own healings signified to Jesus the presence of God's transforming rule: "if it is by the finger of God that I cast out demons, then the kingdom of God has come upon you" (Luke 11:20). In the understanding of the early church it was a natural development to identify him either as God's Messiah or as the Son of man, who was to come again with the clouds of heaven. Note, however, with a view to the later Christian doctrine of the incarnation, that neither the Messiah nor the Son of man was, in Jewish thinking, divine. Each was a human, or perhaps even superhuman, figure who was to be God's servant and instrument in ushering in the kingdom. This role was clearly very special, indeed unique, but it was emphatically not equivalent to being God incarnate.

It seems to have been Jesus' proclamation of the imminent inbreaking of God's rule, a message that the Roman occupying power feared might spark a revolt (such as occurred in A.D. 66 and 132), which led to Jesus' death at the instigation of the religious authorities and at the hands of the Roman occupying power.[3] The words of the disciples in the postresurrection Emmaus story indicate what kind of hopes had centered upon Jesus in the minds of many of his followers. Their thoughts had been "Concerning Jesus of Nazareth, who was a prophet mighty in deed and word before God and all the people, and how our chief priests and rulers delivered him up to be condemned to death, and crucified him. But we had hoped that he was the one to redeem Israel" (Luke 24:19–21). But such hopes of redeeming Israel from Roman captivity were politically dangerous, and it is not surprising that anyone who evoked them was marked in the eyes of the establishment. The ecclesiastical authorities were no more desirous of revolution and disorder than were their Roman overlords.

It seems that Jesus foresaw his own coming martyrdom and also foresaw that it would take place in the Holy City: "for it cannot be that a prophet should perish away from Jerusalem" (Luke 13:33). It also seems that he understood his death as a sacrifice for the good of the people (Mark 10:45; Matt. 20:28). This was in line with the current Jewish belief that the sufferings of the righteous—particularly, in the immediately preceding period, the sufferings of the Maccabean martyrs—worked for the good of Israel. As John Downing concluded, in his study of this aspect of first-century Judaism, "people thought in terms of human beings making atonement for others by means of their sufferings and death."[4] The idea is also illustrated by the following quotation from a second-century rabbi named Shim'on:

> When the righteous are seized by disease or affliction, it is in order to atone for the world. Thus all the sins of the generation are atoned for. When the Blessed Holy One wants to bring healing to the world, He strikes one righteous human among them with disease and affliction; through him He brings healing to all.[5]

But the later Christian notion that Jesus, in his death, was our substitute in bearing God's just punishment or otherwise appeasing the divine wrath or satisfying the divine justice and so enabling a righteous Creator to forgive his sinful creatures is—it seems to me—far removed from the spirit and teaching of Jesus himself. His own understanding of the divine forgiveness is expressed in, for example, the parable of the Prodigal Son. The earthly father clearly represents the Heavenly Father. When his erring son repents and returns home, the father does not say, "Because I am a just father I cannot forgive you until I have first killed my other son to atone to me for your sins." He calls for the best robe and has a great feast prepared, "for this my son was dead, and is alive again; he was lost, and is found" (Luke 15:24). Again, in the Lord's Prayer, Jesus taught his disciples to speak to God directly, as their Heavenly Father, and to ask for forgiveness. There is no mediator, no atoning sacrifice; only the profound and far-reaching requirement that we forgive one another.

After Jesus' death came his resurrection. It is impossible for us today to know the precise nature of the resurrection event. The New Testament evidences are too fragmentary and conflicting to permit more than speculative reconstructions. The only first-person account that we have of an encounter with the risen Jesus, that of Paul on the Damascus road (Acts 26:12–18; cf. 9:1–7), described a bright light and a voice but no physical body. The earliest surviving reference to the resurrection appearances (1 Cor. 15:3–8) includes this Damascus road encounter, and the list is entirely compatible with a series of photisms, luminous phenomena that might take a variety of forms, including that of visions of the glorified Jesus.[6] Later strata of the tradition speak of the empty tomb (Mark 16:6; Matt. 28:6; Luke 24:2–3; John 20:2–9), and of the physical presence of Jesus (Matt. 28:9–10; 16–20; Luke 24:13–49; John 20:14–29; 21:1–22), though aspects of some of these manifestations—sudden appearances and disappearances (Luke 24:31, 36; John 20:19, 26) and difficulties in recognizing Jesus (Matt. 28:17; Luke 24:16)—consist better with visions than with the presence of his raised physical body. In the lengthening tradition the resurrection faith of the church seems to have developed from a certainty of the living presence of Jesus, perhaps mediated by lights or visions or voices, to the story of the return of his physical body to life, his physical presence on earth for forty days (Acts 1:3), and his final bodily ascension into the sky (Luke 24:51; Acts 1:9–11).

However, visions on the one hand and a resuscitated physical body on the other are not the only possibilities. Another is exemplified in at least two recorded resurrection encounters with religiously significant individuals within the past hundred years. These have been recounted by Paramahansa Yogananda (the founder of the still active Hindu movement in the West known as the Self-Realization Fellowship) in his *Autobiography of a Yogi*, first published in 1946.[7] Yogananda wrote in the florid Victorian English that was the literary style of many Indians of his own and earlier generations, but clearly this does not in any way entail that what he said is false. Yogananda's guru, Sri Yukteswar, died on March 9, 1936. Yogananda said that on June 19 of the same year Sri Yukteswar appeared to him in a hotel bedroom in Bombay. He was roused from his meditation by a bright light. "Before my open and astonished eyes, the whole room was transformed into a strange world, the sunlight transmuted into supernal splendor. Waves of rapture engulfed me as I beheld the flesh and blood form of Sri Yukteswar! 'My son!' Master spoke tenderly, on his face an angel-bewitching smile. For the first time in my life I did not kneel at his feet in greeting, but instantly advanced to gather him hungrily in my arms. Moment of moments! The anguish of past months was toll I counted weightless against the torrential bliss now descending . . . " (pp. 414–15). According to Paramahansa Yogananda, Sri Yukteswar spoke with him for two hours before vanishing from his sight, and he has relayed much of what his guru told him during that time (ch. 43). His sudden appearing and bodily presence would seem to have been very like the one recorded of Jesus in the upper room in Jerusalem (John 20:19, 26).

The other resurrection recorded by Paramahansa Yogananda, that of Sri Yukteswar's guru, is said to have occurred in 1895.

> Lahiri Mahasaya's beautiful body, so dear to the devotees, was cremated with solemn householder rites at Manikarnika Ghat by the holy Ganges. The following day, at ten o'clock in the morning, while I was still in Banaras, my room was suffused with a great light. Lo! before me stood the flesh and blood form of Lahiri Mahasaya. It looked exactly like his old body, except that it appeared younger and more radiant . . . (p. 349).

Again, the resurrected guru spoke and eventually disappeared.

Whatever the nature of Jesus' resurrection, inaccessible to us as it is, it launched the Christian church as we know it. Whether without this event Jesus' disciples would have begun again to preach his message and whether that message would have been recorded in Gospels and would have spread far and wide, we cannot know. For it was in fact the conviction of Jesus' continued life as their glorified Lord that inspired his disciples to form a faith-community that was able to capture the Roman Empire and has come to constitute one of the great religious traditions of the world.

In a very early phase of the apostolic preaching, Saint Peter is reported to have proclaimed, "Men of Israel, hear these words: Jesus of Nazareth, a man attested to you by God with mighty works and wonders and signs which God did through him in your midst, as you yourselves know—this Jesus, delivered up according to the definite plan and foreknowledge of God, you crucified and killed by the hands of lawless men. But God raised him up, having loosed the pangs of death, because it was not possible for him to be held by it" (Acts 2:22–24). But later apologists have come to see Jesus' resurrection as a proof of his deity. So self-evident is this connection in popular Christian thought that it must seem paradoxical to question it. Yet the connection is far from self-evident. If we argue that anyone who, being dead, returns to life, is divine; Jesus returned to life; therefore, Jesus is divine, the difficulty will be that according to the Christian Scriptures many other people have also returned to life (e.g., John 11:1–44; Luke 7:11–17; 8:49–56; Mark 5:35–43; Matt. 11:5; 27:52–53; Heb. 11:35). If we then argue that among those who have returned to life Jesus was unique in that he was raised directly by God, we shall be faced with the fact that the early church, who believed that Jesus was indeed raised directly by God, did not infer that he was divine ("a *man* [italics mine] attested to you by God with mighty works and wonders and signs," Acts 2:22). If we now move to what happened to Jesus after his resurrection and argue that he was unique in that, whereas others who had risen from the dead had resumed an ordinary life and eventually died, Jesus did not die but was raised bodily into heaven, we must consider Elijah, who was not divine but who was also taken up bodily into heaven (2 Kings 2:11–12), and the postbiblical story of the bodily assumption of Moses into heaven.[8] Can we then argue that although neither having been raised by God from the dead nor being taken up bodily into heaven indicates divinity, the combination of the two does? Perhaps, but perhaps not. The connection is by no means beyond question.

How then did the historical Jesus develop, in the mind of the church, into the exalted Christ of what was to become traditional Christian faith? The subject is large and complex. The orthodoxy of a century ago and earlier held that no development was necessary: the historical Jesus, as depicted in the fourth Gospel, was already consciously divine, and his message was a summons to be saved by believing in him: "You are from below, I am from above; you are of this world, I am not of this world. I told you that you would die in your sins, for you will die in your sins unless you believe that I am he" (John 8:23–24). This Christ-centered message was for many centuries the foundation of Christian orthodoxy. Since I shall be diverging from that older tradition, on the basis of modern biblical scholarship, I shall cite acknowledged experts in this field.

First, the problem. Students of the New Testament agree that it is extremely unlikely that Jesus made for himself the claims that later Christian thought made for him. To quote Wolfhart Pannenberg:

> In the quest for the historical Jesus, Jesus' self-consciousness was long regarded as the root of his claim to authority; at the same time the self-consciousness of Jesus was understood in a very special sense as the objective knowledge of his own place of honor and community with God. In the Gospels such a self-consciousness is attributed to Jesus. This is done the most clearly in the "I" sayings of John's Gospel. The most important of this group of sayings with respect to content and the clearest in its absence of the usual figurative language is John 10:30: "I and the Father are one." . . . After D. F. Strauss and F. C. Bauer, John's Gospel could no longer be claimed uncritically as a historical source of authentic words of Jesus. Consequently, other concepts and titles that were more intimately connected with Jesus' relation to God came into the foreground of the question of Jesus' "Messianic self-consciousness." However, the transfer of these titles to Jesus . . . has been demonstrated with growing certainty by critical study of the Gospels to be the work of the post-Easter community. Today it must be taken as all but certain that the pre-Easter Jesus neither designated himself as Messiah (or Son of God) nor accepted such a confession to him from others.[9]

Again, Hans Küng accurately summarized contemporary research when he said that "even more conservative exegetes conclude that Jesus himself did not assume any title implying messianic dignity: not 'Messiah,' nor 'Son of David,' nor 'Son,' nor 'Son of God'."[10] Yet the Christian tradition came, in a process that was finally completed in the fifth century, to see Jesus as the eternal preexistent Son of God, Second Person of a divine Trinity, living a human life. How did this happen? There is no single comprehensive answer. In general it seems that the early Christians, seeking to understand and communicate the significance of their Lord, grasped at concepts and titles within their culture and that the usage of these developed under the pressures of preaching and controversy. Consider, for example, the "Son of God" language. The title "Son of God" was common in the ancient world. Oscar Cullmann wrote:

> The origin of the 'son of God' concept lies in ancient oriental religions, in which above all kings were thought to be begotten of gods. . . . In the New Testament period also the Roman emperors were entitled *divi filius*.
> But in Hellenism the expression is by no means limited to rulers. Anyone believed to possess some kind of divine power was called 'son of God' by others, or gave himself the title. All miracle workers were 'sons of God,' or, as one also said, θεῖοι ἄνδρες: Apollonius of Tyana, for instance, whose life is described by Philostratus in a form which is often reminiscent of our Gospels; or Alexander of Abonoteichus, whom we know through Lucian. Used in this sense, the title was quite common. In the New Testament period one could meet everywhere men who called themselves 'sons of God' because of their peculiar vocation or miraculous powers.[11]

And within Judaism:

> In the Old Testament we find this expression used in three ways: the whole people of Israel is called 'Son of God'; kings bear the title; persons with a special commission from God, such as angels, and perhaps also the Messiah, are so called.[12]

In particular the ancient Hebrew kings became sons of God by divine adoption—"You are my son, today I have begotten you" (Ps. 2:7); "I will be his father, and he shall be my son" (2 Sam. 7:14). Clearly, this was metaphorical (or mythological) language. And it is not in the least surprising that Jesus, as a spirit-filled prophet, a charismatic healer, perhaps as Messiah, believed to be of the royal line of David, should have been thought of and should have thought of himself as, in this familiar metaphorical sense, a son of God. What happened, as the gospel went out beyond the Hebraic milieu into the Greek-dominated intellectual world of the Roman Empire, was that the metaphorical son of God was transformed into the metaphysical God the Son, to support which status Jesus had eventually to be declared to have two complete natures, one human and the other divine. As Pannenberg said, "At first the 'Son of God' concept did not express a participation in the divine essence. . . . Only in Gentile Christianity was the divine Sonship understood physically as participation in the divine essence. In the Jewish, also in the Hellenistic-Jewish, sphere, in contrast, the expression 'Son of God' still retained the old meaning of adoption and of

God's presence through his Spirit which was bestowed upon Jesus for a long time. In Mark's Gospel the basic concept of Jesus as the epiphany of the Son of God begins, but represents a conversion into the Hellenistic way of thinking."[13] Purely Jewish concepts, such as the throne (Merkabah), may have provided stepping-stones toward deification. The basic motivation of the early Christian group was to absolutize the one whose impact had so profoundly changed its members' lives, the one for allegiance to whom they were being persecuted, and later, the one in whose name the church had become co-ruler of the empire. It was indeed in this latter period of Christian political ascendancy that the christological and trinitarian doctrines received their fullest scope and became dogmatically solidified as basic articles of faith: the triumphant Lordship of the church was reflected in and validated by the absolute status and authority of the church's Lord.

Notice the parallel in the absolutization of the founder of the Buddhist tradition. Gautama was a human teacher, though one who had attained perfect enlightenment and who accordingly spoke with the authority of firsthand knowledge. After his death he was spoken about in the developing Buddhist literature in exalted terms, frequently as the Blessed One and the Exalted One. Stories of his many previous lives became popular, and legend attributed to him a supernatural conception, birth, and childhood. In later literature he was called *devatideva* ("God beyond the gods," "God of gods") and *Tathagata*. Of this last title T. R. V. Murti says, "The Tathagata as the Perfect Man . . . is the ultimate essence of the universe. His position is analogous to that of God of Rational Theology *(ens realissimum)*."[14]

The later Mahayana doctrine of the Trikaya is comparable with the Johannine doctrine of the Logos and its development of the incarnation idea. As Jesus was the incarnation of the preexistent Word/Son, who was of one substance with the Father in the eternal Trinity, so Gautama was the earthly manifestation of a heavenly Buddha, and all the Buddhas are one in the ultimate reality of the eternal Dharmakaya. Thus, the developed Buddhology of the Mahayana, some five centuries after the death of Gautama, parallels the developed Christology that reached its completion at the fifth-century Council of Chalcedon.

Although comparisons between past events and alternative possibilities are always fraught with danger—for they profess to know what can never be known—a strong case can be made for the functional value of the Nicene/Chalcedonian Christology to the church at that stage of its history. It could well be that its deification of Jesus helped the early Christian community to survive its period of intermittent persecutions and that subsequently, if the church was to be the spiritual, moral, and cultural director of the Roman Empire, and thus of Western civilization, it needed the prestige of a founder who was none other than God, in the person of the eternal Son, who came down from heaven to institute a new human society and who gave to its officers the fateful "keys of the kingdom." However, we are now living in a very different period of history. Christianity has long since ceased to consist of a small persecuted minority—except in certain marginal situations. It has also, since the Enlightenment of the seventeenth century and the rise of modern science, ceased to be the supreme spiritual and intellectual authority within Western civilization. It is now seen as one religion among others in a manifestly pluralistic world. In this very different era the traditional absolutist Christology has become subject to serious criticism, for it now hinders an unqualified acceptance of what is today, within God's providence, the reality of our human situation. In claiming that the life of Jesus was the one and only point in history at which God has been fully self-revealed, it implicitly sets Christians apart from the rest of humanity. In declaring that God has lived a human life on earth, so that here and here only men and women were able to meet God face to face, to hear God speak, and to respond to God in faith, Christianity declares that these fortunate few and their successors have a highly privileged access to the Creator. In the words of Emil Brunner during the high tide of neoorthodoxy, "Only at one place, only in one event, has God revealed Himself truly and completely—there, namely, where He became man."[15] It follows that the Christian religion and it alone was personally founded by God. Must God not then wish all human beings to become part of the church, the body of the redeemed, the saved community? Is not Christianity thus singled out as the one religion that God has authorized, hence uniquely superior to all others? Christian history is indeed full of this assumption— and of its practical outworkings in colonialism, anti-Semitism, the burning of "heretics," and the Western political and cultural superiority complex.

To a growing number of Christians, this assumption no longer seems self-evidently valid. On the contrary, many now see in it a group of human beings consciously or unconsciously asserting their own in-group superiority over the rest of the human race. Further, such exclusivism is now recognized as religiously regressive, for it turns the Lord of the whole universe into the tribal god of Europe and the United States and their spiritual colonies. There is accordingly a move to go behind the projections of the Christian past and to try to recover a more basic and authentic form of Christian awareness. This move is strongly supported by the results of the historical study of the Scriptures and of Christian origins, which show that the Nicene/Chalcedonian Christology lacks the dominical authority that it had so long been assumed to have and that so long constituted the main reason for accepting it.

And so the first major point being made in the contemporary deconstruction of the traditional Christology is that it was not authorized by

Jesus himself. And the second major point—also historical—is that we can discern, at least in very general terms, when and how the deification of Jesus came about and can appreciate that in that religious-cultural milieu it provided a natural way of expressing the legitimate Lordship of Jesus over against the "many 'gods' and many 'lords' " (1 Cor. 8:5) of the Roman Empire.

The third major point is conceptual rather than historical: the developed dogma—that Jesus of Nazareth was both God and man, that he was the Second Person of a divine Trinity living a human life, and that he had two natures, one human and the other divine—has never been shown to have any precise meaning. Every attempt made in the great period of the christological debates to spell out the meaning of the God-man formula proved unacceptable because of incompatibility either with Jesus' Godhead or with his full humanity. For example, one of the most constructive of the early theologians, Apollonius, at the end of the fourth century, holding with a tradition going back to Plato that a human person consists of spirit (*nous*), soul (*psyche*), and material body (*sarx*), suggested that in Jesus the eternal divine Logos functioned as his spirit, whereas his soul (or mind) and body were human. This theory made intelligible the claim that Jesus was both human and divine. But it had to be declared heretical for the convincing reason that without a human spirit Jesus would not have been genuinely human. All of the many other attempts to give specific meaning to the idea of divine incarnation likewise had to be rejected. No way has in fact been found of understanding the literal God-manhood of Christ. All that is left is a "mystery"—in the sense, in this case, of an impressive form of words without any specifiable meaning. The definitive formulation of the mystery adopted by the Council of Chalcedon affirms of our Lord Jesus Christ that he is "truly God and truly man," "consubstantial with the Father in his divinity, consubstantial with us in his humanity": "We declare that in his divinity he was begotten of the Father before time, and in his humanity he was begotten in this last age of Mary the Virgin. . . . We declare that the one selfsame Christ, only-begotten Son and Lord, must be acknowledged in two natures without any comingling or change or division or separation; that the distinction between the two natures is in no way removed by their union but rather that the specific character of each nature is preserved and they are united in one person and one hypostasis. . . ." But of course this does not explain anything. As has recently been said by a historian of that period, "Chalcedon has proved less a solution than the classic definition of a problem which constantly demands further elucidation."[16]

In recent times some theologians—but a decreasing number of those writing in Christology—have continued to affirm the two-natures Christology of Chalcedon; many others have been acutely conscious of its difficulties and have looked for new approaches. These new approaches move in two different directions. One, seeking to remain faithful to the God-man conception that Chalcedon tried to articulate, speaks of God's *kenosis* or self-emptying in Jesus. In this theory the historical Jesus did not have the divine qualities of omniscience, omnipotence, omnipresence, eternality, self-existence, creatorship, or even—in the latest versions— the consciousness of his own deity. For the eternal Son, or Logos, divested himself of these attributes in becoming human. This concept of *kenosis* has appealed to a number of contemporary theologians. The difficulty, however, parallels the difficulty of the Chalcedonian formula, namely that no one has yet succeeded in spelling it out intelligibly. How can God cease to have God's attributes? What can it mean to say that the eternal, self-existent Creator of everything that exists other than God was for some thirty years not eternal, not self-existent, not the Creator of everything that exists other than God? Does it perhaps help to make a distinction and say that although God the Son laid aside his "metaphysi-cal" attributes in becoming a man, he retained his "moral" attributes: goodness, love, wisdom, justice, mercy? At first this sounds more promising. But again questions arise. What does it mean to say that the human Jesus of Nazareth was infinitely loving, good, wise, just, merciful? Let us simplify matters by assuming that all these qualities are aspects of the one central attribute of love, *agape*. What then does it mean to say that Jesus embodied infinite love? Very great love, yes, but *infinite* love? How can a human being embody, incarnate, exhibit, love, or indeed any other quality, to an infinite degree? Surely we must say rather that the historical Jesus possessed, exhibited, incarnated, as much of the infinite divine love as could be expressed in and through an individual human life.

At this point, however, we have come close to the other possible new direction in Christology. If Jesus' life expressed, incarnated, embodied, very great but not infinite *agape*—and if, as we may surely add, all authentic *agape* is a finite reflection of the infinite divine *agape*—we have reached the position that in the life of Jesus the eternal and infinite *agape* of God was mirrored, expressed, lived out, made flesh, incarnated, within the limitations of a particular human life lived at a particular time and place. It is this approach that a number of recent Christologies have sought to make intelligible. Two representative examples are the paradox-of-grace Christology of Donald Baillie and the inspiration Christology of Geoffrey Lampe.

Baillie's book *God Was in Christ*[17] was described by Rudolf Bultmann as "the most significant book of our time in the field of Christology."[18] In this book Baillie proposed that we should understand incarnation in terms of what he called the paradox of grace. This is the paradoxical fact that when we do God's will it is true both that we are acting freely and responsibly and that God, in his supernatural grace, is acting through us. The paradox is summed up in St. Paul's words: "it was not I, but the grace of God which is with me" (1 Cor. 15:10). As Baillie said, the essence of the paradox

> lies in the conviction which a Christian man possesses, that every good thing in him, every good thing he does, is somehow not wrought by himself but by God. This is a highly paradoxical conviction, for in ascribing all to God it does not abrogate human personality nor disclaim personal responsibility. Never is human action more truly and fully personal, never does the agent feel more perfectly free, than in those moments of which he can say as a Christian that whatever good was in them was not his but God's. (p. 114)

Baillie then used this paradox of grace as the clue to the yet greater paradox of the incarnation: that the life of Jesus was an authentically human life and yet that in and through that life God was at work on earth.

> What I wish to suggest is that this paradox of grace points the way more clearly and makes a better approach than anything else in our experience to the mystery of the Incarnation itself; that this paradox in its fragmentary form in our own Christian lives is a reflection of that perfect union of God and man in the Incarnation on which our whole Christian life depends, and may therefore be our best clue to the understanding of it. In the New Testament we see the man in whom God was incarnate surpassing all other men in refusing to claim anything for Himself independently and ascribing all the goodness to God. We see Him also desiring to take up other men into His own close union with God, that they might be as He was. And if these men, entering in some small measure through Him into that union, experience the paradox of grace for themselves in fragmentary ways, and are constrained to say, "It was not I but God," may not this be a clue to the understanding of that perfect life in which the paradox is complete and absolute, that life of Jesus which, being the perfection of humanity, is also, and even in a deeper and prior sense, the very life of God Himself? If the paradox is a reality in our poor imperfect lives at all, so far as there is any good in them, does not the same or a similar paradox, taken at the perfect and absolute pitch, appear as the mystery of the Incarnation? (pp. 117–18)

In other words the union of divine and human action that occurs whenever God's grace works effectively in a man's or a woman's life was operating to a total extent in the life of Jesus.

Baillie's suggestion offers some degree of understanding of what it means to say that the life of Jesus was a divine as well as a human event. Of course, in making the idea of incarnation intelligible in this way Baillie had to discard the traditional Chalcedonian language of Jesus' having two natures, human and divine, and of his being in his divine nature of one substance with the Father. This language has long since largely lost its meaning for the modern mind, and the kind of reinterpretation that Baillie offered is an attempt to bring the doctrine of the incarnation to life in our time, giving it meaning as a truth that connects with our human experience and that is at least to some extent intelligible in contemporary terms. Although few people today use the ancient Hellenic concept of "substance" or find the idea of a person with two natures other than grotesque, all Christians have some experience and appreciation of the reality of divine grace operating in human life. Further, they can connect this reality with the extraordinary events of the New Testament.

In an essentially similar way Geoffrey Lampe, in his book *God as Spirit*[19], used as his clue or model for the understanding of Christ the activity within human life of the Holy Spirit, the Spirit of God, which is, he said, "to be understood, not as referring to a divine hypostasis distinct from God the Father and God the Son, or Word, but as indicating God himself as active towards and in his human creation" (p. 11). The principal activity of God as Spirit in relation to humanity is inspiration; accordingly, the Christology that Lampe presents is "a Christology of inspiration" (p. 96).

> . . . the concept of the inspiration and indwelling of man by God as Spirit is particularly helpful in enabling us to speak of God's continuing creative relationship towards human persons and of his active presence in Jesus as the central and focal point within this relationship. (p. 34)

Again, "The use of this concept enables us to say that God indwelt and motivated the human spirit of Jesus in such a way that in him, uniquely, the relationship for which man is intended by his Creator was fully realized . . . " (p. 11). In this view the Spirit of God has always been active within the human spirit, inspiring men and women to open themselves freely to the divine presence and to respond in their lives to the divine purpose. Indeed "God has always been incarnate in his human creatures, forming their spirits from within and revealing himself in and through them" (p. 23). We must accordingly "speak of this continuum as a single creative and saving activity of God the Spirit towards, and within, the spirit of man, and of his presence in the person of Jesus as a particular moment within that continuous creativity" (p. 100).

This kind of Christology, centering on the activity of the gracious divine Spirit in and through the human Jesus, is in effect the kind that Pannenberg characterized as "probably the oldest attempt to express God's presence in Jesus," namely "by the concept of the Spirit."[20] Before Jesus became deified in the Christian mind and the trinitarian doctrine developed to locate him within the Godhead, the earthly Lord was thought of as a man filled with the Spirit, beginning the fulfillment of the prophecy that in the last days the Spirit would be poured out again. As Pannenberg said, "Through the Spirit, Jesus is not only connected with particular figures of Jewish expectation, with the prophet of the last times, the Son of Man, the Servant of God, or the Messiah, but directly with God himself."[21] Jesus' life was a direct response of obedience to the divine Spirit. It was a special case of divine immanence.

In this inspiration Christology we have not only a return to the original understanding of Jesus in the very early church but an advance to an understanding of him that makes sense in our consciously religiously plural world as it moves toward the twenty-first century.

Both Baillie and Lampe assumed in traditional Christian fashion the "uniqueness" of Christ; they held that in Jesus the paradox of grace was "complete and absolute" (p. 117) or that the working of the Spirit in Jesus was "a perfected form of inspiration" (p. 12).[22] They accordingly assumed the centrality and superiority of Christianity within God's providence. However, their major new departure (the full extent of which they may not have been conscious of) is that the dogma of the unique superiority of Jesus and of the Christian religion no longer follows from the idea of divine incarnation as such. If, with Baillie and Lampe, we see in the life of Jesus a supreme instance of that fusion of divine grace/inspiration with creaturely freedom that occurs in all authentic human response and obedience to God, then uniqueness, supremacy, finality, can be established only by comparative historical evidence. We are no longer speaking of an intersection of the divine and the human that occurs, by definition, only in this unique case but of one that occurs in different ways and degrees in all human openness and response to the divine initiative. Thus the primacy of the Christian revelation no longer follows as a logical corollary from either Baillie's or Lampe's Christology. To see Jesus as exemplifying in his own special degree the paradox of grace, or the inspiration of God as Spirit, is to leave open the further question as to how this particular exemplification stands in relation to other exemplifications, such as those in some of the other great religious traditions. Baillie and Lampe believed that the grace/inspiration in the life of Jesus was unique because it was total and absolute. But the point to be stressed is that such a belief ceases, in the light of this type of Christology, to be a necessary inference from the concept of incarnation itself but must be a judgment based upon historical information. The main question that arises, for any Christian who is familiar with the modern scholarly study of the New Testament, is whether we have sufficient knowledge of the historical Jesus to make such absolute statements as that his *entire* life was a *perfect* exemplification of the paradox of grace or of divine inspiration.

Although this is a matter for inquiry, the inevitable verdict is that we do not have, and indeed cannot have, the volume and quality of historical knowledge that would entitle us responsibly to affirm such absolute qualities. On this issue I quote the New Testament scholar Dennis Nineham. Speaking of such claims as "It is in Jesus, and Jesus alone, that there is nothing of self to be seen, but solely the ultimate, unconditional love of God,"[23] Nineham asked

> Is it, however, possible to validate claims of the kind in question on the basis of historical evidence? To prove an historical negative, such as the sinlessness of Jesus, is notoriously difficult to the point of impossibility. . . . (T)he sort of claims for Jesus we are discussing could not be justified to the hilt by *any* historical records, however full or intimate or contemporary they might be, and even if their primary concern was with the quality and development of Jesus' inner life and character.[24]

In the kind of Christology exemplified in Baillie's and Lampe's work—the basic ground plan of which is also evident in the work both of the older liberal theologians, such as Harnack, and of such recent and contemporary Protestants as the New Testament scholar John Knox and the systematic theologians Maurice Wiles and Norman Pittenger, and also, though much more guardedly and obscurely, in the work of such Roman Catholic thinkers as Karl Rahner, Edward Schillebeeckx, and Hans Küng—there is, I suggest, the basis for an authentically theocentric development of Christianity that is compatible with genuine religious pluralism.

An exposition of the kind of Christian theology of religions that is made possible by such an inspiration Christology lies beyond the scope of this essay, and I have in any case attempted that elsewhere.[25] My purpose here is to present the outline of a Christology or, more precisely, of an understanding of the religious significance of Jesus of Nazareth. I define a Christian as one who affirms one's religious identity within the continuing tradition that originated with Jesus. From its inception this tradition has included a range of Christologies, the kind of inspiration Christology to which I subscribe being one of the earliest, possibly the earliest. A return today, in our pluralistic age, to this simplest, least theoretical or speculative, and most directly experiential understanding of Jesus seems to me to offer great gains, both for the Christian community and for the wider human family.

Critiques

Critique by Stephen T. Davis

Hick's Christology seems to turn on what I will call, speaking radically, a point of sheer luck. That is to say, Hick wants to discard orthodox Christology partly on the grounds that our current awareness of religious pluralism requires our rejection of it in favor of something else. Most fortunately, however, what our theological situation requires turns out to be exactly what was christologically primitive in the church. That is, the earliest views of Jesus in the Christian community are, luckily, precisely what we need today. Thus Hick can have his cake and eat it too—he can propose a Christology that will not entail Christian exclusivism and that (being more primitive) is even more orthodox than the Johannine-Nicene-Chalcedonic variety.

I once met an elderly philosophy professor at a Catholic seminary who when faced with almost any good insight or idea from a modern thinker or movement was inclined to argue that it had already been said, perhaps in an obscure way, by Aquinas. His academic career, I was told, was in fact based on arguing that the best insights of existentialism are to be found already in the Angelic Doctor. The priest who introduced me to him told me privately that almost everyone in the seminary thought this man was at times reading into Aquinas points that were not really there. I am equally suspicious that Hick and the biblical scholars he relies on are reading into the primitive church a Christology that was not really there. More on that later.

The substantive inspiration Christology Hick proposes is quite attractive to me. Although I consider it only partial (i.e., I do not think it says enough about Jesus), it is a serious and incisive proposal. My objections to Hick start much earlier. They concern the assumptions his Christology is based on—assumptions about what New Testament scholarship has shown, about what contemporary religious pluralism requires, and about the logical status of Chalcedonic orthodoxy. In response to Hick, let me make four points, the first three of which relate to these assumptions.

(1)   I absolutely agree that if Chalcedonic Christology is incoherent, it must be rejected. But I have always wondered why Hick so quickly dismisses it as flatly contradictory. (In his essay, of course, Hick charges the Chalcedonic definition only with being mysterious and lacking any specifiable meaning. On other occasions, however, he has rejected it as incoherent or contradictory.) Nicholas Lash once wondered why Hick and the other contributors to *The Myth of God Incarnate* were not more *puzzled* by Chalcedon. Why does Hick not try harder to understand the creed? There are two reasons why I think he should have tried. First, millions of Christians since A.D. 451, many of them presumably fairly bright people, have accepted the claims made at Chalcedon as not only coherent but true. This does not entail that these statements *are* coherent, of course, but it does recommend treating them with care. Second, Hick himself evidently finds *some* paradoxes acceptable, e.g., Donald Baillie's celebrated paradox of grace. Note, then, the following two paradoxes:

a. Jesus Christ was simultaneously truly divine and truly human; and
b. Some acts performed by human persons are done both freely and

responsibly by those human persons and by God's grace acting
through them.

Is one paradox more paradoxical or less acceptable than the other? Perhaps
so. But why? For myself, I can accept both as paradoxes rather than
contradictions, and I suspect that if he tried hard enough Hick could too.
But we can easily see why he is not willing to try to do so. Acceptance of the
second paradox does not raise dangers of Christian exclusivism; acceptance
of the first (he thinks) does. This leads directly to my second point.

(2) I disagree with Hick's claim that our awareness of today's religious
pluralism requires major revisions in Christology. (Having discussed this
point elsewhere, I will be brief here.) It is true, as Hick says, that
Chalcedonic orthodoxy entails a uniqueness, ultimacy, and finality about
the revelation of God in Jesus Christ. I agree: God must want, on some
level, all people to believe in Jesus. Christians do have more ready access to
God than non-Christians do. But that certainly does not entail that God calls
and reaches people only through the Christian religion or that non-Christians are "outside the sphere of salvation." Furthermore, I strongly deny
any necessary connection (as Hick seems to suggest) between orthodox
Christology, on the one hand, and colonialism, anti-Semitism, the burning
of heretics, and Western political and cultural superiority complexes, on the
other. You can consistently hold the one and reject the others.

(3) I disagree with what Hick says about the New Testament picture of
Jesus. It seems to me he accepts uncritically what we might call the
consensus of liberal New Testament scholars about Jesus and Christology.
Of course, on one level, it is perfectly understandable that he—a nonbiblical
scholar—should do so. But, as I argue in my own Christology, this view
ought not be accepted at all, let alone uncritically.

One of the several points on which I dissent from this consensus is the
question of how to decide what to accept as *primitive* or *authentic* or even
true in the New Testament picture of Jesus and what to reject as *later* or
legendary or *accretionary*. I recognize that linguistic arguments about, for
example, the dependence of one New Testament text on another, argue
strongly that one antedates the other. At other points I suspect that some
scholars at times deem late or inauthentic the texts that support the views of
Jesus they reject and baptize as primitive or authentic the texts that tend to
confirm their own views.

In that regard, notice that in places Hick is skeptical about our ability to
know "what really happened" (e.g., the nature of the resurrection event).
At other points he seems sure he knows "what really happened" e.g., that
Jesus was overwhelmingly aware of the presence of a holy and
compassionate God, that Jesus had a strong sense of his own calling from
God, that Jesus was a healer, that Jesus called himself 'Son of man', that

Peter's speech in Acts 2 probably reflects a primitive understanding of Jesus, and that Hick's own inspiration Christology represents a return to an original understanding of Jesus in the primitive church. My point here is just that I doubt this assessment of what we can know and not know. And I note that other New Testament scholars—Martin Hengel, James Dunn, C. F. D. Moule, and others—argue that some of the highest christological notions are present, at least implicitly, in some of the earliest New Testament documents.

Note also that the quotation Hick cites from Peter's speech in Acts 2 (with the term *man* italicized), as if it confirmed his own views, is quite consistent with orthodox Christology. For this Christology too (as all of us know) holds that Jesus was "fully man." It must in fairness be admitted that a few New Testament texts can be (though they need not be) interpreted in an adoptionist direction. But I am not aware that any New Testament scholar has ever located a period or community in primitive Christianity in which Jesus was held to be not just human but *merely* human.

(4) In a way, my deepest problem with Hick's Christology is pragmatic rather than theoretical or theological. Of course I recommend orthodox christological notions because I think they are *true*, not just *useful*. Nevertheless, I am dubious that any view that subtracts from Christology all notions of uniqueness, ultimacy, and finality will be sufficient to carry the Christian community through the next two thousand or two hundred or even twenty years. Hick recognizes the functional value of Chalcedon in its day; I think Christianity needs this or similar notions today. The day may again come when, in the face of rising secularism, Christians will be a tiny minority or, in the face of totalitarian political regimes, even a persecuted minority. Christianity will survive, in my opinion, only if it keeps its distinctives.

In conclusion let me note that Hick's Jesus is essentially a guru. Jesus is, to be sure, a guru who gets an A+ on the scale of religions Hick developed in his notable article "On Grading Religions." But I think what the Christian community needs (and this has been virtually the unanimous testimony of Christians throughout history) is not a guru but a Savior.

Critique by James M. Robinson

John Hick quite rightly begins with the difficulty posed by the problem of the historical Jesus: "how relatively little certain knowledge we have of him"; "our assured information about him is very limited"; "our all too scanty historical information." This modern consensus functions, however, not so much as a limitation on what Hick wants to say (for that, Jesus is not really crucial) as an aid in his polemic against traditional claims. To him it poses acutely the question "whether we have a sufficient knowledge of the historical Jesus to make such absolute statements as that his *entire* life was a *perfect* exemplification of the paradox of grace or of divine inspiration."

To speak about Jesus, Hick introduces a method he describes as trying "to imagine ourselves as first-century persons encountering Jesus of Nazareth. *Imagine* is the right word, even though it must be imagination under the broad control of historical evidence." Aided by "our knowledge of other religiously impressive people," we are to produce "imaginative reconstructions of the historical Jesus," which "say something about us as well as something, hopefully something that is historically well-founded, about the Jesus who was a part of public human history." Thus Hick adds "my own imaginative reconstruction" to "our imaginative pictures of him."

The obscurity of this method is equaled by that of some of its results, modest though they are: "He must have been a religiously very impressive person"; "his awareness of the overwhelmingly evident reality and presence of God"; "the divine creativity flowed through his hands in bodily healing and was present in his personal impact, with challenging and re-creating power, upon people"; "Jesus, as a spirit-filled prophet, a charismatic healer, perhaps as Messiah . . . should have thought of himself as, in this familiar metaphorical sense, a son of God."

Such formulations of theological method and its results may be as clear as can be obtained in our latter day, but they do suggest that one is in too much of a glass house to speak loudly of the traditional Christology that "has never been shown to have any precise meaning," "an impressive form of words without any specifiable meaning." "But of course this does not explain anything."

Hick's method and its results are indeed to a considerable degree free of the metaphysical language that "has long since largely lost its meaning for the modern mind." But a language analyst should recognize that language is not rendered intelligible merely by being freed of most of its metaphysics. To paraphrase a statement Hick quotes about Chalcedon, he himself "has proved less a solution than the [modern] definition of a problem which constantly demands further elucidation." God talk, even such sanitized God talk as Hick presents, is not academically intelligible until it is translated into language that really communicates with modern scholarship in one form or another (since of course we live in a pluralistic academic as well as a pluralistic religious world).

It is the premise of Hick's paper that it does stand at such a threshold. This is also true of the two examples he gives, Donald Baillie's Christology of the paradox of grace and Geoffrey Lampe's Christology of inspiration. Hick works on them to improve them in the direction in which he wishes to move. But both are still saturated with the traditional language of the church, which is familiar and thus understood within the church in the sense that Christians have their own religious experience in such familiar language. But this does not make of it modern scholarly language. Being able to empathize with it is not the same as being able to understand it.

Rudolf Bultmann's praise of Donald Baillie's book as "the most significant book of our time in the field of Christology" need not be put in question as an apocryphal quotation introduced into the tradition by Baillie's brother John, to whom it is ascribed. Rather it would be a further indication that such a Christology does invite explication in modern language. For Baillie, God was in Christ "in refusing to claim anything for Himself independently and ascribing all the goodness to God." This is recognizable in the New Testament but also as dialectic theology. It is a point of departure for a modern Christology. But it is only a beginning. Bultmann would naturally have developed it in the language of the existentialistic interpretation that he advocated and that, to his distress, Karl Barth had abandoned in midstream for a neoorthodox vocabulary. Thus there would be for Bultmann an irony in that the massively impressive and christocentric *Church Dogmatics* is in fact surpassed by the relatively modest but much more promising *God Was in Christ*. Today scholarly media other than those used by Bultmann are more up-to-date. But in one way or the other Christology, to be meaningful, must be more than nonmetaphysical and more than churchly God talk.

Critique by John B. Cobb, Jr.

I am struck by the extent of my agreements with John Hick in his christological reflections. These are centered on our shared appreciation for John Baillie and also our shared view that the model he used for understanding the incarnation opens the way to other steps. Those steps include the abandonment of all absolutist language with respect to how perfectly Jesus lived by grace and recognizing that the question of how fully persons in other traditions have lived by grace is left open.

Within the bounds of what is explicitly said, I have to strain to find clear disagreements. As in Robinson's essay, I am unhappy with the treatment of Nicea and Chalcedon. Brunner did explicitly hold to the impersonal humanity of Jesus, and Hick is correct about the consequences. But Nicea and Chalcedon can support a quite different view (this is not really important to Hick's argument, so I will not pursue it).

The points at which I am uncomfortable with Hick's views are at the fringes of this essay and have been developed by him elsewhere. Because they do appear here, even if at the fringes, and because the issues are important, I will lift them up for discussion.

Hick states that once we have recognized that grace works in all, the fact that its working is especially manifest to Christians in Jesus Christ does not support Christocentrism. Indeed, he argues that these views lead to theocentrism. For several reasons, I do not find his proposals helpful.

First, in strictly orthodox terms, Christocentrism is already theocentrism. It is only because Christ is God that faith can be centered in Christ. Since this language may be confusing in the context of Hick's essay, let me use language closer to his. By Christocentrism, I mean something like centering in grace. Grace is of God and is indeed, in Baillie's view and mine, God. It is God as efficaciously present in creatures, especially human ones. If shifting from Christocentrism to theocentrism means anything here, it means shifting from God as grace to God as transcendent, from the Second or Third Members of the Trinity, perhaps, to the First, or even from the Trinity as a whole to the Godhead. It is because I understand Hick's proposal of a shift from Christocentricity to theocentricity as a shift from a focus on grace as God's creative and redemptive activity in the world to a transcendent noumenal reality devoid of all attributes that I strongly oppose it. What we need is a shift from a bad Christocentrism to a good one.

Second, Hick supposes that the shift from Christocentricism to theocentrism allows a more open and positive view of the merits of other religious traditions. In an obvious sense this can work for theistic traditions. That is, if one makes central what these traditions have in common, then what distinguishes them becomes relatively unimportant. But Hick seems to think that theocentrism also provides common grounds with nontheistic religious traditions. I do not agree. In response to the obvious objection that making God central does not provide common ground with those who deny the reality of God, Hick argues that "God" is only one way of conceiving the ultimate reality, so that this ultimate reality, not God, becomes the common ground. This ultimate reality must be conceived as that which is pointed to by the names *Brahman* and *Nirvana*, as well as *God*. To avoid favoring one tradition over others, we must recognize the ultimate reality as devoid of all the characteristics that distinguish Brahman, Nirvana, and God. Hick proposes that it is noumenal in the Kantian sense, so that all that is positively affirmed about Brahman, Nirvana, and God in the great religious traditions applies only to phenomena. My own view is that far from satisfying the religious needs of all three traditions in this way, we end up with a position that all would consider contradictory to their deepest convictions.

Third, the quest for commonality behind differences also expresses itself in comments about Jesus. Hick seems to think that if we can see that Jesus is to be understood as one in whom God's grace was powerfully effective or as one who was inspired by God, we can and should apply the same view to other great religious leaders. As one who believes that God's grace works in all and through all, I cannot entirely disagree. Yet this approach can blind us to the true diversities. Buddhists do not understand Buddha as having lived by divine grace or as having been inspired by God. To insist that this is, nevertheless, the correct way of interpreting the Buddha's work does not reflect the open appreciation of other traditions for which Hick rightly calls. Is it not better to listen carefully to what others say and learn from them than to impose our categories upon them? I am interested in the radical distinctiveness of Jesus as incarnation of God and in the radical distinctiveness of Gautama as the Enlightened One. I am not interested in seeing both under a single rubric. Strong affirmations of Jesus' distinctiveness, even of his uniqueness, do not conflict with deep appreciation for the distinctiveness, or uniqueness, of others.

Fourth, I am doubtful that a return to the "simplest, least theoretical or speculative, and most directly experiential understanding of Jesus" offers the gains Hick expects. This is partly because I do not think we can recover the historical Jesus or the most directly experienced Jesus apart from theory and speculation. More significantly it is because I see more promise in a forward-looking approach. Such an approach requires a continual reshaping of the memories by which our Christian identity is constituted. But it seeks to enter into modes of understanding that cannot be found in the past. For this we need to learn from the whole of Christian history. For example, as we confront the wisdom of India and China today, we can learn from both the successes and the failures of the early church in its confrontation with the wisdom of the Greeks. One thing we will learn is that bold speculation has its place in appropriating new wisdom. Hick engages in bold speculations in discussing the noumenal ultimate and the phenomenal God. These do not arise out of direct experiential understanding of Jesus. Although I believe that more fruitful speculations are needed and possible, I commend Hick's willingness to speculate.

Critique by Rebecca D. Pentz

In his essay John Hick challenges us to deconstruct our traditional Christologies and return to the "simplest, least theoretical and speculative, and most directly experiential understanding of Jesus." Hick finds such an understanding in his inspiration Christology. I accept Hick's challenge, but I find that my own "most directly experiential understanding of Jesus" is quite different from Hick's.

Hick begins by asking whether we should begin with the historical Jesus or with what he calls the idealized Christ. It seems to me that if we are to take his challenge seriously we must start with neither. I for one do not directly experience the historical Jesus, though I am informed by reading others' encounters with him. Nor do I experience an idealized theological Christ. I experience Jesus himself now, as he saves me, as he empowers me, as he nurtures me. I pray to Jesus and he responds. I ask for his help, and he infuses me with his Holy Spirit. I listen to him, and he makes me sensitive to the oppression and suffering around me. Integral to my experience of Jesus is his position as God. I experience him as my present Lord and Savior.

I do not think I am alone in this experience. Certainly one of the reasons the early church came to affirm Jesus' deity is that its members too, prior to any developed Christian theology, experienced Jesus after the resurrection as present with them as their reigning Lord. Oscar Cullmann, one of Hick's "acknowledged experts," argued in *The Christology of the New Testament* that the members of the early church experienced fellowship with Jesus in their worship and communion and that the confession *Kyrios Christos* and the Aramaic prayer *Maranatha* expressed their conviction based on these experiences that Jesus was their absolute, divine Lord. So the members of the early church did not deify Jesus because so doing added prestige and survival power to their group. Rather they *experienced* Jesus as reigning in power; they *experienced* him as God. And they made their confession on the basis of this experience.

I would be naïve to assume that what I have said proves that Jesus is God. My experience of Jesus as God does not make him God any more than Hick's experience of Jesus as an inspired man makes Jesus just an inspired man. The experiential methodology Hick recommends will not prove anything. Besides, much more would need to be said about what it means to say that we experience Jesus *as* God, or *as* anything, for that matter. So, enough for experiences. Let me turn to some objective theology, treating briefly Hick's objection to the doctrine of the atonement.

In treating the atonement I do not mean to imply that Hick's other theological claims are unobjectionable or unimportant. For example, I cannot agree with Hick that the doctrine that Jesus is both God and man "has never been shown to have any precise meaning" or that we are "irresponsible" if we affirm with Baillie and Lampe that Jesus was unique. I have chosen to focus on the atonement because this doctrine is central to any Christology and because I think a feminist Christology provides special insight. In fact, feminists often have trouble with the doctrine of the atonement. Many feminists deny that Jesus' death had anything to do with God's plan of salvation, arguing instead that his death was merely the lamentable result of his conflict with human authorities. Hick argues that Jesus' teachings about the nature of God—he quotes the parable of the Prodigal Son—reveal that God does not require a mediator or an atoning sacrifice in order to forgive.

Hick's objection here is unfounded, even on Hick's own parsing of

Jesus' teachings. Earlier in his essay, Hick mentions another aspect of Jesus' teachings about his Heavenly Father. According to Hick, Jesus describes God "both as the loving Heavenly *Abba* who welcomes home the prodigal son and also as the holy and righteous One who makes a total and absolute claim upon human beings." Hick fails to mention God's holy righteousness when he discusses the atonement; yet, God's righteousness is just as important as his love, especially vis-à-vis the atonement. Let me explain.

My own understanding of the atonement is based on women's experience of childbirth: Jesus suffered just as a mother does to give us a new birth. It is my understanding of a mother's love that helps me make sense of why Jesus had to die. The Bible teaches us that the pain of childbirth is a result of and an integral part of the brokenness of the world after the fall. Certainly Jesus' pain is a result of the fall. But there is more to be said.

When a child goes wrong, a mother suffers. She suffers, not because some divine justice or godly wrath requires her suffering. She suffers because she loves. But, and this is the point Hick misses in his comments on the atonement, if the loving mother is also a holy and righteous mother she cannot in her suffering pretend to the world and to herself that the misdeed never occurred. To do so would compromise her own righteousness and jeopardize her child's moral development. So, instead, with words and actions she communicates to the child the fact that misdeeds have consequences.

Neither can the holy and righteous God ignore sin. He too communicates dramatically that sin has consequences. The cross, at least in part, is the righteous God's shout to the world: "Sin cannot be ignored!"

Even more must be said, and the parable of the Prodigal Son says it. There is no doubt that the mood in Jesus' parable is celebrative. The father rejoices when he sees his bedraggled son, even before the boy verbally expresses his repentance. Rather than chastising the boy, the father kills the fatted calf and throws a party. All this does not mean that the Prodigal Son's sin does not have consequences. The boy has squandered his inheritance; the money is gone. He has misused a period of his life; that time is now irrecoverable. And his return home destroys family harmony. Who bears the brunt of these consequences? The father. It is the father who must continue to support the family. It is the father who goes to make peace with the elder brother. The father does not deny that sin has consequences. Rather, he takes those consequences upon himself. Just so, God the Father does not deny that sin has consequences. He takes them upon himself. Here is the mystery of the cross. God's rule is that the consequence of sin is death. Rather than changing this rule, rather than killing those of us who sin, God allows his own Son to be killed.

Is God able to forgive us outright just as the father forgives the prodigal? *Certainly he is able.* But because he is holy and righteous, he screams out against sin. And because he is loving, he takes the consequences of sin upon himself.

Following hundreds of years of theology, I would never claim to have hit upon a complete and perfect theory of the atonement. But an analysis of a mother's love gives me two helpful clues. Loving mothers suffer. Good mothers are honest about sin. At the cross God showed us exactly what Jesus taught us—that God is *both* loving and good.

Hick's Response to Critiques

On reading the critiques, my own as well as the others, I realize that we are a fairly contentious lot! I only hope that any overly polemical tone arises from a sense of the critical importance of the subject as well as from our own personal clumsinesses in dialogue. I also hope that this response will not at any point be needlessly sharp—but that must be for the reader to judge. I shall respond to my colleagues in alphabetical order.

John Cobb's criticisms are not for the most part directed against an inspiration or grace Christology but against the wider pluralistic interpretation of religion in terms of which some of us see the relationship between Christianity and the other great world religions. In this connection he criticizes two different theories, both of which he ascribes to me. One of these (hereafter referred to as "the theory") I am happy to acknowledge and defend; the other (which I shall refer to as "the misunderstanding"), I am glad of the chance to repudiate.

To deal with the misunderstanding first, this is the theocentric view that the different religious traditions of the world, including the nontheistic ones, represent acts or revelations of a personal God. This is a view that I do not hold. Nor indeed do I describe my position as *theocentric*; in fact I have very seldom used the term, though it is difficult to avoid it altogether since it seems to have become established as a label for the view—to which I do subscribe—that the Christ event was only one of a number of authentic manifestations of the divine reality, the Real. The disadvantage of the term *theocentric* is its ambiguity. Sometimes, as generally in Roman Catholic writings, it has embodied the assumption that the ultimate reality is a personal God; here Cobb rightly points out that in strictly orthodox terms Christocentrism is already theocentric, since Christ is identified as God. Sometimes, however, as in my own occasional uses of the term, theocentrism is linked with the understanding that *God* is our Christian term for the ultimate reality, it being thus far an open question whether that reality is personal or nonpersonal or, in a sense, both. (For this last option see, e.g., my paper "Is God Personal?" in F. Sontag and M. D. Bryant, eds., *God: The Contemporary Discussion* [New York: Rose of Sharon Press, 1982].)

Because the term *theocentricism* is in this way ambiguous, I have generally opted not to use it; I prefer to speak, not of God, but of the Real. At the same time I have sometimes, in the context of intra-Christian discussion, and when the nontheistic traditions were not in view, spoken of God-centeredness in contrast to Christ-centeredness and Christianity-centeredness. Thus the two titles *God and the Universe of Faiths* and *God Has Many Names* could well, if taken by themselves, suggest the more usual and more restricted usage. In using our Christian term for the ultimate reality in the titles of books addressed to the Christian community I seem to have given rise to a misunderstanding, and I am glad to have the opportunity now to identify it as such.

A repudiation of the misunderstanding carries with it a repudiation of what Cobb builds upon it: "Hick seems to think that theocentricity also provides common grounds with nontheistic religious traditions." I do not think that. What I do think is embodied in the theory that Cobb accurately introduces when he says that "Hick argues that 'God' is only one way of conceiving the ultimate Reality." I have suggested that in order to affirm the basic authenticity of the different forms of religious experience, theistic and nontheistic, we have to postulate an ultimate reality, which is differently conceived, experienced, and responded to through different religiocultural "lenses." (The hypothesis is briefly outlined in my critique of Rebecca Pentz' essay.) Cobb objects, "My own view is that far from satisfying the religious needs of all three traditions [Hinduism, Buddhism, and Christianity] in this way, we end up with a position that all would consider contradictory to their deepest convictions." However, the hypothesis is not intended to satisfy first-order religious needs. For most people, these are met within one's own tradition in its concrete particularity. It is designed to satisfy the intellectual need to understand the worldwide religious situation of which one's own tradition is a part. Accordingly the Real, *an sich*, is not the object of a cult. It is the ultimate reality that we postulate as the ground of the different forms of religious experience and thought insofar as these are more than human projections. We should thus not expect to find the concept of the Real, *an sich*, within the religious discourse of the particular traditions (although there are some interesting pointers in that direction); for it functions not within that discourse, but in the metadiscourse that we call the philosophy of religion. Here we stand, in thought, outside the different traditions, seeking to understand the relationship between them.

One of the merits of the pluralist proposal is that it frees us to notice and to be fascinated by the wealth of differences within the phenomenology of religion. I am under no such temptation as Cobb supposes to insist that Buddhists must understand Gautama as having lived by divine grace or having been inspired by God. Grace and inspiration belong to the theistic sphere of thought and experience. Gautama was not inspired by God but was one who "attained to Enlightenment." But he and Jesus—according to the pluralistic hypothesis—lived in a transformed relationship to the Real through different but authentic ways of conceiving, experiencing, and responding to the Real; and the influence of each upon others has been to draw them into the transformation of human existence from self-centeredness to Reality-centeredness.

I begin here to touch upon large and complex issues, going far beyond anything discussed in my essay, which is within specifically Christian theology. See my new book, *Problems of Religious Pluralism* (London: Macmillan; New York: St. Martins Press, 1985), which treats some of these issues.

Steve Davis helpfully numbers his critical comments, so that I can respond to them in the same order.

(1) He invites us to consider these two statements:

    a. Jesus Christ was simultaneously truly divine and truly human; and

    b. some acts performed by human persons are done both freely and responsibly by those human persons and by God's grace acting through them.

He then asks: if the second of these paradoxes is acceptable, why not the other also? The second is what Baillie calls the paradox of grace, a paradox that arises within Christian experience. The paradox is something that happens; and I imagine that virtually all Christians, including Davis, accept that it happens, even though we do not understand it. The question in the first paradox is *whether* it happens. If it does, it must of course be accepted. But the God-manhood of Jesus, with his divine and human natures, is not an observed fact; it is a humanly constructed theory. The question is whether it is an intelligible and supportable theory. I have argued that it is not. Davis' statement that "millions of Christians since A.D. 451, many of them presumably fairly bright people, have accepted the claims made at Chalcedon as not only coherent but true" is, I venture to think, misleading. For the millions of Christians, many of them highly intelligent, who have recited the Chalcedonian Creed down the centuries have not professed to understand what it means to say that a historical human being was God—to understand, for example, whether his brain was human but his mind divine, and so on through all the familiar conundrums. They have regarded the idea as a mystery—meaning that it is to be believed without being understood. But in our more historically minded age we have become acutely conscious that the Chalcedonian definition was not divinely revealed but was a human formulation. And its long success resides precisely in the fact that it has no clearly specifiable meaning. People who have rashly attempted to spell it out have ended up being condemned as heretics. The lesson of history is that the mystery is much better left a mystery. Indeed we see in Davis' own essay how perilous it is to infringe this rule. He is led onto very dangerous ground and would, in the days of high orthodoxy enforced by the Inquisition, probably have been burned at the stake before me!

(2) Is there not something disturbing, arbitrary, and dubiously intelligible in Davis' joint assertions (a) that there is a uniqueness, ultimacy, and finality about the revelation in Jesus Christ, so that God wants ("on some level") all people to believe in Jesus and so that Christians have more ready access to God than non-Christians, and at the same time (b) that God calls and reaches non-Christians through other means than the Christian religion and that they are within the sphere of salvation? We have to ask: is it or is it not necessary for salvation that people come to God through Jesus? If yes, then non-Christians *are* outside the sphere of salvation (which Davis denies). If no, then it does not ultimately matter whether people come to God through Jesus or by some other path (which, however, Davis does not show any sign of accepting).

Concerning the side effects of traditional Christian exclusivism it is true, as Davis says, that there is no "*necessary* connection" between the Christian claim to absolute truth and a consequent superiority, and the phenomena of colonialism, anti-Semitism, the burning of heretics and witches. But there *is* an actual historical connection, as I am sure Davis must be aware.

(3) The New Testament evidence. It is true that I am not primarily a biblical scholar. (Davis and I are philosophers who have also had seminary training.) On such questions as whether Jesus taught that he was God incarnate, or the divine Son, the Second Person of the Trinity living a human life, I accordingly rely on the broad consensus of current biblical scholarship. As I read the literature, the contemporary consensus is very clear that the historical Jesus did not teach this. Davis seems to understand the literature differently. At this point I refer the reader to what James Robinson—who is not only a New Testament scholar but a very eminent one—writes in his critique of Davis' essay.

(4) Davis believes that Christianity needs to hold on to uniqueness, ultimacy, and finality if it is to survive. Of course, in one sense this is tautologically true: if a form of Christianity that insists upon its own unique superiority is to survive, it must continue to insist upon its own unique superiority! In fact Christianity has never been an unchanging monolith; it is a long history of gradual change. It looks as though Christianity is now

gradually becoming conscious of being, not the one and only path, but one of several paths of salvation. Davis apparently assumes that in that case Christianity will die out. This seems to me unwarrantably pessimistic. Perhaps Christians can learn to live with the fact that we are not a uniquely privileged and preferred group, but part of God's universal human family. At any rate it is manifestly true, whether we like it or not, that Christianity *is* one among several great historical contexts of salvation. Let us trust the truth and await its consequences with confidence.

More generally, I suggest that the theologian's task is to try to make sense of facts, not to look for ways of closing the Christian mind to facts that demand new thinking. This applies both to the facts revealed by our greatly expanded contemporary awareness of the wider religious life of the human race and to the results of modern biblical scholarship.

I now turn to Rebecca Pentz. The relevance of experience to Christology deserves a little unraveling. The sense in which an inspiration or grace Christology can be said to be not only the likely earliest but also the "simplest, least theoretical and speculative, and most directly experiential understanding of Jesus" is that inspiration/grace is a reality given within Christian experience. We are, sometimes at least, conscious of the power of divine grace or inspiration in our lives. Accordingly, to apply this category in our understanding of Jesus, as Baillie suggested, does not require philosophical constructions such as the concepts of the Logos or of the Trinity. An inspiration Christology is based insofar as possible on human experience and avoids insofar as possible human speculations. This is the intention of the phrase I quoted. It is not, as Pentz suggests, that my "experience of Jesus as an inspired man" opposes her experience of him as God.

It is of course proper for her to bear witness to her own experience of Jesus as one to whom she prays, who empowers, nurtures, and sensitizes her and infuses her with his Holy Spirit—integral to which experience, she says, is "his position as God." In other words, she experiences the presence of Jesus; and her attitude toward him and his effect upon her are such that she is convinced that he is God. Anyone's account of a personal religious experience is to be attended to with great respect, for experience is the lifeblood without which religion can become, and has often become, purely formal. But when it is produced in support of a theological dogma, we are entitled to examine it and to note any elements of theory or dogma that may have entered into the formation of the experience itself. People equipped with different sets of religious ideas and images tend to have correspondingly different forms of religious experience. Thus, beyond the borders of Christianity great numbers of people, ancient and modern, have experienced particular human figures, both living and dead, as divine and as their Lord and Savior—though usually with at least an implicit qualification that such a person (usually a king or a guru) is "wholly God" rather than "the whole of God." Within Christianity, Roman Catholics sometimes experience the Mother of God as one to whom they pray and who empowers, nurtures, and sensitizes them and infuses them with the Holy Spirit. Pentz' form of Christian experience is a very Protestant one, apparently embodying a special trinitarian doctrine to the effect that the Holy Spirit is Jesus' Holy Spirit. One can very easily see that the kind of analysis so persuasively presented by Steven Katz and others (Steven Katz, ed., *Mysticism and Philosophical Analysis* [New York: Oxford University Press, 1978]) applies to her report. Each of these different forms of religious experience, including Pentz', is in my view formed partly by the impact of the divine reality upon human beings in their different religiocultural situations and partly by the categories and images supplied by those contexts. She is right, then, in holding that such experiences, even though accepted as authentic points of contact with the divine reality, do not prove that Jesus is God. They show that Jesus constitutes *her* image of God.

The rest of Pentz' critique is devoted to the doctrine of the atonement. (She might, incidentally, like to check the accuracy of her quotation that it is "irresponsible" to affirm Jesus' uniqueness.) Here, though using interestingly the analogy of a mother's love rather than the more traditional analogy of a father's love, she repeats the old Protestant penal-substitutionary atonement theory. As she summarizes it, "God's rule is that the consequence of sin is death. Rather than changing the rule, rather than killing those of us who sin, God allows his own Son to be killed." I have to confess that this theory is to me morally and spiritually repugnant; and it seems to me audacious indeed to suggest that it is supported by the parable of the Prodigal Son! Surely the message of the parable is that God can and does fully and freely forgive and receive as beloved sons and daughters all who genuinely repent of their sins. There is no suggestion that the father has to let someone be killed to atone for the Prodigal's sins. Nor does the Lord's Prayer suggest any condition other than that we seek God's forgiveness and in turn learn to forgive one another. Indeed, forgiveness that has to be bought by full payment of the debt is not forgiveness. Pentz presents the picture of a God who does not forgive but whose pardon is bought when some person—guilty or innocent—receives the appointed punishment. Jesus presented the picture of a God who performs the miracle of forgiveness in response to genuine, humble, sorrowful repentance. Then, he says, there is joy in heaven!

Finally, James Robinson. He comments on the method that I have followed. He thinks that the very limited results that I derive from the New Testament evidence, interpreted partly in the light of our knowledge of other outstanding religious persons, suffers from as great obscurity as does the traditional Chalcedonian Christology. This response seems to me to include an element of exaggeration. Is it really so obscure to hold that Jesus must have been a religiously very impressive person, with an awareness of the overwhelmingly evident reality and presence of God, who performed acts of healing, and who may well have thought of himself as, in the familiar Hebraic metaphor, a "son of God"? This is of course a *religious* interpretation of Jesus. But Robinson does not mean by an "academically intelligible" interpretation one that avoids religious presuppositions, for his own suggested Sophia Christology shares a religious presupposition. The traditional two-natures Christology, on the other hand, although it of course also involves a religious presupposition, is—it seems to me—obscure in the further sense that it has never yet been intelligibly explicated. Thus, although I am sure that the kind of inspiration Christology that I present can be improved in a number of ways, particularly in its relation to the detailed New Testament evidence, I am not sure that "obscurity" is the problem.

Robinson approves Donald Baillie's christological attempt in *God Was in Christ*. Indeed this book emerges today as a key work for modern discussions, meriting Rudolf Bultmann's high praise, which is not apocryphal but appears in a subsequently published letter. Bultmann wrote, "*Es is* (sic) *das bedeutendste Buch unserer Zeit über das Thema der Christologie*" (see n. 18 in my essay). I fully agree with Robinson that the paradox-of-grace Christology (as also the parallel inspiration Christology of Lampe) needs to be developed in modern language; indeed it was to this task that I was endeavouring to make a contribution in my essay.

2 Jesus Christ: Savior or Guru?
STEPHEN T. DAVIS

I

One of the most striking texts from the fourth Gospel tells of an encounter between Jesus and a Samaritan woman at a well. It ends with the villagers of Sychar declaring of Jesus: "we have heard for ourselves, and we know that this is indeed the Savior of the world" (John 4:42). I believe these villagers were correct; I too hold that Jesus is the Savior of the world. In my contribution to this book I try to show why.

Although I remember as a child hearing some of the stories about Jesus, I first saw myself as one who believed that he was the Savior of the world after I, as a teenager, encountered Jesus in a conversion experience. As I began to read the Bible, listen to sermons, and speak with other Christians, I remember forming the definite impression that Jesus must have been an extraordinary person. There were several reasons for this impression.

First, I remember being convinced that Jesus must have been an attractive person who had a flair for leadership and an aura of charisma. Like most strong leaders, he must have been a great polarizer of people—they seem in the Gospels either to love him and follow him loyally or else to hate him and plot against him. He does not seem to have been the sort to inspire neutrality.

Second, I remember thinking that Jesus must have been an enigma to many of his contemporaries. He must have struck people as being strangely different from other folk; they couldn't figure him out or place him in a category. Once, when some hardened temple officers were sent by the authorities to arrest him, they were dumbfounded by his words. They returned to their superiors, gasping, "No man ever spoke like this man!" (John 7:32–46).

Third, I remember noting that Jesus seemed a loving, concerned, compassionate person. The story of Jesus and Zacchaeus (Luke 19:1–10) is one of the earliest I remember hearing about Jesus, and it made a deep impression on me, even as a child, that the Son of God would make friends with an ostracized tax collector. Jesus' love extended to all sorts of people, rich and poor, educated and ignorant, righteous and sinful, sophisticated and crude. I remember feeling how strange and unexpected it was that the Lord seemed to love and accept all the people he met, just the way they were, even his deepest enemies.

Fourth, I remember being impressed with Jesus' apparent facility for changing people. Almost nobody met Jesus and remained the same as before. Some changed for the better: Peter, an ignorant fisherman, became the courageous leader of the church. Saul, a persecutor of Christianity, met Jesus in a vision on the road to Damascus and became Paul, the greatest missionary and theologian the church has known. Others changed for the worse: the man we call the rich young ruler came to Jesus anxiously seeking salvation but left him rejecting salvation when he learned how dearly it would cost (Matt. 19:16–22). An obscure man named Judas, of whom otherwise no one today would ever have heard, met Jesus, made a decision, and became infamous for an act of betrayal that history will never forget.

I count myself as one of those who has been changed by Jesus. I am convinced that I was once on a wrong path that was leading nowhere and that in Christ I found the right path. I have a strong sense of having been created, guided, forgiven, and redeemed by God in Christ; that, I suppose, is much of what makes me a Christian and engenders in me an interest in Christology.

II

Soon after my conversion, I joined a church of a mainline Protestant denomination (the same denomination in whose historical descendant I am now an ordained minister). As a member of that denomination, broad and inclusive as it was and is, I soon became aware of theological pluralism. Lots of theological options were available. People interpreted the Bible differently. How was one to decide what to believe?

Even more than in those innocent days, we live today in a time of theological pluralism. Many Christian theologies are available today, and many Christologies. However, it seems to me that all the available christological options can be divided into two categories, what I will call maximal and minimal Christologies. A maximal Christology is based upon or presupposes or argues for (even though it may struggle with) the classical doctrine of the incarnation from Nicea and Chalcedon (i.e., Christ is "truly divine and truly human" and "two natures in one person"). A minimal

Christology does not presuppose or accept this notion and indeed is offered as an alternative to it.

Many (not all) minimal Christologies seem to me to revolve around at least some of the following six points.[1]

(1) The Bible is a wholly, or at least primarily, human book. No doctrine of biblical inspiration or trustworthiness is accepted; the Bible is to be viewed and treated like any other ancient text.

(2) A great variety of distinct and inconsistent Christologies can be found in the New Testament, but the classical doctrine of the incarnation is not one of them. In addition, some sort of quasi-evolutionary explanation is given of the rise of "high" Johannine Christology and of the classical doctrine.

(3) The classical doctrine of the incarnation is incoherent. On purely logical grounds it is to be rejected.

(4) There never has been a universally accepted Christology in the church. What we find in the history of the church is the same kind of christological pluralism that exists in the New Testament. As John Hick says, "there is nothing that can be called *the* Christian doctrine of the incarnation."[2]

(5) The classical doctrine of the incarnation is to be rejected not just because of its logical incoherence but because it has had dire pragmatic consequences; it has, for example, helped foster Christian exclusivism vis-à-vis other religions, or male domination of women, or anti-Semitic attitudes.

(6) Accordingly, what the New Testament writers say or were *trying* to say about Jesus can best be captured via a minimal Christology.

Naturally, the Christology proposed can take many shapes, but nearly always the humanity and the teachings of Jesus are stressed. In fact, some minimal christologists like to claim ownership, as it were, over the humanity of Jesus; maximal Christologies, they claim, always entail some form of Docetism. Jesus is said to be a man who perfectly reflects the presence of God, or a man who is uniquely chosen by God to express and symbolize God's love for us, or a man gifted by God with love and wisdom and self-sacrifice, or a man whose exemplary life and unparalleled teachings still inspire men and women to live godly lives and to alter oppressive structures of society.

In sketching my own Christology, I try to reply to many (but for lack of space, not all) of the criticisms that minimal christologists have raised against the classical doctrine of the incarnation. In the concluding section, I mention the deepest reason I have for rejecting minimal Christology.

III

In A.D. 451 the Council of Chalcedon declared that Jesus Christ is

> at once complete in Godhead and complete in manhood, truly God and truly
> man, consisting also of a reasonable soul and body; of one substance with the
> Father as regards his Godhead, and at the same time of one substance with us as
> regards his manhood; like us in all respects, apart from sin; . . . one and the
> same Christ, Son, Lord, Only-begotten, recognized in two natures, without
> confusion, without change, without division, without separation; the distinction
> of natures being in no way annulled by the union, but rather the characteristics
> of each nature being preserved and coming together to form one person and
> subsistence.[3]

This is the dogma I have been calling the classical doctrine of the
incarnation. It constituted something of a consensus in Christendom from
the time of Chalcedon till recently. Some aspects of what the fathers were
trying to say are difficult to grasp, especially for us today. The concepts from
Greek ontology that form the metaphysical underpinnings of the doctrine
are particularly intractable. Few people today have any idea what a
hypostatic union is (the term typically used for the unity of divinity and
humanity in Christ); the many subtle ancient uses of the word *substance* are
now almost impossible to sort out and explain to nonexperts; and even the
one important metaphysical term that we recognize, *person*, was used by the
fathers in a different way from the way we use it.

Nevertheless, the main idea the fathers were driving at is quite simple.
It is that Jesus Christ is one person, truly divine and truly human. That is,
Jesus Christ is one person with two natures, a divine nature and a human
nature. The natures are neither confused nor separated in him. Nor are they
merged or amalgamated—divinity and humanity are far too different for
that. Nor are the two joined so as to convert the one into the other—that
cannot happen either. Nor are they fused so as to produce a third, or hybrid,
nature. The two are united in the person of Jesus Christ "without confusion,
without change, without division, without separation."

Notice that the classical doctrine is primarily negative. It makes no
attempt to explain, for example, how one person can have two natures (let
alone a divine and a human nature); it merely insists that that is what Jesus
Christ has. The mystery, the paradox, of the incarnation stands unresolved.
What the fathers did, I believe, was set a boundary. Certain heresies and
errors (adoptionism, Docetism, Ebionism, Arianism) are ruled out; any
Christology that affirms that Jesus Christ is "truly divine and truly human"
and has "two natures in one person" is allowed.

Should the classical doctrine still be believed by Christians today? I believe it should. Of course, like any exercise in theology (which is after all a human discipline) the words of the fathers at Chalcedon are fallible. They can never have scriptural authority for Christians. Thus, we must leave open the possibility that some theologian will find a doctrine superior to the classical doctrine. As for me, however, I do not believe any past theologian has done so, and I doubt that any current or future theologian will do so either. I confess to a strong belief that the church was led to the classical doctrine by the Holy Spirit (although, even if I am right, that *by itself* does not settle the question whether the classical doctrine ought to be normative for us today). As I argue later, the theological costs are far too high if we deny either the divinity or the humanity of Christ's person.

IV

My early impressions of Jesus (mentioned earlier) and the classical doctrine of the incarnation defined at Chalcedon were based upon what we might call a precritical reading of the four Gospels. But one of the facts of our age is that the Gospels are subject to rigorous and searching historical-critical scholarship. Surely this fact is the single most important factor distinguishing Christian faith in the twentieth century from Christian faith in, say, the fifth or the sixteenth century. Surely all those who intend to do Christology today must first make their peace with the historical-critical study of the New Testament.

My own view is that the historical-critical study of the Bible is to be strongly encouraged. I have no problem with the various methods New Testament scholars have been using to illuminate biblical texts—source criticism, form criticism, redaction criticism, structuralism, etc. I have no doubt that such methods are both helpful and necessary. I am not a proponent of the theory that the Bible is "inerrant"[4]; the Gospels contain inconsistencies that I am quite unable to harmonize sensibly. I do, however, hold a "high" view of scriptural authority and reliability. Accordingly, I am suspicious of many of the more radical conclusions some historical-critical scholars have been reaching about the Gospels.

(1) One of the reasons for my disquiet concerns what appears to be a near-axiom of contemporary Gospel scholarship. It can be expressed like this: what we encounter in the Gospels is not Jesus himself (i.e., the actual events as they occurred, say, in A.D. 29 or 30) but the Christian church's understanding of Jesus, say, in the 70s or 80s or 90s, when these books were receiving final form; ergo, many of the events recorded in these books did not occur as described.

Is this axiom worthy of belief? Well, part of it surely is. I have no difficulty accepting the idea that the Gospels are indeed expressions of the faith of the Christian church and that accordingly we do indeed come in contact there with the consciousness of the church at the time they were written. But what I do not see is how that fact entails that in the Gospels we do not *also* come in contact with Jesus himself, with events that occurred in A.D. 29 or 30. The point can be generalized. In reading any historian's work about any figure or period of history, we do naturally enough come in contact with the consciousness of the historian at the time the work was written. But surely if the historian has done a worthwhile job of writing history, we also come in contact with the person or period written about. I do not wish to be interpreted as claiming that the Gospels are entirely or even primarily works of history. Nevertheless, I believe these books bring us into contact with Jesus himself, that is, with what he said and did.

(2) A second reason for my disquiet about some of the more radical conclusions of contemporary New Testament scholarship concerns the unity of the New Testament. Reacting against an almost a priori assumption of biblical unity in the so-called biblical theology movement of a few years ago, contemporary biblical scholars seem to me to have gone overboard in the other direction. Contradictions in the Bible are sought out with inquisitorial zeal; any attempt at harmonization of two apparently inconsistent texts is seen as laughably unsophisticated; one sometimes feels it is considered almost uncouth to use a text, for example, from the fourth Gospel to illuminate a Pauline text, or vice versa; and it seems to be assumed that there is almost no such thing as "the New Testament view" of this or that.

The issue of biblical unity and disunity becomes relevant to my concerns in this essay at the point of the contemporary insistence that many Christologies exist in the New Testament. It is now widely held that the New Testament contains many competing and mutually inconsistent interpretations of Jesus, that harmonization is impossible, and that accordingly no one orthodox biblical Christology is normative for all believers.

Once again (in my opinion), some of this is right and some wrong. Surely there *are* different christological emphases in various New Testament texts, and facile harmonization is to be avoided because it can cause us to miss the richness and variety of Christology in the New Testament. We need to respect the differences among the portraits and interpretations of Jesus. But I believe that the various interpretations are mutually consistent, are best seen as related insights that developed about Jesus among different persons and communities, and are best expressed in terms of the classical doctrine of the incarnation. It is, I think, a telling fact that many theologians from the second century (e.g., Ignatius) onward, most of whom were presumably not obtuse, were sufficiently impressed by the unity of the various New Testament pictures of Jesus to claim strongly that they can be synthesized in the notion of incarnation.

Furthermore, it seems to me evident that what might be called a "New Testament picture of Jesus" does exist. Despite differences of emphasis, all the New Testament texts seem to me to agree on various crucial points about Jesus. As William Wainwright has recently convincingly argued, the Gospels agree: (a) that Jesus is uniquely related to God; (b) that Jesus is the unique revealer of God; (c) that Jesus is Savior; (d) that Jesus has certain personal characteristics (e.g., strength of purpose, compassion, obedience to God); (e) that Jesus is teacher; and (f) that Jesus is identical with the risen Christ.[5]

(3) A third reason for my disquiet about some of the conclusions of contemporary New Testament scholarship concerns the life of Jesus. A rough and fuzzy but nevertheless real consensus about the life of Jesus seems to emerge among the more radical New Testament scholars. Here are the main facts many of them would claim we can know about Jesus: He was a Palestinian Jew from Nazareth who became a public figure in first-century Palestine, through a ministry of preaching, teaching, and healing; under the influence of Jewish apocalyptic thinking he preached the kingdom of God and came into conflict with leading Jewish groups such as the Pharisees and Sadducees; though ministering mainly in Galilee, he eventually came to Jerusalem, where he was arrested, tried, and crucified; some time later his disciples began preaching that he was alive and had been raised from the dead.

My difficulty is not in accepting that these are facts; I am quite prepared to do so. My difficulty is in seeing how anybody can claim that this is *all* (or almost all) we can know about Jesus. I have never been able to understand how these minimum facts are sufficient to explain the existence of the Christian church and the traditions about Jesus that we find in the New Testament and in the early church. Why, for example, would anyone hold that the relatively innocuous figure described here was God incarnate? Surely scholars are rationally obligated to posit a "life of Jesus" that would go at least some way toward explaining why the church so quickly arrived at notions such as sinlessness, preexistence, divine Sonship, and unity with God. Surely more needs to be said about Jesus than what is said in the consensus described earlier.

(4) A fourth reason for my disquiet about the more radical conclusions of contemporary New Testament scholarship follows immediately from the third. It concerns the intense speculation about the sources of and influences on New Testament Christology. Many scholars seem strongly committed to the assumption that Jesus was an entirely human figure and that notions such as preexistence and divine Sonship were arrived at years later through a long and complicated quasi-evolutionary process primarily involving embellishments in the

tradition due to the influence of other cultures and religions. A mere Jewish prophetic teacher who was deeply committed to God eventually became a preexistent being, ontologically one with God.

The *minimum* point to be made here is that those who argue for some such scenario have yet to make a compelling case. Despite the best efforts of certain scholars to find pre-Christian parallels to and influences on the classical doctrine (and some such efforts surely merit high marks for imaginativeness), no assured parallels and influences have been found. Even if parallels were located, the assumption of extensive pagan syncretistic influence on pre-Pauline Christology seems to me implausible in the extreme.

The *stronger* point, however, is that nowhere in the New Testament or in any of the sources or layers of tradition that supposedly antedate and influence it has any scholar discovered a purely human Jesus. Scholars such as C. F. D. Moule, Martin Hengel, and others have convincingly argued that even the most elevated christological notions are very old indeed. Hengel, for example, argued that the title "Son of God" was applied to Jesus between A.D. 30 and 50.[6] Moule argued that some of the "highest" Christology in the New Testament is present, either explicitly or by implication, in the Pauline epistles, the earliest datable documents in the New Testament.[7]

(5) A fifth reason for my disquiet concerns the frequently made claim that the early Christians were quite blasé about the facts of Jesus' life; what they were interested in was not history but proclaiming the *kerygma*; the only facts about Jesus that were preserved were those that furthered the evangelistic, liturgical, or apologetic ends of the church. But this assumption seems to me both a priori improbable and irreconcilable with the evidence. It is a priori improbable because the people who believed in Jesus, or were being encouraged to believe in Jesus, would naturally have been quite curious about what he said and did. It is irreconcilable with the obvious and intense interest the early church had in writing gospels, especially in writing detailed Passion narratives. The four Gospels record all manner of items about Jesus that seem, as far as I can tell, either unrelated to or even at cross-purposes with the needs of the church in the period A.D. 50–90.

For these five reasons (and others), I do not share the deep skepticism that many New Testament scholars today exhibit toward the Gospels. I accept as accurate the basic New Testament picture of Jesus; the documents are faith-statements, to be sure, but reliable nonetheless. My method, then, both in this essay and elsewhere, is to trust the Gospels as reliable witnesses to Jesus except in instances in which there is compelling reason not to do so.

V

Why would God choose to become incarnate in human flesh? What was the purpose of the incarnation? My own view is that there were three main purposes. First, the incarnation was designed definitively to show us what God is like, especially that God is loving. Second, the incarnation was designed to make it possible for us to come to know God; apart from Jesus Christ, I claim, people can have only a hazy knowledge of God. Third, the incarnation was designed to defeat all the forces in the world that are God's enemies—forces such as sin, death, suffering, and despair. (I do not claim it would have been impossible for God to have accomplished these ends in any other way than through incarnation. I do claim that incarnation is the route God chose in order to accomplish them.)

"God became a man"—that is the doctrine. If so, the incarnation means first that Jesus Christ is a *person*, a real living human person. Jesus Christ is not an idea, an ideal, an emanation from God, a divine influence, a principle, a lifestyle, or an ethical system. These notions are ruled out because what God became was a man ("and the word became flesh and dwelt among us").

If God became *a man*, then we have here the decisive ruling out of all forms of Docetism. Jesus Christ was a human being. He had a human body; he got hungry and thirsty and tired (John 4:6); he was tempted (Matt. 4:1–11; Heb. 4:15); he wept when a friend died (John 11:35); he was not omniscient, expressing at one time ignorance of who had touched his garment (Mark 5:30) and at another time of the date of the parousia (Mark 13:32); lastly, he died (Mark 15:36).

But if it is *God* who became a man, then we also have here the decisive ruling out of all Arianism. Jesus was a man, but not a mere man, not a man *simpliciter*. He was a man who was also God. (Arius himself would have denied that Jesus was merely human; nevertheless, by the term *Arianism* I mean views that make Jesus merely, or entirely, human.) But why would anybody want to claim such a bizarre thing as this? Why would anybody want to say Jesus was God incarnate? As a general answer to these questions, Moule said: "the impact made by Jesus on his own and the next generation was such as precludes an estimate of him as no more than a man."[8] I agree with this sentiment and wish now to explore what characteristics of Jesus might have led his contemporaries and near-contemporaries to such an assessment.

I will cite four reasons that I believe convinced many such people that he was the divine Son of God.[9] Accepting the Gospel accounts, as I nearly always do, I find them convincing as well. Doubtless, none is a strict proof, but all seem to me strong indications. First, and perhaps foremost, Jesus seemed to assume for himself the divine prerogative of forgiving sins (see Mark 2:5, 10; Luke 7:48). All of us as moral agents own the prerogative to forgive sins *that have been committed against us*, but only God (or God incarnate) can *forgive sins*.

Second, the intimate, almost blasphemous way Jesus addressed God (often translated *"Abba!* Father!"—something perhaps analogous to our English expression "Daddy") indicates at least a uniquely close relationship to God. I suspect the amazement caused by this novel form of address was the reason the church remembered and recorded it.

Third, Jesus spoke "with authority," not citing sources or precedents or famous sages. He spoke, not as if he were speaking *on behalf of God* (he did not say "Thus saith the Lord"), but as if he were God, delivering the truth to human beings. As J. A. T. Robinson said, "This is epitomised in his characteristic and distinctive form of address, 'Amen, I say to you'. . . . While a pious Jew concluded his prayer with an 'Amen', . . . Jesus prefaces his words with an 'Amen', thus identifying God with what he would say."[10] I think it highly significant that Jesus assumed for himself the authority to reinterpret and even overrule the Old Testament law (see Matt. 5:21–48; Mark 2:23–28), again something no mere human being could have done.

Fourth, Jesus claimed to be divine, and his earliest interpreters accepted that claim. I recognize that it is a commonplace of contemporary New Testament scholarship that the historical Jesus (as opposed to the Jesus of the Gospels) said remarkably little about himself—what he spoke about (so it is said) was not himself but God. Apart from an a priori assumption that Jesus simply *could not* have said such things, I see no rational way of ruling out as inauthentic Jesus' claim to be "the Christ, the Son of the Blessed" (Mark 14:61–62), which the high priest took to be blasphemy. Notice also this statement from Matthew's Gospel: "All things have been delivered to me by my Father; and no one knows the Son except the Father, and no one knows the Father except the Son and anyone to whom the Son chooses to reveal him" (Matt. 11:27; see also Luke 10:22). "He who has seen me has seen the Father," said Jesus to Philip in John's Gospel (14:9), the sort of statement that twice earlier in this Gospel had led to charges of blasphemy (5:18; 10:30–36). Again, apart from an ideology that says that no such strong Johannine statements can be authentic, I see no good reason to deny they were said by Jesus. Notice also such typical Pauline affirmations of Jesus' divine Sonship and incarnation as Romans 1:3–4; 8:3; Galatians 4:4; 1 Thessalonians 1:10.

Does the New Testament actually teach that Jesus was God incarnate? Frances Young and Don Cupitt have said no.[11] They have admitted that it teaches Jesus' divine Sonship, preexistence, nearness to God, mission from God, and eschatological return as judge; Jesus is God's chosen agent, a transcendent human being—but not God incarnate. Surely these two scholars are being contentious. Where in the New Testament do we find the claim that Jesus is (merely) "a transcendent human being"? Although few people want to claim that Jesus went about saying "I am God" (and I surely do not claim he did so), there are places in the New Testament where Jesus' status as God incarnate is evidently being affirmed, e.g., John 1:1, 18; 20:28, 31; Philippians 2:6–7; Colossians 1:15–19; 2:9; 1 John 5:20. (Depending on how one solves the textual problem, Heb. 1:8 might be included; and depending on how one solves the grammatical problem, Titus 2:13 might be included.)

Furthermore, I argue that the best way for God's aims in the incarnation (already discussed) to be achieved would be for Jesus to be "fully divine and fully human." First, why should Jesus have been "fully human"? (1) Pure God in our midst would only dazzle and frighten us; we would not understand what God wanted to show us or say to us unless God were at least partially veiled, incognito. (2) God wanted to declare as fully as possible his love for us and solidarity with us; the incarnation means that our fate is intimately (rather than remotely) tied to God; because he was fully involved and immersed in human weakness, Jesus Christ can empathize with us and be our redeemer (Heb. 2:17–18; 5:2; 4:15). (3) God cannot die. Accordingly, Docetism in any form is unacceptable.

Second, why should Jesus have to be "fully divine"? (1) We human beings are incapable of saving ourselves. If we are to be reconciled to God, God must do the reconciling. (2) We human beings cannot defeat death. If death is to be overcome (along with God's other enemies), God must do the overcoming. (3) If Jesus were a mere human being, he would in the end amount to nothing more than a great religious hero or genius among all the others. There is in my opinion no compelling reason to believe or follow one guru rather than another apart from purely subjective ones ("My guru speaks to me; your guru leaves me cold"). Some gurus of course speak the truth, but even they teach truth that is not intimately connected to their person or personal authority. Even the opponents of incarnation recognize that if Jesus is God incarnate there is a nongainsayable finality about him and his path to God. Accordingly, Arianism in any form is unacceptable.

VI

There is no doubt that the classical doctrine is puzzling, mysterious, paradoxical. Its defenders admit as much. But is the doctrine also contradictory or incoherent? Let us define an incoherent statement as one that either does not make sense ("the green running huge beneath a never") or that for logical reasons cannot possibly be true ("Jones is simultaneously both taller and shorter than Smith"). Critics of the classical doctrine have frequently claimed that it is incoherent. The latest of them is John Hick. In *The Myth of God Incarnate* he said that it has no clear content and thus no nonmetaphorical meaning. The doctrine "remains a form of words without assignable meaning. For to say, without explanation, that the historical Jesus of Nazareth was also God is as devoid of meaning as to say that this circle drawn with a pencil on paper is also a square."[12]

As it is stated, Hick's criticism is remarkably crude. For one thing, Christian theologians typically do offer an explanation when they set out the doctrine. (I see myself as providing such an explanation of the classical doctrine in this essay.) For another, Hick seems to assume that we know enough about the properties of divinity and humanity to see that so far as compossibility is concerned, they are on a logical par with squareness and circularity, and that surely can be doubted. Nevertheless, though I disagree with it, I am inclined to think that wisdom can be found in the neighborhood of Hick's objection. Let me try to state a more nuanced version of it.

First, some definitions. Let us say that an *accidental property of X* is an attribute that X has but can fail to have and still be X (e.g., right-handedness, for me). Let us say that an *essential property of X* is an attribute that X has and cannot fail to have and still be X (e.g., three-sidedness for a triangle). Let us say that a *common property of a kind K* is an attribute that all members of K have (e.g., for humans, never having lived on Mars). And let us say that the *nature of K* is all the common properties of members of K that are essential properties of those members of K (e.g., for a circle, being a closed geometrical figure and having all points equidistant from the center).

Now let us list some properties of God and human beings:

God	Human Beings
1. Being necessary	1′ Being contingent
2. Living forever	2′ Living only for a finite time
3. Being omnipotent	3′ Being non-omnipotent
4. Being omniscient	4′ Being non-omniscient
5. Being incorporeal	5′ Being corporeal

Now I am in a position to restate Hick's objection in a slightly more sophisticated form. If properties 1–5 are essential to God and (in part) make up the divine nature; and if properties 1′–5′ are essential to all human beings and (in part) make up human nature; and if the classical doctrine (which includes the "truly divine and truly human" clause) says that Jesus Christ must simultaneously have all the members of both sets of properties; and if it is logically impossible for any being simultaneously to have all the members of both sets of properties (i.e., if you have the 1–5 properties, you can't have the 1'–5' properties and vice versa); then the classical doctrine is incoherent.

Naturally the obvious questions are these. How do we go about deciding what properties of human beings are essential to them (and thus help constitute human nature)? How do we go about deciding what divine properties are essential to God (and thus help constitute the divine nature)? I am certainly prepared to grant that 1'–5' are properties of human beings; with the possible exception of 2', that much seems obvious. I am also prepared to grant that 1–5 are divine properties (as—so I believe—Christianity teaches). But why must I affirm that 1'–5' are *essential* properties of human beings and that 1–5 are *essential* properties of God?[13] Hick's argument (as reconstructed by me) depends on the assumption that these properties are essential properties, but why should we admit as much?

Of course many would claim that one who does not have the 1'–5' properties is not really human. Perhaps, in some sense, this is true. Many theologians in the tradition have held that God would not be the being God is or would not be divine if God did not have the 1–5 properties. Perhaps, in some sense, this too is true. It is also surely true that like all beings, both God and human beings must have at least *some* essential properties; e.g., both must have a nature. Note here that those who, like Hick, criticize the classical doctrine on the grounds that it is incoherent assume we know that certain properties are essential to God and that certain other incompossible properties are essential to human beings. But perhaps this is not true, or at least not true in the sense the criticism requires.

Again, the important question is this: how do we go about deciding which properties of a given being are essential and which are accidental? In cases involving ideal and mathematical objects (circles, sets, etc.) the decision is sometimes not difficult. For concrete entities such as human beings, it is rarely easy. As a Christian, I accept the classical doctrine: I strongly believe that Jesus Christ is "truly divine and truly human." Thus I am inclined to deny that the properties listed in the chart are *essential* properties of God and human beings, respectively (or at least essential in the sense Hick's criticism requires). In fact, Christian theology has always considered Jesus Christ both the preeminent revealer of God and the model human person. I claim that looking to the incarnation of Jesus Christ is one fruitful way (perhaps the best way) of finding out about divinity and humanity, of finding out which properties of God and human beings are essential and which are accidental. If Jesus Christ is "truly divine and truly human," then perhaps the properties listed are either not essential properties or else are compossible.

To carry further, with an acute suggestion from Tom Morris,[14] perhaps the 1'–5' properties are essential properties of *being merely human*. But this is not what Christians want to say about Jesus Christ in the incarnation. Perhaps the 1–5 properties are essential properties of *being divine simpliciter* (i.e., being divine without also being human). Nor is this what Christians want to say about Jesus Christ in the incarnation. They want to say he was *truly human* but not *merely human, truly divine* but not *divine simpliciter.*

What would have to happen in order for God to remain divine and to become a man? Naturally, a complete answer to that question is beyond my knowledge. But *one* of the things that would surely have to happen would be that God would have to give up whatever divine properties (accidental ones of course; the essential ones cannot be given up if God is to remain God) are inconsistent with being human. It would also entail God's not assuming whatever accidental human properties are inconsistent with being divine. The whole picture depends on there not being any essential divine properties that a human being cannot have and on there not being any essential human properties that God cannot have.

One christological theory in the history of theology says something much like this, and it is called kenosis. The theory was devised in the nineteenth century (though its roots go back much further than that) and was skillfully defended by such theologians as Thomasius, Dorner, Gore, and Weston.[15] It was also roundly criticized,[16] and although some of the criticisms of early versions of the theory are surely apt, kenosis seems to be making a twentieth-century comeback among a small but able group of theologians. The name and the essence of the theory derive from the great christological hymn of Philippians 2:6–11, where Paul says of Jesus Christ: "who, though he was in the form of God, did not count equality with God a thing to be grasped, but emptied himself [the Greek term Paul uses here is a derivative of the word *kenosis*], taking the form of a servant, being born in the likeness of men."

The idea, then, is that Jesus Christ was "in the form of God" as the Logos, or the Second Person of the Trinity and that at a certain point in human history he voluntarily and obediently "emptied himself" both of the divine glory and of certain divine properties; he then took on "human form," i.e., became a human being. This of course is not the only possible exegesis of Philippians 2, but it is at least one traditional interpretation. It would be a mistake to believe that a biblical basis for kenotic theory can be made only from Philippians 2. Note also John 17:4–5, where Jesus prays: "I glorified thee on earth, having accomplished the work which thou gavest me to do; and now, Father, glorify thou me in thy own presence with the glory which I had with thee before the world was made." What exactly is being said here? Possibly several things—first, that Jesus Christ once had divine glory and complete oneness with the Father (cf. John 17:11, 20–26); second, that at the time of his prayer (i.e., during his earthly ministry) he did not possess the fullness of divine glory; and third, that he looked forward to regaining it.

Martin Hengel[17] argued that the notion of kenosis is also to be found in the New Testament paradox of the humiliation of the Son of God in his scandalous death on a cross. The entire epistle to the Hebrews, he says, can be interpreted as a commentary on the Philippians hymn. And Lucien J. Richard, in a fascinating recent book, used kenosis as a key to unlock not just the incarnation but the nature of God and all of God's dealings with human beings. He too has seen kenosis in the concept of Jesus' finitude and powerlessness and in the fact that on the cross God withdrew from him ("My God, my God, why hast thou forsaken me?"). Jesus died the death of a criminal or slave, but this caused the centurion to make the statement that can be considered the climax of the Gospel of Mark: "This surely was the Son of God." "This extremity of emptiness" experienced by Jesus, Richard said, "enabled him to become the vessel of God's fullness."[18] Kenosis makes sense, Richard said, only if it is rooted in the entire divine life; kenosis as self-emptying and self-giving love is a basic character of God (see 2 Cor. 12:9) and is the essential way God relates to human beings.

Can kenosis be used as an explanation (in Hick's sense) of the incarnation? I believe so. Of course we cannot use kenosis (or any other theory) to remove the mystery of the classical doctrine. As Brian Hebblethwaite said, incarnation is a baffling act of a being whose essence we will never fully understand; it is highly unlikely, therefore, that we will ever completely grasp the incarnation.[19] Nevertheless, a kenotic explanation of the incarnation might say something like this: in the incarnation Jesus Christ "emptied himself" by giving up those divine properties that are inconsistent with being truly human while retaining sufficient divine properties to remain truly divine; he gave up those common human properties that are inconsistent with being truly divine but retained sufficient human properties to remain truly human. In the incarnation, then, Jesus Christ was not *a mere human* but truly human; he was not God *simpliciter* but truly God. Perhaps one cannot simultaneously be a mere human and truly divine; and perhaps one cannot be God *simpliciter* and truly human; but perhaps it is possible to be "truly divine and truly human."

What does it mean for God to "give up" a property? Well, as long as the property in question is accidental, I see no problem. We certainly give up properties constantly, e.g., the property of having long hair whenever we cut it, the property of being seated whenever we stand, the property of being undefeated whenever we lose. "God gives up property p" would roughly mean, then, that at a given point God has property p but at a later point, of God's own free choice, does not have property p. Suppose, for example, that God is in fact omniscient but that God could still be the being God is or could still be divine if God were slightly less than omniscient (if there were, say, some things God does not know). That is, suppose omniscience is a property of God, but an accidental one. Then "God gives up the property of omniscience" means that at one point God is omniscient and that at a later point God voluntarily becomes non-omniscient.

Residing in the neighborhood of kenosis are many theological aberrations from which kenosis must be distinguished. For example, kenosis is not a theory that so qualifies the divinity of Jesus Christ that it becomes part of his humanity. Nor does it make Jesus Christ a kind of demigod by enlarging his humanity with a few divine properties.[20] Nor does it imply that the Logos, shorn of many of its divine attributes in the incarnation, is temporarily excluded from the Trinity.[21] Nor is the theory correctly described as follows: "He who formerly was God changed Himself temporarily into man, or exchanged His divinity for humanity."[22] These are misunderstandings. Kenosis (at least as I defend it) affirms that the Logos, the Second Person of the Trinity, was fully present in Jesus Christ in the incarnation *as the Second Person of the Trinity*. To deny that is to deny that he was "fully divine."

More often than most christological theories, kenosis seems to be subjected to ridiculous and bizarre criticisms. (Several are found in Goulder, especially pp. 44–45, 54–55; they have been patiently and competently answered by Brian Hebblethwaite.) In a criticism often cited, William Temple[23] charged kenosis with having left the universe without any control from the creative Word of God during the period of Jesus' earthly life—since the Word was fully incarnate in the man Jesus during that period, who was guiding, controlling, sustaining, the universe? In reply, we might wonder what Temple himself did whenever he was going to have to be away from the office for a few days. I suspect he planned ahead, made arrangements, settled matters ahead of time. Does not Temple's criticism illicitly assume that God is unable to act in analogous ways? Of course I speak somewhat anthropomorphically here, but surely if God has foreknowledge and is omnipotent (as most Christians believe) this sort of thing would have been no big problem.

VII

Two objections to the version of kenosis I have been defending do, however, need to be considered in more detail. I will discuss them in turn.

The first objection might run as follows: If a given property (omniscience, for example) is an essential property of *God simpliciter*, it must also be an essential property of any being who is *truly divine*. That is, if omniscience is essential to God *simpliciter*; and if any being who is God *simpliciter* is divine; and if any being who is "truly divine" is divine; then omniscience is essential to any being who is "truly divine." But since kenosis affirms both that God incarnate was truly divine and that God incarnate was not omniscient, it follows that kenosis is incoherent.

Of course the defender of kenosis need only reply that the argument is invalid. Why must a being who is "truly God," i.e., who can truthfully be described as divine, have all the essential properties of a being who is God *simpliciter*, i.e., who is "truly divine" without also being "truly human"? What is true is that if God incarnate is "truly God," then God incarnate must have all the properties that are essential to being divine (whatever precisely they are). But why must this being have all the same essential properties of any being who is God *simpliciter*?

Suppose there is a heavenly body that we can describe as "the morning star *simpliciter*"; i.e., suppose the heavenly body that we call the morning star is not in fact identical to any heavenly body that we describe in another way (e.g., "the evening star"). If so, I suppose that this heavenly body that we are calling the morning star *simpliciter* not only has the following property but has it essentially—*not being identical to the evening star*. But, as all of us know, the heavenly body that we call the morning star *is* in fact identical with the heavenly body that we call the evening star. So there is no such heavenly body as the morning star *simpliciter*. I argue, then, that in order truly to be the morning star, a heavenly body not only need not have the mentioned property essentially—it need not have it at all. The heavenly body that we call the morning star does *not* have the property of *not being identical to the evening star*, because the morning star is in fact identical with the heavenly body that we call the evening star.

Similarly, the believer in kenosis would argue that (trinitarian considerations aside) there simply never has existed and never will exist a being that we ought to call *God simpliciter*, i.e., a being who is God without also being at some time or another incarnate in a man. God does exist, of course, a being who can truthfully be described as divine, and this being is the only divine being that has ever existed or will exist. And this one unique divine being is a being who is also at one time or another incarnate in a man. What knowledge we have of God, then, is not knowledge of God *simpliciter*, for such a being does not exist and cannot be known. The knowledge of God that we have is knowledge of a being who is eternally truly divine and at some time or another both truly divine and truly human. The objection to kenosis that we are considering, then, errs in taking supposed properties of God *simpliciter* and then asking whether those properties can be had by God incarnate.

The second objection to kenosis can be stated as follows: Surely some properties can be "given up," e.g., properties such as having long hair, being seated, being undefeated; and possibly some properties (those involving the exercise or nonexercise of some ability) can be given up, e.g., omniscience, omnipotence; but some properties quite apparently cannot be given up. These are what we might call time-indexed properties or properties one has because of events that occurred in the past, e.g., properties such as *not having been created, having existed in the sixteenth century, being the Creator of the heavens and the earth.* Without arguing that these properties are essential to any being who has them (they may or may not be), the point is that they are "ungiveupable," i.e., any being who has them at one temporal point has them at all other or at least subsequent temporal points. Thus kenosis, which says that Jesus Christ is truly human and truly divine, must be an incoherent theory because it makes no sense to say, for example, that Jesus of Nazareth gave up the property of *having been created* in order to be truly divine or that the Logos gave up the property of *not having been created* in order to be truly human. If no being can simultaneously have both these properties; and if these properties are properties of human beings and of God, respectively; and if both these properties are "ungiveupable" in the sense mentioned; then the notion of incarnation is incoherent.

In reply to this objection, the defender of kenosis will want to refer to a traditional way of making christological affirmations, that Jesus Christ has some properties *as* God and some *as* a human being. In fact, the Chalcedonic creed itself seems to imply something of the sort: "of one substance with the Father *as regards his Godhead,* and at the same of one substance with us *as regards his manhood"* (italics mine). This way of making christological affirmations has been explored in a preliminary way by Peter Geach,[24] who calls them reduplicative propositions. He distinguished what we ought to say that God *simpliciter* can do from what we ought to say that God *as God* or God *as a human being* can do. In sentences such as "A as P is Q," Geach says, we are not to think of Q as a predicate attached to the complex subject "A as P"—rather, we ought to read the sentence as "A is, as P, Q." Thus we can sensibly say things such as "Jesus Christ is, as God, unable to die" and "Jesus Christ is, as a human being, able to die" without nonsense.

There are dangers here, of course: if the notion is pushed too far, Christ might seem divided into two persons, one of which was and the other of which was not able to die. To divide Christ would be to fall prey to the Nestorian heresy, condemned at the Synod of Ephesus in A.D. 431. And if the unity of Christ's person is stressed, the following objection might arise: "Well then, is the one person Jesus Christ able to die or not? Surely it must be one or the other. Let's have your answer. If he is able to die, he is not divine; if he is unable to die, he is not human."

Suppose a certain person named Malan is both mayor of the town and athletic director at the local college. (Similar to an example given by Geach, this one describes an actual person known to me.) Malan does have certain rights and responsibilities as mayor (e.g., signing into law resolutions passed by the city council) and certain rights and responsibilities as athletic director (e.g., signing checks paid out of the athletic department budget). Someone might then ask: "Well then, is this one person Malan able to sign bills into law or not?" In one sense the answer is yes—the one person Malan does have that ability. But in another sense, the question is ill-formed. It ought to ask: "Does Malan, as mayor, have that ability?" Then of course the answer is yes (just as the answer to "Does Malan, as athletic director, have that ability?" is no). Similarly, the objection raised at the conclusion of the last paragraph is ill-formed. In one sense (a sense that will lead to paradox), the one person Jesus Christ both was and was not able to die. Better, however, to say: he was, as human, able to die; he was not, as divine, able to die.

The analogy between my Malan example and the incarnation is not exact, of course. The main difference is this: there seems no great logical or metaphysical difficulty in an athletic director's also serving as mayor, but there is a very great logical or metaphysical difficulty in God's becoming a man. Thus, sentences such as "The athletic director of the college signs bills into law in this town" seem, though puzzling, logically possible. But sentences such as "The Second Person of the Trinity is able to die" seem both puzzling and logically impossible. Nevertheless, I will stand by the claim that when the sentence is well-formed ("The Second Person of the Trinity is, as a man, able to die") it is true.

The theory of kenosis, then (which, in my opinion, is not the only promising way of doing orthodox Christology), helps us grope toward an explanation of the incarnation. It helps provide a sense in which we can legitimately (although admittedly somewhat paradoxically) say: "Jesus Christ is truly divine." It helps provide a sense in which we can legitimately (although admittedly somewhat paradoxically) say: "Jesus Christ is truly human." I have been trying to provide such senses. Looking at Jesus, Christians do indeed want to say about him, "he is divine" and "he is human."

VIII

In this concluding section I wish to consider briefly three implications of the Christology I have outlined.

(1) I promised earlier to mention the deepest reservation I have about all forms of minimal Christology. Minimal Christology would be a perfectly acceptable theological option, in my opinion, if Christianity were at heart an

ethical system and if the Pelagian notion were true—that we can save ourselves by hard spiritual effort. But Christianity is not primarily an ethical system—it *involves* an ethic, to be sure. But at heart it is a set of beliefs and deeds that form our feeble response to a surprising and quite undeserved act of infinite love that God has performed on our behalf.

We are not able to save ourselves, no matter how hard we try. The Protestant Reformers were quite correct on that point. We are in *bondage*, and the Jesus of minimal Christology is anything but the (or even *a*) redeemer from bondage. Of course we do desperately need spiritual teachers these days, and we do desperately need supreme examples of openness to God—minimal Christology provides both. The truth is that we need far more than this—what we need is not a guru but a Savior. The classical doctrine of the incarnation, recognizing as it does that Christianity is a religion of *grace*, provides this. That is to me the deepest reason why it is to be preferred to all versions of minimal Christology.

(2) John Hick said: "If Christ was (literally rather than metaphorically) God incarnate, it would seem clear that the religion which he founded must be intended to supersede all other religions."[25] Here Hick is surely correct. If the classical doctrine is correct, then doubtless Jesus is, after all, "the way, and the truth, and the life" (John 14:6), and doubtless it is true that "there is salvation in no one else" (Acts 4:12). The incarnation is of cosmic rather than local significance, in my view; any human being who is reconciled to God is reconciled through Christ. One of the main objections global theologians have to absolutistic interpretations of Christianity is that these interpretations imply that non-Christians are "outside the sphere of salvation." That of course does not follow. The view that no non-Christian can be saved is not taught in the Bible; few Christians of even a conservative persuasion hold it; nor do I hold it.[26]

Christianity is a metaphysical and theological system, not a set of discrete gems of heavy spiritual wisdom from which we can pick and choose. (The same can be said, I suspect, about most of the other religions of the world.) So the emerging discipline known as global theology is, in my opinion, untoward. To attempt a syncretistic amalgamation of the "best insights" of various equally valid and valuable religious systems is ill-advised.

(3) In the New Testament a strong connection is made between Jesus' status as Son of God and his resurrection from the dead (see Rom. 1:3-4). We live in a world in which messiahs, gurus, and holy people proliferate. (In southern California, where we contributors to this book live, they seem to proliferate geometrically.) In such a world, how can we know whom to believe? Which messiah is the true Messiah? Paul's answer (through Luke) to the Athenian philosophers was that Jesus is the man whom God has

appointed and "of this he has given assurance to all men by raising him from the dead" (Acts 17:31). Many messiahs have commanding personalities. Many gurus are full of spiritual wisdom. Many holy people recommend noble lifestyles. But none of them has been resurrected from the dead.

Of course Jesus is not the only person to have been raised from the dead. Others (Lazarus, the daughter of Jairus) are mentioned in the Bible. Such stories appear in other religions too, and perhaps some of them are true. I am willing to believe that God performs miracles in other contexts than the Christian context. But these raisings were of an entirely different character than Jesus'. These people were restored to their former earthly life; they were *resuscitated*. Jesus was transformed into what Paul calls a glorified body. He was raised never to die again. He lives today. He was *resurrected*. In my opinion, Jesus is the only person in the history of the world ever to have been resurrected from the dead.[27]

If Jesus had not been raised, Christianity would not exist today. He would have ended up a fine teacher of religion and ethics—like Socrates or Gandhi, perhaps—but not the Savior of the world. I believe the resurrection was God's way of pointing at Jesus and saying: *He* is the one you are to believe. *He* is the Savior. *He* is Lord.[28] The resurrection of Jesus from the dead was a graphic way for God to repeat what the villagers of Sychar had said about him—"this is indeed the Savior of the world."[29]

Critiques

Critique by James M. Robinson

My first concern with this essay stems from the testimonial in the opening pages, which leads to the invidious distinction between maximal and minimal Christologies. Then Davis informs the reader that God is on the maximalist side of the argument: "I confess to a strong belief that the church was led to the classical doctrine by the Holy Spirit." In spite of the format of this book, which has been designed to produce fruitful dialogue and expedite progress in our mutual thinking, I am very discouraged about the possibility of real dialogue. I feel quite helpless to say anything that would really make a difference. Only if it were recognized that all our essays are merely human intellectual efforts, that all of us are equally near to or far from divine help, that dogma is (to quote Karl Barth) an eschatological concept rather than a fourth–fifth century achievement, would such an enterprise be more than an exercise in tolerance and politeness.

Because I am the biblical scholar on the panel, my concern is focused on the Bible. Davis recognizes that "rigorous and searching historical-critical scholarship" is "one of the facts of our age." He indicates that his readers "must first make their peace with the historical-critical study of the New Testament." Such study "is to be strongly encouraged." "Such methods are both helpful and necessary." This is in spite of the fact that Davis' conversion experience was "based upon what we might call a precritical reading of the four Gospels." Thus, again, Davis informs us that he has come out on the side of the angels.

But a disquieting note is immediately struck by his suspicions "of many of the more radical conclusions some historical-critical scholars have been reaching about the Gospels." "Contemporary biblical scholars seem to me to have gone overboard in the other direction" from the traditional emphasis on the unity of the Bible, even with "inquisitorial zeal." They have fallen into "deep skepticism." To this may be contrasted Hick's comment: "Again, Hans Küng accurately summarized contemporary research when he said that 'even more conservative exegetes conclude that Jesus himself did not assume any title implying messianic dignity: not "Messiah," nor "Son of David," nor "Son," nor "Son of God." ' " Surely it is a fact that the course of biblical scholarship in the twentieth century has been characterized by an increasing acceptance of the historical-critical method and its results by the more scholarly wing of evangelical and Roman Catholic scholarship. It is a distortion of the situation to describe anything to the left of Bible college exegesis as radical. Mainline biblical scholarship of our time, from Harvard to Claremont, is what Davis dismisses with his battery of pejorative terms.

In spite of their inquisitorial tactics, the radicals "have yet to make a compelling case. Despite the best efforts of certain scholars to find pre-Christian parallels . . . , no assured parallels and influences have been found. Even if parallels were located, the assumption of extensive pagan syncretistic influence on pre-Pauline Christology seems to me implausible in the extreme." Even if it is permissible to abstract away from the invidious language that tends to caricature critical scholarship into a position with which no scholar would want to identify ("extensive pagan syncretistic"), one may conclude that we are not here invited to reasoned argument that could hope to change a mind. "My method, then, both in this essay and else-where, is to trust the Gospels as reliable witnesses to Jesus except in instances in which there is compelling reason not to do so." "Accepting the Gospel accounts, as I nearly always do, I find them convincing as well." To be sure, Davis reassures us that he is on the side of the scholarly community: "I am not a proponent of the theory that the Bible is 'inerrant.' " But it is simply not possible to accept a method of scholarship and then pick and choose among the results of that method on the basis of a faith-commitment.

Such invidious caricature of the biblical scholarship of our time hardly reflects the commitment to love for which Jesus is so rightly famous. It actually sounds much more like "You shall love your neighbor and hate your enemy." But it is the Dead Sea Scrolls, not the New Testament, that contain a text entitled "The War of the Sons of Light against the Sons of Darkness." In the academic community Christian love shows itself first and foremost by the avoidance of caricature, invidiousness, and other such facile argumentation, or, put positively, Christian love is a real seeking to present empathetically and fairly the position with which one disagrees but with which one wishes to enter into fruitful dialogue. Only then can an academic community be a Christian community.

In concluding, I wish to read into the record a few methodological statements going back to the beginning of modern biblical scholarship, from the preface to the third edition of the commentary on the Gospel of John of 1840 by Friedrich Lücke, the pupil and friend of Schleiermacher:

> I have used industriously the newest exegetical works on the Gospel and been glad to learn from them. Also the most recent, sharper treatises about its genuineness and reliability I have worked through attentively and, as much as I was able, tested impartially. You will find that, though unshaken in my conviction, I have nonetheless been glad to acknowledge truth and right on the opposing side. In fact it in no way helps to hide from oneself and others weaknesses and deficiencies in the historical and exegetical grounds of faith, once they have become perceptible. Hidden, covered-over deficiencies are the most dangerous. Only what is real and true, only what is genuinely sound, stands the test of faith and of science. And so I have for the sake of truth given up much that seemed to me untenable, no matter how dear it had become to me . . . . The word of revelation is to me just as precious as to anyone who professes it. The more I understand it, the more it becomes my life's sole light. But in understanding it, where I have to learn from others, I seek the truth and receive it, when it makes sense to me, from anyone, unconcerned whether the person in whom I find it is a rationalist or a pietist or something else, my friend or my foe. This is my orthodoxy. It is not up to me to avenge, precisely because the word of revelation says: But you, why do you judge your brother? But I will continue now as I always have in free research, without all kinds of consciously taking sides and supporting a party, to give honor to the truth according to my best conviction, wherever I find it, and each time to express honestly my conviction according to the degree of its certainty.

My concern is that "encountering Jesus" not be blocked by the confines of evangelical theology. The irony is indeed that the outcome would be a deficient Christology: behind the proto-orthodox facade of the New Testament lies a remarkable person that all of us would do well to know much better.

Critique by Rebecca D. Pentz

Davis' kenotic defense of the classical doctrine of the incarnation is straightforward and surprisingly uncomplex. In the incarnation God adopts the properties essential to being human while retaining those properties that are essential to being God and giving up any accidental properties that are incompatible with being human. The crucial issue of course is whether the set of properties essential to being God and the set of properties essential to being human are compossible. Davis suggests that we have no good reason to assume that they are not and that in fact since Jesus is "the preeminent revealer of God and the model human person" we should look to Jesus to determine which properties are essential to Godhood and humanhood. I am sympathetic to this defense but somewhat dubious as to whether it can be worked out in detail.

My first question arises in regard to Davis' heavy use of a distinction he borrows from Tom Morris, the distinction between being "merely human" and being "truly or fully human." Morris claimed that being *fully human* is to have all the essential properties of humanhood and that being *merely human* is to be fully human *plus* having some limitation properties such as contingency. These limitation properties are essential to being merely human—all mere humans must have them—but they are not essential to being fully human. To count as fully human, Jesus did not need to have them. Morris' distinction is helpful in that it explains our intuition that contingency is an essential property of humanhood. Morris has admitted that contingency is a common property of all created, mere humans—all created humans are in fact contingent. But he argued correctly that this fact alone does not entail that contingency is an essential property of being fully human. First, a common property is not necessarily an essential property. To use Morris' example, spending some time on the surface of the earth is a common property but not an essential property of humans. An individual who is born, lives, and dies on a space station still counts as human. Second, even if some property is essential to being a mere created human, we cannot immediately infer that it is essential to being fully human. It is this second inference that does the work for Morris. He realized that our intuition that contingency is an essential property is strong, so he allowed that contingency is an essential property of being merely human. But his distinction between being merely and being fully human blocks the conclusion that contingency is an essential property of being fully human.

Davis adopts Morris' distinction and applies it to God. He suggests that God *simpliciter*, i.e., "a being who is God without also being at some time or another incarnate in a man," may be for example essentially omniscient and incorporeal, but that these properties are not essential to being truly God. I suppose that Davis uses this distinction to account for the traditional theological position that properties such as "being omniscient" and "being incorporeal" are in fact essential properties of God, just as Morris has used the merely human/fully human distinction to explain our intuition that being contingent is essential to being human. Davis' distinction, however, is not parallel to Morris'. Morris' distinction makes use of the fact that Jesus is not the only human, that there are created, mere humans as well. And it makes sense to say that these created, mere humans have different essential properties from a fully human Jesus. But there is no God *simpliciter*, according to Davis. And since no God *simpliciter* exists, Davis cannot say to the traditional theologians, "You were just thinking of God *simpliciter* with all of his essential properties," as Morris said to his objectors, "You were just thinking of mere humans with all of their essential properties." In short, all Davis' talk of God *simpliciter* does nothing to explain the traditional position that God is essentially omniscient, incorporeal, etc., a position that Davis would claim is a mistaken one. If it is not wrong, his kenotic Christology is in jeopardy; omniscience and incorporeality are incompossible with the limitations of a finite bodily human.

Second, I have a puzzlement related to my first question. I am puzzled by Davis' treatment of the first objection to kenosis, the objection that an essential property of God *simpliciter* must also be an essential property of a being who is truly divine. At first it sounds as if Davis is making Morris' move, namely, that two separate sets of properties are essential to being divine—those of God *simpliciter* and those of a being who is truly God—and that one need not have all the essential properties of the former to count as truly God. Jesus, who is truly God, need not have the essential properties of God *simpliciter*. But because in Davis' view there is no God *simpliciter* and thus there is only one set of properties essential for divinity, the only real issue seems to be whether or not omniscience, incorporeality, etc., are essential properties of God. Theologians who believe that God *simpliciter* exists think that those properties are essential; theologians such as Davis think that they are not.

It strikes me that the real force of this first objection comes when *God simpliciter* is used, not in the sense that Davis identifies in this essay, but in the sense Davis adopted in *Logic and the Nature of God*. In *Logic and the Nature of God* Davis told us that God *simpliciter* is God with all of the divine properties, including those that would dazzle and frighten us (p. 124). This usage is parallel to Morris'. There is a God *simpliciter*, i.e., God in all of his glory with all of his properties, as well as a being who is truly God but who lacks some of the essential properties of God *simpliciter*, i.e., Jesus. Or to use language closer to Morris', there is a being who is fully divine as well as a being who is merely divine, the latter having all of the properties essential to full divinity *plus* some glorifying properties. And, I take it, the glorifying properties are essential to mere divinity but not to full divinity. With this usage, however, I find it very difficult to answer Davis' first objection. How can we say that Jesus need not have all of the *essential* properties of God *simpliciter*, if Jesus and God *simpliciter* are one? Morris' distinction just does not seem to be adaptable to one God. In short, Davis' use of Morris' distinction puzzles me.

My third question is undoubtedly the most pressing one. If the traditional list of essential properties is incorrect, which properties are essential to being truly divine? Kenotic Christologies have often been criticized for jeopardizing the divinity of Jesus. Davis tries to safeguard Jesus' divinity by affirming that he retains the properties essential to divinity. But which properties are these?

Let me press this point a bit further. If one takes Augustine's list of the attributes of God (ch. 15 of *The Trinity*)—the negative attributes of eternity, immutability, ingenerability, incorruptibility, and incorporeality, the metaphysical attributes of omnipotence and omniscience, and the moral attributes of perfect goodness, perfect justice, and perfect mercy—and if one adopts Davis' methodological principle that we should look to Jesus to see which attributes are essential to God, one would think that the moral attributes might be the ones that could be essential to being divine and also compossible with being human. John Hick argues in his essay that the moral attributes are not compossible because no human being can be infinitely good, just, and merciful. I see no reason that "perfect goodness" must mean "infinite goodness." I would appreciate hearing Professor Davis' position on this issue.

In sum, I am quite interested in a kenotic Christology, but I am concerned about how much of the traditional doctrine of essentiality must be relinquished and about which attributes are in fact the essential ones. I am looking forward to Professor Davis' further thoughts on these matters.

Critique by John B. Cobb, Jr.

Much of this paper I have read with pleasure and a sense of warm agreement. I share Davis' rejection of what he calls minimal Christology. I share his affirmation of incarnation as central to Christian faith. I share his appreciation of Nicea and Chalcedon as basically faithful to the New Testament witness. I want to think christologically in continuity with them. I like also Davis' point that "kenosis as self-emptying and self-giving love . . . is the essential way God relates to human beings."

But I find much that is objectionable in Davis' explanation of incarnation. Indeed, it helps me to understand why so many contemporaries have rejected Nicea and Chalcedon. If Davis' account of incarnation were the required understanding of those affirmations of the church, I would agree that they must be rejected as mythological. They require an unacceptable worldview and have disturbing existential implications.

If I understand Davis correctly (I hope that I do not), he affirms that one Person of the Trinity surrendered some divine properties, including, I assume, omnipresence, and existed for some years only as the divine aspect of the divine-human Jesus. Davis answers the questions about the metaphysical functions of this divine Person by saying that he made advance preparations for the leave he took from heaven. I cannot harmonize this extraordinarily anthropomorphic way of thinking of the Logos with any classical or contemporary doctrine of the Trinity. The idea that the relations among the Persons are such that one can be separated from the others in this way is shocking to me. This whole imagery seems to fit better with Zeus' becoming a bull than with Christian thought about the incarnation.

I do not want to deny that some language in the Scriptures and the creeds can lead to this kind of speculation. But it is precisely this strain that supported Arianism. I fear that Davis' use of this label to refer to those who affirm that Jesus was a mere man has blinded him to the real heresy properly called Arianism. As Davis admits, Arius certainly did *not* affirm that Jesus was a mere man. Indeed, he denied the true humanity of Jesus. Jesus was for Arius a superhuman creature, the first and greatest of all creatures, who took on human form. That such a creature would cease to be in heaven and for a time exist only in human form on earth could make sense in the thought world of the time and is not necessarily unintelligible today. The kenotic hymn was one scriptural source of this heresy. Any language that speaks of "the preexistence of Jesus Christ" as if what was preexistent were somehow to be distinguished from God or already included Jesus' creatureliness, moves us conceptually in an Arian direction (it in fact supported the widespread acceptance of Arianism in the early church). The effort to harmonize all scriptural Christology led in the early church, even among the opponents of Arianism, to applying the rhetoric about a preexistent superhuman creature to the Logos, which became flesh, and the same harmonizing has the same consequences in Davis. However, the early church, after struggling for a century to overcome Arianism, was more careful than Davis in its formulations. I am quite sure that the bishops assembled at Chalcedon would have anathematized much of Davis' proposal.

It remains true, as Davis says, that the creed is much clearer about what is to be rejected than about the positive conceptual explanation of the incarnation. It may be that many of the bishops would also have anathematized Baillie's explanation, which I much prefer to that by Davis. However, I think the Antiochene wing, at least, would have found it quite congenial. In Baillie's account it is clear that God is truly, constitutively present in Jesus. The God who is present has all the characteristics that God everlastingly has. But for true God to be truly present does not mean that every characteristic of God characterizes the one in whom God is present. Everyone agrees to this when we speak of the presence of the Holy Spirit in our lives or of the working of grace within us. Baillie showed that we can understand the Chalcedonian formula in continuity with this. Chalcedon reaffirmed the Nicene point against Arius that the divine that is truly constitutive of Jesus' person is truly God—not a preexistent divine being distinct from God or separable from God. Baillie affirmed this too. Also, the human that is constitutive of Jesus is truly human, indeed, rendered fully human by the constitutive presence of God. Jesus is one person constituted by the union of the divine and the human.

In one respect Davis is probably closer to the Chalcedonian bishops than I am. Like him, most of them probably thought that what had happened in the incarnation in Jesus was metaphysically different from what happened elsewhere. They probably thought that Christianity supersedes all other ways of salvation. But these were not the issues before the council. The issue was whether Jesus had a fully human nature. And the bishops said he did. We are not bound by their formulation to particular metaphysical views. I believe we are encouraged to emphasize the radical uniqueness of Jesus—of his mission, his way, the work in which God was present in him—but that need not involve a metaphysical difference. The effort to explain the difference as metaphysical has produced many of the christological heresies and led finally to the, to me, highly offensive doctrine of the impersonal humanity of Jesus. To revere Jesus as the incarnation of God and as Savior of the world need not entail this. Nor need it entail a failure to learn from all the other great traditions of the world the universal truths that they have apprehended in their diverse histories.

Critique by John Hick

Traditional Christology, with its Christ, who is the one and only Lord and Savior available for all human beings, is under criticism from several directions. It is therefore instructive to see what an able philosophical mind, with conservative theological convictions, can do to reestablish it.

In the limited space available, I shall concentrate upon the second and more philosophical section of Stephen Davis' essay. His defense of the Chalcedonian Christology is reminiscent in its structure of that of a defense lawyer who argues (a) that his client did not commit the act of which he is accused and (b) that if he did commit it he is still not guilty because he was legally justified in doing so. Here the charge is that the idea that Jesus was both God and a man is incoherent—like the idea that a particular circle is also a square. In response Davis argues (a) that it is possible that no incompatible divine and human attributes are involved in the incarnation and, later, (b) that even though some incompatible divine and human attributes are involved they belong respectively to "Jesus as God" and "Jesus as man" and so do not conflict with one another. Thus in the end the defense depends upon the second plea—which, I believe, proves to be unsustainable.

But let us first see how Davis is led onto this difficult ground. He notes that some divine and human characteristics are manifestly incompatible; for instance, God cannot die, although a human being can.

He then invokes the distinction between essential and accidental properties. The essential properties (or attributes) of X are the ones that X cannot cease to have without ceasing to be X; the accidental ones are those that X can cease to have while still being X. According to Davis, God has both essential and accidental properties. The question then is whether, for example, the inability to die is an essential or only an accidental divine attribute. Davis claims that we do not know whether any divine attribute (including the inability to die) is essential. Accordingly we cannot look at Jesus, observe that he did not have that attribute, and conclude that he was not God incarnate. Nor can we conclude, more radically, that some essential divine attributes are such that it is impossible for them to characterize a historical human being.

Let us now apply this essential-accidental distinction to some of the attributes of God as defined in the central Christian tradition: the "moral" attributes of being unlimitedly good and unlimitedly loving, and the "metaphysical" attributes of being uncreated and of being the creator *ex nihilo* of everything that exists other than God.

Note that what is distinctively divine about the moral attributes is their infinity or unlimitedness. Human beings can be good and loving, but only God is infinitely so. Are these, then, *essential* divine attributes? If so, God cannot set them aside in becoming a man, and the man whom God becomes must have these infinite qualities. But is it coherent to say that Jesus of Nazareth was *infinitely* good and *infinitely* loving? Surely the characteristics of any finite human individual *must* be finite. God as the human Jesus of Nazareth would thus only be able to incarnate as much of the divine goodness and love—and likewise, wisdom, mercy, justice, knowledge—as could be expressed in the thirty or so years of a human life lived within a particular earthly setting. But then, rather than describe such a historical figure as God incarnate, would it not be more natural to describe him as a human being who was, within the particular circumstances of his time and place, responsive and obedient to God, doing God's will, open to the inspiration of God's spirit—perhaps even, as a judgment of faith going beyond the historical evidence, *totally* responsive, obedient, inspired, as Baillie and Lampe proposed?

If, on the other hand, infinite goodness and love are *accidental* properties of God, then God in becoming man can become finitely good and loving—as, surely, Jesus must have been. But the cost here is that God's goodness and love are now insecure because they are merely accidental properties. Perhaps God has been infinitely good and loving for the past few thousand years but was not so before that and may again not be so in the future. This is a religiously disturbing thought.

As for metaphysical attributes, it is (as Davis acknowledges) impossible that God, having the property of being uncreated, should at some point in time cease to have it. It is likewise impossible that if God has the property of being the creater *ex nihilo* of everything other than oneself, God should discard that property. These divine attributes are not capable of being set aside in a divine *kenosis*. This is the burden of the second objection that Davis considers to the kenotic theory: such properties are, as he says, "ungiveupable." They must become incarnate in Jesus if Jesus is God incarnate. On the other hand, they are manifestly not compatible with being a created human being.

In response to this objection, Davis appeals to the idea that Jesus as God had certain properties (such as being the uncreated creator and being unable to die) and that Jesus as man had certain incompatible properties (such as being created and being able to die). So Jesus as God was uncreated, the Creator of all, immortal, infinitely good and loving; as man he was created, not the Creator of all, mortal, and only finitely good and loving.

Davis is clearly conscious of the dangers that beset this move. He says cautiously that "if the notion is pushed too far, Christ might seem divided into two persons, one of which was and the other of which was not able to die." And he seeks to avoid this very evident peril by distinguishing Jesus *as* God and Jesus *as* a human being, the distinction being analogous to that between Malan *as* mayor of the town and Malan *as* athletic director of the local school. In one role Malan has the property of, for example, being authorized to sign checks on the athletic department account, which in his other role it would be illegal for him to do. But the incompatible attributes of being able and being unable to sign these checks belong to different roles and thus do not conflict with each other. Likewise, in his role as God, Jesus is immortal, Creator of all, infinitely loving; in his other role as a human being, he is a mortal creature, finite in love.

I suggest that this analogy cannot save from unacceptable implications the theory that Jesus had two complete natures exhibiting incompatible attributes. In the case of Malan we have two social roles performed at different times by the same personal unity of consciousness, memory, and will: Malan functioning as athletic director in the afternoon can of course remember what he has done as mayor in the morning. But does Davis really want to apply this model to Jesus? It would entail that while acting as a human being Jesus could remember what he did as God when he created the heavens and the earth and when he did all the things recorded of him in the Old Testament. But could such a being intelligibly be described as "truly human"?

It is the incompatible attributes—such as being Creator of all and not being Creator of all, being infinitely loving and not being infinitely loving—that keep the two natures apart. The same personal unity of consciousness, memory, and will cannot both remember and not remember being the Creator of everything else that exists and cannot both be and not be infinitely loving. We therefore have to press the question whether Jesus had one consciousness or two. If one, was this a divine consciousness (consciously omniscient, omnipotent) or a human consciousness (with a merely human knowledge, power, and love; sometimes tired, tempted, misinformed)? If Jesus had a divine consciousness, can we coherently say that a person who conversed with him was conversing with an authentically human being? Or, if Jesus had a human consciousness, can we coherently say that one who conversed with him was conversing with God? On the other hand, if Jesus had two consciousnesses, did these alternate, so that sometimes those around him were conversing with a human being and sometimes with God? And is someone who is only sometimes human "truly human"?

It seems to me that in defending the Chalcedonian Christology Davis has set himself an impossible task and that the great skill and resourcefulness that he has devoted to it only emphasize how impossible the task is.

Davis' Response to Critiques

I enjoyed reading the criticisms of my colleagues and learned from what they had to say. What I have tried to present in my essay is but one of several promising ways of understanding, explaining, or defending orthodox Christology. (David Brown, in his excellent recent book *The Divine Trinity*, explored in detail both kenosis and more traditional approaches, and argued that both can be coherent.) So in response to remarks made by Cobb and Hick, I do not suppose that my own view is the required Christology for those who want to be orthodox. Would the fathers at Chalcedon have liked my proposals? Cobb thinks not, and perhaps he is right. Who can say? The important questions, in my opinion, are (1) is what I say consistent with what they say? and (2) have I found a way of defending the most important truths they were struggling to preserve? I like to think the answer to both questions is yes.

Since Robinson's critique has an entirely different character from the other three, let me begin with it. It is difficult to know what to say or where to begin, since Robinson attributes to me attitudes I am not aware of having. Where did he find *hatred* in my essay? Was my language really *invidious*? Where did he get the impression I reject all biblical scholarship to the left of what is practiced in Bible colleges? As a matter of fact, I am comfortable at very many points with much of contemporary biblical scholarship; as I made clear, its more radical conclusions—especially those that are relevant to Christology—are what I want to deny. At any rate, I want to reject any attempt to discredit evangelicals as unscholarly obscurantists and as full of hatred for theological liberals. That is a caricature at least as exaggerated as the one of which Robinson has accused me.

Let me now say something in response to three of the specific points Robinson makes.

(1) He seems to think I am too dogmatic in my christological beliefs and too ready to condemn those who disagree. He is offended by what he sees as my subtle attempts to imply that God is on my side of the debate, as if my essay were something more than a mere human intellectual effort. Let me then own that my essay was not divinely inspired and is probably full of errors (many of which have surely been caught by my colleagues in this volume). It is just that I naturally think the views I have put forward are correct (do the other contributors to this volume not have similar opinions about their own views?). I do not (at least I hope I do not) hold to my views *no matter what*. I hope I would be prepared to change my mind if a convincing case were made that I should do so.

All the contributors to this book are members of two communities—the community of scholars and the community of believers. In most instances the values of the two groups need not conflict. In our own ways, all of us are members in good standing (so to speak) of both groups. At certain points, however, the values of the two groups can stand in tension. In the university the only accepted authority is human reason, all beliefs are tentative, and scholars hope by their joint efforts to shed light on intellectual (in this case, theological) problems. In the believing community (as I understand it, at least) people accept other authorities besides human reason, and they are committed to a gospel that they hold to have been revealed rather than discovered. I would like to suggest (with the deepest respect for Jim Robinson and with no offense intended) one truly foundational difference between his methodology and mine in this book. Robinson seems to me to lay greater stress on the first set of values; I lay greater stress on the second. In fact, I want to be quite explicit about this: if I ever had to choose between membership in one community or the other, it would take me about three seconds to opt for the community of believers.

(2) The criticism from Robinson to which I feel most open is that of having caricatured, rather than depicted accurately, contemporary biblical scholarship. I am not quite ready to plead guilty and issue *mea culpa* statements, but what he says is surely possible. It is hard for a rank outsider to capture accurately the methods and conclusions of any scholarly movement, especially one as diverse and pluralistic as contemporary biblical scholarship. (I know that this is true because I have reacted similarly to papers by theologians condemning "analytic philosophy.") But I think Robinson is wrong that one cannot accept a method of scholarship and then on the basis of a faith commitment choose to accept some of its conclusions but not others. As long as good reasons can be given for what is accepted and what is rejected (i.e., on behalf of the faith commitment), why cannot a person consistently do that very thing? Why cannot I, for example, accept the method of New Testament scholarship but reject some of the conclusions Robinson reaches on the basis of that method?

Keep in mind that in my essay I am trying to criticize, not the current state of New Testament scholarship on Christology, but its extremes. Nevertheless, if what I have said contains an element of caricature, that is a serious error on my part. The only point on which Robinson makes this general criticism specific concerns my charge that some scholars posit "extensive pagan syncretistic" influence on pre-Pauline Christology. Perhaps the term is overblown, but the idea is not. One need only read some of the recent attempts to explain how the church so quickly arrived at the high Christology of the kenosis hymn or at Johannine Christology (attempts written by people unprepared to accept those Christologies) to grasp my point. Some scholars do point to the influence that other religions or religious movements had on early Christians in order to solve this mystery, do they not? (A remarkable example of this sort of effort, but not by any means the only one, is Michael Goulder's second essay in *The Myth of God Incarnate*.) It is true, however, that Robinson himself does not take the pagan influence route; he solves the problem in terms of the influence of hymnic ecstasy.

(3) By far the most interesting part of an interesting critical essay is Robinson's concluding sentence. Here is another foundational difference between the two of us. He thinks Jesus is *hidden behind* the New Testament (and can be located, like the ore to be found somewhere in the mountain, only by the most careful use of the best available tools). I think Jesus is *revealed by* the New Testament (and the careful use of the best available tools helps us grasp that revelation more clearly). In the light of Robinson's methods, I cannot help wishing he had explained *why* he thinks Jesus was a remarkable person and *why* he thinks all of us would do well to know him better.

Hick and Pentz raise questions about essential predication, and they are good questions. To Pentz I need to say that I do not feel responsible for explaining how certain early theologians arrived at the theory that all God's properties (or at least properties such as omnipotence, omniscience, incorporeality) are essential properties. Despite my denial that any being correctly describable as God *simpliciter* (i.e., God who is never at any time incarnate in human form) exists, it may well be that these theologians were mistakenly thinking of God as such a being. God *simpliciter*, let us say, possesses a certain set of properties 1–n, which are jointly sufficient for being divine; a being who is "truly God" in the Christian sense possesses all the 1–n properties *plus* the extra property of being at one time incarnate in a human being. Thus (contrary to the conclusion Pentz reaches), I hold that there *are* two separate sets of properties sufficient for divinity—it is just that only the second set is in fact instantiated. Any being who possessed only the first set of properties would definitely be divine—but no being ever does. The only God who exists *was* at one time incarnate in a human being.

It is surely a necessary truth that every actual being possesses at least some essential properties—which properties of God, then, are essential? I do not know, and I am not sure why Pentz thinks I am supposed to know. I suppose it would be the properties (whichever they are) that are consistent with the incarnation, properties such as *being divine*, *being self-identical*, *existing*.

Exactly why do I doubt that God is essentially omnipotent, omniscient, incorporeal? The first is an epistemological reason, and the second is theological. The epistemological reason is simply that I do not know how anyone could know that God is, say, essentially omnipotent or essentially good. That God possesses these properties essentially is surely not a datum of revelation. As far as I can tell, the biblical writers knew little of the distinction between essential and accidental properties. Would God no longer be the very being God is or no longer be divine (depending on whether we are talking about a *de re* or *de dicto* necessity) if there were one act God logically could perform but somehow was not able to perform or if there were one morally unjustified act God once performed? But the theological reason is far more important—it is simply the fact (so I take it) of the incarnation. If Jesus was God; and if Jesus was non-omnipotent; then being omnipotent is not essential to God.

Hick suggests that my notion of God's possessing these properties merely contingently makes them insecure, and that thought (he says) is religiously disturbing. What is true here is that if God is, say, merely contingently perfectly morally good, then it is logically possible for God to sin. God could still be the very being God is or could still be divine if God sinned. True enough. Now, as I argued in *Logic and the Nature of God*, there may be compelling religious reasons for holding God to be contingently rather than essentially morally good. Why praise God for God's goodness toward us if God is logically unable to behave in any other way toward us? Furthermore, my own view is that God's goodness is (as Nelson Pike once put it) a firm and stable aspect of God's character. It is logically possible for God to sin, but God will not sin.

For example, what are the chances that one fine day Mother Teresa will leave the church, embrace the notion that poverty is the poor's own fault, and move to Las Vegas with a secretly amassed fortune? I do not expect such an event to occur, and I'm sure no one else does either—even though Mother Teresa is quite possibly free to do these very things. And whatever the chances that this event will occur, they are almost infinitely lower for God's sinning. God's perfect moral goodness is perfectly secure.

Cobb's point about the Christology of Arius is one that I accept; perhaps my use of the term *Arian* for any Christology that in effect makes Jesus merely or entirely human is not the best choice. I do not agree, however, that my reply in terms of "advance preparations" to Temple's criticism of kenosis commits me to anything like Arianism or to a Zeuslike theology. I agree that my reply is an anthropomorphic answer to an anthropomorphic criticism. But I am not at all sure why Cobb thinks my reply entails some kind of crude separation of the trinitarian Persons. Have I said that? Nevertheless, we do at times find it necessary to speak anthropomorphically about God, do we not? Temple himself was doing so when he asked the kenoticists: "Who was governing the heavens and the earth when the *Logos* was temporarily incarnate in Jesus?"

My answer is to ask why there had to be (so to speak) an active governor during that period if God is omniscient and omnipotent; why could not God have arranged it all ahead of time (as some extreme Calvinist theologians apparently think God does in *all* events)? This reply is also anthropomorphic, but is it unacceptably so? (I notice also that David Brown, whose book I read only after writing my main essay, answers this objection to kenosis in terms of the social model of the Trinity, to which he thinks consistent kenoticists are committed in any case. I find Brown's argument convincing.)

The concluding paragraph of Cobb's critique has caused me to do some thinking. I share his rejection of the doctrine of the impersonal humanity of Jesus, and I am glad Cobb wants to affirm the radical uniqueness of Jesus. But it troubles me that Cobb does not want to affirm that Jesus was metaphysically different from the creatures.

Let me propose some definitions. Let us say that a given being is *unique* if that being possesses a property that no other being possesses. Thus, the shortest mathematics professor in Claremont (whoever in fact he or she is) is unique. Let us say that a given being is *radically unique* if it possesses a property that no other being possesses or ever has or ever will possess. Perhaps Roger Maris' record of sixty-one home runs in one major league season will never be broken—if so, Maris (as the one who possesses the property of having set that record) is not just unique but radically unique. Now of course all beings are radically unique in terms of some of their properties, especially those related to self-identity. Cobb himself is radically unique in that it is impossible for any being other than Cobb to possess the property of "being identical with John Cobb, the eminent Claremont process theologian who is a contributor to this book." Nevertheless, most of us are not radically unique in terms of very many of our properties that are not related in some such way as this to self-identity.

I suspect that Cobb would be happy to affirm that Jesus is unique (in the sense I have defined in the preceding paragraph). Would Cobb also affirm that Jesus is (as I define the term) radically unique (in terms of properties not directly related to his self-identity)? I am not sure. Did Jesus possess any properties that no other being ever has or will possess? I surely think so. In fact, I think Jesus was not just radically unique but *metaphysically different* from all other beings. Let us say that a given being A is *metaphysically different* from all other beings if A is radically unique in A's ontological status or kind. That is to say, no other being ever has or will share A's ontological status. This is precisely what I want to affirm about Jesus (in my essay I have tried to explain why such an affirmation is important). No other being ever has been or will be both truly divine and truly human. Cobb does not want to affirm that Jesus is metaphysically different, and that remains a truly basic difference between our Christologies. (I am, however, delighted to note Cobb's statement: "for true God to be truly present does not mean that every characteristic of God characterizes the one in whom God is present." This is one of the main points I have tried to establish in my essay, and it goes a long way toward answering Hicklike objections to incarnation.)

Hick and Pentz ask about Jesus' possession of moral properties such as perfect goodness. Hick argues that what makes such properties distinctively divine is their infinity or unlimitedness. But (he asks) how can a finite human being be *infinitely* good or *infinitely* loving (or *infinitely* anything, for that matter)? The word *infinite* may mean several things, and I am often suspicious of its use in theology. The term is if anything a metaproperty rather than a property; some theologians do speak of God as simply infinite, but that expression does not seem to me to mean anything clear. God may indeed be infinitely this or infinitely that, but even here we must tread carefully. I believe the proper use of the term *infinite* in theology is to say that a given being possesses a given property to an infinite degree only if that property possesses, so to speak, an intrinsic maximum or limit. No being can possibly be *infinitely tall*; for every inch in height we can imagine a tall person as being, we can always imagine another person an inch taller. And though I have no space to explore the matter here (as I have done elsewhere), I believe that properties such as being powerful and being knowledgeable have intrinsic maximums, so the idea that God is infinitely powerful and infinitely knowledgeable makes sense.

But I am not at all sure that moral goodness has an intrinsic maximum. It seems to me that no matter how good we imagine a given person as being, we can always imagine a person who performs slightly more good deeds or deeds slightly more beneficial in their effects. Even if the notion of infinite goodness does make sense, Jesus was clearly not infinitely good. There were lots of good deeds that as far as we know he never bothered to perform, e.g., healing all the sick people of Jericho, feeding all the hungry of Egypt, preaching his message to the needy of Tibet. This is why I am much more inclined to say that Jesus was *perfectly morally good*, which the New Testament interprets in terms of sinlessness (see Heb. 4:15). This is, I believe, a unique divine property, or at least a property no other human being possesses, and is thus one of the properties that influences toward the notion of incarnation the persons who believe Jesus had it. But (Hick suggests) once we give up infinite goodness for Jesus, is it not more natural for us simply to describe him as a very morally good human being, a mere human who was perhaps even *totally* obedient to God? Yes, it surely would be more natural to do so—obviously, this way of talking would avoid the thorny paradoxes associated with the notion of incarnation. But (so I have been arguing in this book) it would not be true.

Hick is right to point to the limitations of my Malan analogy; as I have pointed out, it will indeed lead to unacceptable implications if pushed too far. And in answer to Hick's concluding point, I strongly opt for the view that Jesus had (like all other nonschizoid human beings) just one consciousness and that it was a human consciousness. Jesus may or may not have been aware of also being divine: people who reject the notion of incarnation naturally deny he was conscious of anything of the sort; those who affirm incarnation can and do disagree about the matter. It does not particularly bother me whether Jesus was or was not conscious of being something other than a mere human being. Either can be consistent with my own understanding of the incarnation. But (Hick asks) if Jesus' one consciousness was a human consciousness, can we coherently say he was God? Of course we can. Jesus was a human being with a human consciousness who was also truly divine. That, at least, is the notion I have been trying to defend in this book.

I continue to find it helpful to make a distinction between those theologians who try to *reinterpret* Chalcedonic Christology and those who simply *reject* it. Sometimes the difference between the two is a fine line. In my view Donald Baillie (whose name has come up several times in this book) fits in the first group. For reasons I have pointed out in my essay, I want my christological work to fit in that category too.

3 Can Jesus Save Women?
REBECCA D. PENTZ

I think I have always been a feminist. My mother worked outside the home because she loved it. My father encouraged his daughters to achieve just as enthusiastically as he encouraged his son. There was never any doubt when we were growing up that not just boys but girls too should strive for their best.

I have not always been a Christian. I became a Christian as an adult after years of searching for the truth in philosophy. In becoming a Christian I embraced what is sometimes described as a patriarchal, antifeminist religion. Yet I did so without relinquishing my feminism. How that is possible takes some explaining.

Perhaps what takes the most explaining is how I can accept Jesus, a male, as my Lord and Savior. In fact it has been Jesus' very maleness that has been used as a bludgeon to oppress and demean women. Religious history is dotted with arguments such as the following: Women cannot be priests because there must be a physical resemblance between the priest and his Lord. The female sex must be the inferior sex because God chose the male sex for his incarnation. Christ is head of the church; Christ is male; the church is female. This sex role should extend to individual male and female persons; i.e., males should be the head of females. Such arguments have led to feminist outcries such as Mary Daly's "the idea of a unique divine incarnation in a male, the God man of the 'hypostatic union' is inherently sexist and oppressive. Christolatry is idolatry." Or more pithily, "Since 'God' is male, the male is God."[1]

In this essay I shall not argue with Daly and others like her who say Jesus' maleness has been used oppressively, for I am afraid it has. But I shall argue with the conclusion these feminists draw that women must therefore give up Christianity. I shall argue that following Jesus does not require relinquishing feminist principles. Furthermore, I think I can show this theologically. Specifically, I shall suggest that an orthodox Christology does not contradict feminism.

Feminist criticisms of traditional Christologies have focused on two concerns: can women accept the God whom Jesus reveals? can Jesus himself be a model for women? These questions fall within the scope of what the tradition has called the work rather than the person of Christ. They ask how Christ functions rather than who he is and how his deity and humanity relate. I too shall focus therefore on the work rather than the person of Christ as I attempt to respond to these feminist concerns. My discussion is divided into three sections: Jesus' revelation of a transcendent Father, Jesus as a model for humans, and Jesus as Savior.

I narrow my scope to the work of Christ with some trepidation. I agree with Karl Barth that treating just the work of Christ opens one to the question "Couldn't this work be accomplished by something more or less than a divine-human person?"[2] I think this question can be answered, though I shall not attempt to do so here. Let it suffice to say that I accept the biblical record as authoritative; therefore, I accept its testimony that Jesus is Lord, Jesus is God. But I also think it is important to consider seriously the questions that feminists have raised about the work of Christ. What if these feminists are right and Jesus' twofold revelation, his revelation of who God the Father is and his revelation of who humans are to be, is oppressive and demeaning to women? Then perhaps feminists should be looking for Goddess religions or joining witch covens. Or at the very least they should not be Christians. For if Jesus' work is sexist, if no Christology is compatible with feminism, then there is no place for feminists in Christianity. My goal is to show that this is not true. My goal is to show that an orthodox Christology need not be sexist and that an orthodox Christian woman can find within her religion the vision and the strength to be all that she can.

I

The first feminist objection to Jesus' revelation of God arises before we even get to the content of this revelation. If God's unique self-revelation is in a male, must we conclude that God himself is male? Absolutely not. Even though theologians do slip into this error, the biblical picture of God is overwhelmingly of a being who transcends sexual categories.[3] God is personal, but God is neither a male nor a female. God has both masculine and feminine characteristics, but it is blatant anthropomorphism to conclude that God is therefore either a man or a woman.

Even if God is not a male, are not the characteristics of the God whom Jesus reveals nevertheless abhorrent to feminists? Some feminists answer yes. The controlling image Jesus used to describe God is "transcendent Father," and to some feminists this image communicates an oppressive patriarch, the top dog in an oppressive hierarchy. Once again Daly leads the charge. The divine Patriarch is the one who controls this world and keeps human beings "in a state of infantile subjection."[4] There are two red flags for feminists in this description: *control* and *hierarchy*. Feminists are opposed to any hierarchy in which one person is set up over and controls the other. Wilson-Kastner calls for the healing of the divisions of hierarchy, the dualisms of male/female, dominance/submission, spirit/matter, reason/intuition, "which divide, separate, cause pain, and support oppression and lack of communication with the other. . . ."[5] So hierarchy and control are bad, and the transcendent Father of Jesus is the one who controls everyone from the top of the whole despicable patriarchal hierarchy.

Christian feminists have responded to this critique by pointing out that Jesus was opposed to social hierarchies. Elisabeth Schüssler Fiorenza catalogued Jesus' teaching against patriarchal hierarchies.[6] She identified three categories of antipatriarchal teachings. First, according to Fiorenza, the main intent of several of Jesus' teachings on marriage and divorce is to attack patriarchal marriage structures, with their hierarchy of male over female (see Mark 10:2–9 and Mark 12:18–27). Second, Fiorenza listed a group of afamilial teachings that state that the natural patriarchal family bonds are destroyed in Jesus' company so that whoever does the will of God is a brother or a sister (Mark 3:32–35, Matt. 10:35–39, Mark 10:29–31). Third, Fiorenza listed a group of antidominance sayings that criticize people who try to exalt themselves (Matt. 23:5–12, Mark 10:14–15, Luke 22:24–27, Mark 9:33–37).

Mark 10:42–45 is typical of this group:

> "You know that those who are supposed to rule over the Gentiles lord it over them, and their great men exercise authority over them. But it shall not be so among you; but whoever would be great among you must be your servant, and whoever would be first among you must be slave of all."

In Christ's community there will be no hierarchies in which one male lords it over all others. The old patriarchal rule must go.

I applaud the Christian feminists who point out that Jesus was opposed to the patriarchal structures of his time and that he called for a new form of community structure. But we do have to be careful to avoid concluding from this fact that Jesus was opposed to hierarchy in general. Certainly Jesus advocated at least one hierarchical structure, the one with him and God the Father at the top. Let us look at one of Fiorenza's antidominance sayings, Matthew 23:7–12. The scribes and the Pharisees love

> being called rabbi by men. But you are not to be called rabbi, for you have one teacher, and you are all brethren. And call no man your father on earth, for you have one Father, who is in heaven. Neither be called masters, for you have one master, the Christ. He who is greatest among you shall be your servant; whoever exalts himself will be humbled, and whoever humbles himself will be exalted.

Fiorenza aptly pointed out that given this text there can be no patriarchs on earth who claim to have ultimate authority—that role is reserved for God the Father. But of course this also entails that there is a hierarchy in the grand scheme of things, with God the Father at the head. Is this not just what the radical feminists such as Daly object to? Yes, it is, and it is just this objection that is unfounded. Let me argue for this conclusion by making a few observations about the notions *hierarchy* and *power*.

A hierarchy is simply a system of organization by ranks, grades, or classes. This system is offensive because the ranks often become static and because certain groups of people, typically minority groups, are relegated to the lowest positions. Furthermore, the groups that do hold the top positions use their power to oppress those beneath them. They use their power *over* as power *against*.

Power need not be exercised in this way. Power *over* need not be power *against* but can be power *for*. Let me explain. Mary Lou Retton is a world-class gymnast who won the gold medal in the women's all-around event at the 1984 Summer Olympics. Her coach is Bela Karolyi, a Romanian who also coached Nadia Comaneci. For a year before the Olympics, Retton lived away from her family at a secluded gym and had two long workouts every day. Karolyi had power over almost every aspect of Retton's life. But this power over was not power against; this power was not used to oppress or tramp down. This power was used for Retton to help her achieve the perfection she desired. Karolyi exercised power over and power for. I think we see this model of power over and power for repeated in many aspects of human life. The teacher, the mentor, the master tradesperson have power over their subordinates, but they use this power for the benefit of their subordinates. This is the road to excellence. The people with knowledge and skill use their power to bring along the less knowledgeable and less skillful.

I suggest that this is the kind of power the transcendent Father of Jesus has. There is no doubt that the transcendent Father has power *over*. He has this power over by virtue of two facts. First, he is *Pantokrator*, Ruler over all. He holds the top position in the hierarchy. Jesus indicates God's position at the top when he refers to God as "Lord" and "the Most High." Second, God has ability commensurate with his position. He is omnipotent and therefore has the ability to control all those beneath him. Jesus indicates this ability when he refers to God as "Power." In short, Jesus reveals that God has both the position and the ability to exercise power over. And by so doing he raises both the red flags of the feminists—God is at the top of the hierarchy, and he has the ability to control.

Furthermore, and in this respect God's power exceeds any power of a human mentor, God has the right to total control over us. He is our Creator, and as Creator he has the right of total control. Any creator has this right over his or her creation. This essay is my creation; I may submit it to friends for criticism, or I may file it in my big green file cabinet and never let another person see it. One or the other of these fates may be the better one, but as creator I have the right to choose. Similarly, God as our Creator has the legitimate right to handle his creation as he sees fit.

Legitimate power can be oppressive power, so we need one more factor in the mosaic. God has the position to control, he has the ability to control, he has the right to control, but he exercises this ability only for our benefit. His power *over* is power *for*. And Jesus could not make this "forness" clearer. Jesus teaches us again and again that God is the loving Father who searches for the lost sheep, who welcomes home the prodigal, who bears the load of the poor, the oppressed, the outcast. Jesus' fate testifies to God's beneficence even more clearly than his teachings. "He who did not spare his own Son but gave him up for us all, will he not also give us all things with him?" (Rom. 8:32). "For God so loved the world that he gave his only Son" (John 3:16).

Here too God exceeds anything a human mentor can accomplish. Earthly mentors are limited in knowledge and skill; therefore, some of their judgments are unintentionally harmful. They are also limited in goodwill; therefore, some of their judgments are intentionally harmful. But the God whom Jesus reveals has none of these limitations. He is omnipotent. He lacks no skill. He is omniscient. He knows what is best for us in every set of circumstances. He is perfectly loving and never lacks in goodwill. This last difference between God and human mentors is quite significant for women. Too many oppressors have claimed to wield power over women "for our own good"; in fact they wield power for their own good. These oppressors would never sacrifice their only begotten sons in order to save their adopted daughters.

The good news does not end here. We feminists must notice two further points. Even though God has controlling power over us, he does not dominate us. This is another aspect of his power over but power for. His power over us would not really be for us if he controlled every aspect of our lives. If Karolyi held Retton's hand on the balance beam every step of the way, Retton would never develop. If he boosted her over the horse vault, she would never become strong. Part of his wisdom as a trainer is knowing when to step back, knowing when to let her succeed on her own and when to let her fail on her own. God too respects our freedom both to succeed and to fail—to a frightening extent, given the magnitude of the failure he allows. So, since God's power over us is for us, he steps back and lets us exert our own power.

In this stepping back, and this is the second point, he never deserts us. His power is always available to those who ask (Acts 1:8; Eph. 3:14–21; Phil.

4:13). Although he never coerces us, he always helps us if we but ask.

Is this the kind of hierarchy and control that a feminist should object to? I think not. Certainly the transcendent Father of Jesus has the position at the top of the hierarchy, and he has the ability to control all beneath him. But, and this is the significant point, he exercises this control only for our benefit. His power *over* is power *for*. At this point I think Fiorenza's point deserves reemphasizing: because God sits at the top of the hierarchy, no human patriarch who may be tempted to oppress may aspire to this position. God alone is Lord.

I think we women can learn something from this analysis of power over and power for. I think we women have a tendency to shun power, and certainly we should shun power that is used oppressively. We should shun static hierarchies in which men "lord it over" and lock women and other oppressed people into demeaning roles. But this does not mean we should shun all power. Power can be used to ennoble, to enlighten, to empower. This is the power properly exercised of the teacher, the mentor, the coach. This is the way God chooses to exercise his almighty power. This is the power that women should strive to attain.

In sum, Jesus' transcendent Father is not someone we feminists need to reject. He is not an oppressive patriarch (though, admittedly, oppressive patriarchs have ruled in his name). Rather he is like a woman who is looking for a lost coin and who will not be satisfied until it is found. When it is found, she cannot contain herself but calls in all her neighbors to celebrate and rejoice (Luke 15:8–10). Like such a loving, caring woman is our transcendent Father.

II

Jesus points above to his transcendent Father, and he points below to us. Much work has been done in Christian feminist scholarship to show, first of all, that Yahweh can be spoken of as having feminine as well as masculine characteristics, though in fact he transcends all gender, and second, that Jesus' *Abba* is open and loving, not oppressive. But Christianity also claims that Jesus is the perfect human and thus reveals who we ought to be. This latter claim has not been adequately discussed and has in fact driven some feminists from Christianity. How can a male who has had only male experiences reveal who I as a woman should be? How can a male be a perfect model for females?

I have some sympathy for this attitude. In my own experience I find that I do not pray to Jesus but to God the Father. Furthermore, I have always felt a special kinship with Mary. As a new Christian I was more taken with the

Magnificat and its example of obedience than I was with Jesus' perfect obedience and his acceptance of the cross. The very first Scripture I memorized was the Magnificat. I was moved by Mary's praise of God, and I identified with her exuberance at having been chosen. Having become a Christian as an adult, I too felt blessed, chosen, and special that God had regarded me.[7]

Mary has touched other women as well. In discussing the cult of Mary, Fiorenza claimed that "on an *emotional, imaginative, experiential* level the Catholic child experiences the love of God in the figure of a woman."[8] When Jesus is divinized and God patriarchalized, it is Mary who presents the human face of God. Even Mary Daly has grudgingly admitted that the example of Mary has been uplifting for Christian women, though I disagree with her analysis of why this is so.[9] The fact is that we as women can be moved by things that do not move men. Of course, there is a large area of commonality between a woman's experience and a man's, but because women alone bear children and are still the primary caretakers of children, our experiences as women can be radically different from a male's. Given these differences and others, we may approach problems differently, intuitively value different things, have different worldviews, and respond empathetically to different models than men.[10] Because Mary, as a woman, shares these differences, I am beginning to think that Protestants have missed out by shunning all Mariology. I shall not venture to comment on the extent to which Mary should be a symbol for the church nor to what extent she models for the church the creature's role in redemption, but I do think that Protestants have been too quick to exclude Mary and other women as spiritual models. Catholic girls have not only Mary to look up to but the women saints as well. To this extent their heritage is much richer. Perhaps women need female models such as Mary and the saints, and perhaps men need male models such as David and Barnabas. We do relate most emphathetically to our own sex.

Recognizing the need for female models for women does not entail that Jesus cannot be our model as well. When Jesus, after washing his disciples' feet, states that he is acting as an example for his disciples, I think he is also providing an example for women. Women too should serve others. Interestingly, when Jesus confronts women one-to-one, he does not call them to servanthood. He never washes a woman's foot and tells her to do likewise. Rather he models different kinds of behavior when he is dealing with women alone. Let me explain why this may be so by examining an interesting article by Valerie Saiving.

In "The Human Situation: A Feminine View" Saiving developed a critique of contemporary theology. Saiving argued that there are particularly masculine as well as particularly feminine sins. She began with the premise I have suggested, that in some fundamental ways female experience is different from male experience. She then argued that because of this different experience, women have strengths and weaknesses that are different from those men have. For example, a woman is more secure in her sexuality. Even a little girl is a woman in a way in which a little boy is not a man. Biology continues to reinforce the girl's security. She begins to menstruate; she bears children; she goes through menopause. Each of these is a very dramatic reminder of her womanhood. Men have fewer built-in biological indicators. Men therefore have more to prove. Driven by their anxiety, men commit the sins of pride, will to power, and exploitation. But they also have a built-in discontent that helps them to achieve more and to be more creative. Women, on the other hand, find it easier to be self-giving and sacrificial. We experience self-transcending love in our relationships with our children. But we too face temptations. We tend toward "triviality, distractibility, and diffuseness; lack of an organizing center of focus; dependence on others for one's own self-definition; tolerance at the expense of standards of excellence; inability to respect the boundaries of privacy; sentimentality, gossipy sociability, and mistrust of reason—in short, underdevelopment or negation of the self."[11] Saiving concluded by criticizing contemporary theology because it teaches self-sacrifice rather than encouraging creativity and excellence, because it speaks only from and to the male experience.

Saiving limited her discussion to contemporary theology, but what about Jesus? He was a male and therefore had only male experiences. Look at the temptations. Jesus was not tempted to be self-demeaning and trivial. Jesus was tempted to abuse power. Jesus was tempted by things that tempt males, not things that tempt females. Can we not then argue that his preaching, like that of contemporary theologians, speaks only to males and not to females, that he calls men away from power and to self-sacrifice but has nothing to say to women? Or even worse, that Jesus' message to women is detrimental to us because it encourages us to continue in our self-demeaning sin, to be even more self-giving, never finding an identity of our own or striving toward excellence? A Saivingesque challenge to a feminist Christology is much more threatening than the mere fact that women feel a special sisterhood with Mary.

In response to this challenge, I shall examine three of Jesus' encounters with women—his encounter with the Samaritan woman (John 4:7–30), with Martha (Luke 10:38–42), and with an unidentified female in a crowd (Luke 11:27–28). The story of the Samaritan woman is a familiar one. Both the woman and the disciples are astounded that Jesus would break the social taboos and talk freely with a woman. The content of the conversation is even more astounding. For whatever reason, the woman is living with a man out of wedlock. The road to her current living arrangement has been a rocky one. It is strewn with five husbands. Jesus points out this fact but does not dwell on it. He does not tell her that if she only had been a more obedient wife she would not be in such straits. Instead he discusses theology with her. He speaks to her of the living water and of the correct way to worship. Then he reveals to her who he is: "I who speak to you am he," the Messiah. This woman then becomes the first evangelist to Samaria and an effective one at that: "Many Samaritans from that city believed in him because of the woman's testimony" (John 4:39). Does Jesus tell the Samaritan woman to be more self-sacrificing? No, self-sacrifice is not even discussed. Does he tell her to keep her mind on her chores? No, he ignores her chores, speaking of the living water of God rather than of drinking water from a well. By the end of the conversation, her consciousness has been so raised that she forgets her chore altogether. She leaves her water jar at the well. In short, Jesus stretches the Samaritan woman's mind, encouraging her to move beyond thoughts of physical water and the physical location of worship to thoughts of salvation and the Christ. Jesus calls her beyond triviality to fulfillment.

Jesus gives the same sort of message to Martha. Martha has been driven to distraction by the demands of getting a big dinner on the table for Jesus and his whole crew of disciples while her sister Mary lazes at Jesus' feet. Finally she can take it no more and asks Jesus to send her sister in to give her a hand. Is that not a woman's place anyway? Jesus' response is no. By listening to Jesus teach, Mary has made the right choice. A woman is not defined by her housework. She too must seek after truth and salvation. To echo Saiving, Martha is guilty of triviality, distractibility, and diffuseness; Mary has found a center of focus.

The third encounter takes place in a crowd scene. A woman calls out a compliment: "Blessed is the womb that bore you, and the breasts that you sucked!" Jesus retorts: "Blessed rather are those who hear the word of God and keep it!" Jesus rejects this attempt to exalt Mary for being a baby bearer and child nurturer. These activities are not the highest calling of a woman. A woman's true identity is not found in her relationship to her children, as tempting as that means of self-definition may be to her. A woman's true identity is found in relationship to God.

In each of these encounters Jesus calls women from particularly feminine sins to excellence. He does not tell them, as he tells the rich young ruler, to sacrifice all they have. He does not heap scorn upon them, as he does upon the Pharisees, for their pride, their self-righteousness, their will to power. He does not pull them up short, as he does James and John for their attempt to seize the privilege of sitting one on his left, one on his right. He teaches them. He calls them from their concerns with their everyday womanly chores, from their earthy womanly experiences, to a focus on the kingdom of God.

In sum, in these encounters with women Jesus does not call them to be self-sacrificing, to be servants. This does not mean that Christian women need not be self-sacrificing. Nor does it mean that we need not be servants. What it does mean is that Jesus realizes that women may find it easy to be self-sacrificing and therefore do not need to be nudged in that direction. Women do not find it easy, however, to give up household chores in order to think theologically. We do not always have the self-esteem necessary to say no to the men in our world in order to say yes to the kingdom. So Jesus applies pressure in these areas rather than urging women to greater self-sacrifice.

Furthermore, if a woman in her self-sacrifice is self-demeaning or if her self-sacrifice is a response to oppression, she cannot truly be a servant in the manner of Jesus. When Jesus serves others, he does so from the immense abundance of his personal strength. When Jesus washes the disciples' feet, he does so as their "Lord and Teacher," a position he reminds them of. Jesus is a servant because he freely chooses to be. Therefore, if a woman is to follow Jesus' example of servanthood, she too must serve from an abundance of ego-strength. She too must serve freely. When Jesus encounters women, he does not call them to servanthood but to selfhood, because without this selfhood they cannot freely give of themselves as Jesus freely gave of himself.

Is Jesus a model for women? Yes, in that women should be self-sacrificing servants. Furthermore, Jesus calls women, just as he calls men, to focus our lives on the kingdom of God. "Blessed are those who hear the word of God and keep it." But Jesus realizes that hearing and keeping God's word requires effort in different areas for women than it does for men. And Jesus encourages women in the areas in which we need encouragement.

III

As important as I consider Jesus' function as a model (I do not think we can be Christians without striving for a life of servanthood, a life that takes seriously in action Jesus' teaching about and treatment of the oppressed), I do not consider it the most important dimension of his work. Jesus' lifework culminated in his death on the cross and his subsequent resurrection. And this death and resurrection are not-to-be-repeated and not-able-to-be-imitated acts of salvation.[12] Jesus Christ may be our model, but he is more importantly our Savior. His death and resurrection save us from sin, restore us to God, and free us to be all God created us to be.

These words may sound like a sexist cliché to feminist ears. Certainly male theologians again and again point to Christ's acts of salvation, which were accomplished in his death and resurrection, as the primary work of his incarnation. In the prologue to his Christology in the Third Part of the *Summa Theologica*, Thomas Aquinas described Jesus as "our Saviour," who came "in order to save His people from their sins." Thomas argued that it was necessary for the restoration of the human race that the Word of God should become incarnate, and agreed that the purpose of the first coming of Christ was for the remission of sins.[13] John Calvin stated in the *Institutes* that "The sole purpose of Christ's incarnation was our redemption,"[14] and Karl Barth developed a Christology of reconciliation with Jesus as the "Reconciler of all men of all times and places."[15] Even more recently, Wolfhart Pannenberg identified Jesus' office as calling people to the kingdom of God and imparting salvation to them.[16] In short we find it reiterated throughout the history of male theology that the main work of Christ is to be our Savior, a task he accomplished in his death and resurrection.[17]

If the male theologians are right and Jesus Christ is our Savior, we feminists must ask the question Rosemary Ruether asked in *Sexism and God-Talk*: "Can a male savior save women?"[18] Ruether answered in the affirmative by developing a Christology of Christ the liberator, or as she called it in another work, a Christology of the prophetic iconoclastic Christ.[19] In this Christology, Jesus' main work is to renounce hierarchy and domination, to serve and empower the oppressed. Christ's effectiveness as liberator is independent of his maleness, so Ruether concluded that his maleness, theologically speaking,"has no ultimate significance."[20] I can agree with much in this Christology. Christ does call for a new social structure. Christ is a liberator of the oppressed, and women are frequently the most oppressed of the oppressed. But I do not think we need to resort to a Christology modeled exclusively on a prophetic iconoclastic Christ in order to find a justification for Jesus as the Savior of women. I contend that feminism is consistent with the more traditional view of Christ the Savior, the view that Jesus' death and resurrection vanquished sin in such a way that all humans can escape from captivity to sin while being empowered to be the persons they were created to be in relationship to God eternally. I do not offer a theological theory as to how Jesus' death and resurrection usher in this freedom and unleash this power, but I do suggest that this is a freedom and a power that feminists need to embrace.

If a male Savior is to save women, three conditions must be met. The male Savior's act of salvation must be intended to cover women. His act of salvation must be effective. And women must be able to accept his offer of salvation.

Given that Jesus is the male Savior, I think all three of these conditions have been met. First, Jesus clearly intended his salvific work to include men and women. He offered the Samaritan woman the living water of salvation. He stated that harlots and tax collectors will precede the elders and chief priests into the kingdom of God (Matt. 21:31). He told the parable of the Great Supper, to which all are invited (Matt. 22:1–14). He predicted that in the end times two women will be grinding and one will be taken (Matt. 24:41). He healed women. He accepted women into his band. He appeared to women first after the resurrection. There is no doubt that Jesus held values affirmed by feminists today and that he intended his salvific work to include women. Furthermore, the Bible claims that God the Father intended Jesus' death and resurrection to save women. One of the main themes of the pastoral epistles is that God desires all to be saved (e.g., 1 Tim. 2:4, 4:10, Titus 2:11). John 3:16, which Luther called "the Gospel in miniature" sums it up: "For God so loved the world that he gave his only Son, that whoever believes in him should not perish but have eternal life." The requirement is belief, not gender.

Second, if both God the Father and Jesus intend that Jesus' salvific acts save men and women and if in fact these acts are effective in saving men, I can think of no good argument for concluding that these salvific acts are not effective in saving women. I can think of no good argument for the conclusion that an omnipotent God's intentions are thwarted for women when they are not thwarted for men. Even granting the significant differences between men and women, any argument that God's intentions are thwarted only for women must show that these very differences tie God's hands. It does not even seem plausible that the sins of triviality and diffuseness are more intractable than the sins of pride and exploitation of others, particularly for an omnipotent being. So if God intends to save both men and women, and in fact he does save men, then in fact he does save women. Notice that I have not argued that Jesus' salvific acts are effective for men, though I am convinced they are. I merely contend that if Jesus' death and resurrection save men, they save women too.

Third, and this part of the argument is just as important as the first two, I do not think that Jesus' maleness need stand in the way of us as women accepting his offer of salvation. In a sense we humans play a part in our own salvation. Faith is the human side of salvation. We need to accept God's offer in order to be saved; he respects our freedom to reject him. Wolfhart Pannenberg said it this way: Jesus promises salvation to those who accept his message of the coming of the kingdom of God and who seek community with him.[21] John 3:16 puts in the rider "whoever believes." Our response is necessary.

But if this is true, some feminists might claim that women cannot respond to a male Savior and therefore Jesus cannot save women. In this instance the differences between men and women are significant. If women cannot accept the offer of a male Savior but men can, then women, unlike men, cannot be saved. But women can accept this offer. Let me explain. First, it has been clearly documented that while Jesus was on earth women did respond to him.[22] Second, if we contemporary women understand what kind of Savior we are dealing with, I do not think we will feel alienated from him.

There are saviors and there are saviors. In New Testament times the title "savior" was not reserved for God alone. It was also applied to men, particularly to rulers and emperors who granted some special favor to a city or to an individual. For example, the Roman Emperor Hadrian was often dubbed "savior." What kind of savior was Hadrian? Although more cultivated and more widely traveled than most Roman emperors, Hadrian was taken with self-aggrandizement, calling himself Hadrianus Augustus after the great Caesar Augustus and proclaiming the beginning of a golden age on his coinage. He even wrote his own autobiography, not all of it true, to record his reign in the best light. He was an unpredictable man whose whim determined who would be benefited and who would be squelched. He fell in love with a twenty-year-old boy whom he deified upon the boy's early death. His reign began with the execution of four opponents and ended with the execution of two, and some accused him of poisoning his wife. Hadrian was not the kind of savior that women would find it easy to relate to.

Jesus was not that kind of savior. Jesus was not self-aggrandizing. He "emptied himself, taking the form of a servant" (Phil. 2:7). Jesus did not execute others. He "became obedient unto death, even death on a cross" (Phil. 2:8). In fact Jesus' execution is the act that saves us. How a death can save us is hard to understand. But a parallel exists in an experience shared by many women but never experienced by a single man. Jesus' death on the cross is perhaps best understood as an act of mothering. This is the way many medievalists understood it. St. Anselm described Jesus' death in terms of childbirth:

And if you had not died, you would not have brought forth.
For longing to bear sons into life,
You tasted death,
And by dying, you begot them.

We find the same thought expressed by the thirteenth-century prioress Marguerite d'Oingt:

Ah, who has seen a woman give birth thus!
And when the hour of birth came, they placed
You on the bed of the Cross. And it is not astonishing
your veins ruptured, as you gave birth in one single day,
to the whole world![23]

Julian of Norwich, the fourteenth-century anchoress, is famous in feminine literature for her repeated references to "Mother Jesus." She too likened the crucifixion to childbearing.

> We realize that all our mothers bear us for pain and for dying, and what is that? But our true mother, Jesus—All love—alone bears us for joy and for endless living, blessed may he be! Thus he sustains us within himself in love and hard labor, until the fulness of time.[24]

Patricia Wilson-Kastner identified the significance of "Mother Jesus":

> No one can pray to Jesus our Mother without being jarred into a recognition that the maleness of Jesus is quite accidental to his meaning as Christ. In the crucified one, masculine/feminine distinctions break down just as the language of male-Father, female-Mother falls into insignificance. In Jesus the dualities of sex stereotypes and roles are overcome in the perspective of the work of redemption.[25]

I agree with Wilson-Kastner's analysis but would like to push the point even further. It is not just that Jesus' maleness is accidental to his meaning as Christ. The very act by which he saves us, his death on the cross, is best described in human terms by the feminine metaphor of childbirth. On the cross Jesus brings forth new life. He makes possible our transformation from creatures subject to sin into creatures free in God. As Jesus tells Nicodemus (John 3:3), this transformation is more like a birth than a liberation, because of the radical discontinuity between the old self and the new self. In a spiritual sense, Jesus is our birth mother. Like a birth mother, Jesus suffered in order to give us this new life. He labored on the cross. In short, Jesus' salvific act on the cross was in many ways parallel to an experience that only women have. It was an act of suffering to bring forth new life. It was an act of childbirth. It was not the act of an alien patriarchal male deity.

Jesus' mothering of us does not end with his death on the cross. As Julian pointed out, Jesus continues to nurture us like a mother. He feeds us with himself in the sacrament of communion. He lets us make mistakes for our own good, just as a wise mother does.[26] He wants us to seek him out when we are in need so that he can give us the power through the Holy Spirit to overcome the obstacles that confront us now, both in our personal lives and in our attempt to continue his battle against oppression and injustice. What kind of savior is Jesus? He is a mother who gives us birth and who nurtures us and strengthens us in love.[27] Certainly we as women can relate to this kind of savior.

What I have tried to argue in this essay is that the Jesus of orthodox Christianity and the claims of moderate feminism are not in conflict. I can imagine many reasons why one would reject Christianity and its claim that Jesus is the Christ—perhaps one has trouble with the authority of the

Scripture, or one is scandalized by the particularity and exclusiveness of a God-man. I have not of course argued that Christianity is true. I have merely assumed it. I have argued that there is one reason which is not a good reason for rejecting the claims that Christianity makes. And that reason is that Jesus is a male. Neither Jesus' revelation of a transcendent Father nor his own maleness should prevent anyone, man or woman, from accepting Christianity, for neither of these factors conflict with feminist values or insights. In fact in my own experience it has been my belief in this transcendent Father and in this male human-God that has been decisive in my journey toward wholeness and self-esteem. Jesus has saved me.

Critiques

Critique by John B. Cobb, Jr.

It is difficult to respond to a testimony in any way but appreciation for the sharing. It is difficult for a man to respond to a woman's account of women's experience and women's needs in any way but by learning. It is especially difficult to be in the role of critic when so much that is said is simply illuminating and when the conclusions are those one wants to support.

I too believe that Jesus can save women, and I hope the time will come when this question will be laid to rest. The types of arguments Pentz has confessionally given should speed that time. Nevertheless, I think that Pentz has not responded to the legitimate concerns of some women. With considerable hesitation I shall suggest ways that the response could be strengthened.

The most obvious issue is at the level of language. It does not bother Pentz to use exclusively male language for God. She knows that God is in fact neither male nor female and that God has both male and female characteristics, and knowing that, she has no objection to the male language. Perhaps she even prefers it. Whatever her reason, she uses it consistently.

I think the time might come when male language will not be problematic. But that time seems to me quite far in the future. At this time the term *Father*, not balanced by *Mother*, and the repeated use of the male pronoun, do bother some women who, like Pentz, believe that Jesus can save women and do put off others who might, with other rhetoric, be attracted. Also, some of us men have found that changing language has a more than trivial effect on our understanding of God. Although we would always have denied that God is male in any literal sense, our existential experience of God has been affected by the language of the church. We do not live by concepts as much as by images. Feminists have forced us to recognize that. It is much, much too early to suppose that this lesson has now been assimilated and that we can return to exclusively male language with impunity.

It seems to me that the question of whether a male Savior works for women requires other levels of exploration in addition to the ones at which Pentz makes rich contributions. Many women have been brought up to think that their fulfillment will come through a male. As long as they retain this assumption, they cannot attain the fully woman-identified status that is an important part of female wholeness. If the Heavenly Father takes over the role of fulfillment where the earthly one failed, the deeper shift will not have occurred. That does not mean that nothing of healing and saving significance will have occurred, but something important will still be lacking. The same may be true if the savior figure is the male Jesus.

Pentz is not ignorant of that lack. Indeed, she sees the importance of female models for women, such as Mary and the women saints provided by the Catholic church. She sees Protestantism as impoverished in this respect. But more is needed here.

More generally, Pentz seems much more satisfied with traditional forms of Christianity than I am. She knows, of course, that there have been many abuses, especially male sins against women. But she does not seem to view these as indicative of anything deeply wrong with inherited forms of theology, including the biblical images. My view, on the contrary, is that there has never been a satisfactory form of Christianity. It has always been patriarchal and anti-Jewish, for example, in ways that should not be repeated. The fact that Christians look to the future for fulfillment rather than to the past makes Christianity, for me, a saving faith. I am freed from the need to defend anything in the past, either my personal past or the collective past of that community and tradition from which I derive my identity. I am free, therefore, to seek a form of Christianity that is truly saving of both women and men rather than to claim that it already exists. Of course, I do not seek salvation in discontinuity from the way that God's saving power has worked in the past. But I see that power as having again and again freed people from bondage to the forms that Jewish and Christian life and thought have taken, and I see it working now in the same way, especially through feminists.

One point on which Pentz's commitment to traditional language and thought seems incongruous for a feminist (at any rate, it disturbs me personally) is with respect to power. She rightly points out that God never coerces us, that God's power is for us, that it is enabling, enlightening, and empowering. But it seems quite important to her also to state that it is power *over* us and that God is omnipotent.

Of course, a great deal in the tradition supports her. Also a great deal in the Bible. But in the New Testament, outside the book of Revelation, there is surprisingly little. God's power in the New Testament is neither revealed as omnipotent nor spoken of in those terms. It is, of course, sufficient, but that is quite a different matter. The renewal of an emphasis on omnipotence and its quite new and questionable philosophical elaboration belong to the church and tell us more about the needs and imagination of church writers than about what is revealed in Jesus or affirmed by Paul. Now that the problematic character of this rhetoric has been widely noted, one wonders why a feminist Christian is so insistent upon it. Why, in an essay like this, when the main points lie elsewhere, is God's omnipotence so insistently emphasized and reemphasized? Why is our relation to God treated like that of an essay to an author? Does this express a sense of total dependence on the Father that may still need to be transcended? I am not sure. But I do believe that it is important to go on from the status of slaves to that of friends.

Critique by John Hick

The basic feminist accusations against traditional Christian theology and the traditional churches, as formulated by contemporary feminist theologians and briefly summarized here by Rebecca Pentz (and also by John Cobb and James Robinson in their essays), seem to me also to be well founded. I am therefore extremely interested to see whether the interpretation of religion that appeals to me and that I have adumbrated elsewhere (e.g., *God Has Many Names* and *Problems of Religious Pluralism*) is open to these same objections. On the face of it, it is not. For my own interpretation seems to be congruent with feminist insights in that (a) it is incompatible with any conception of the Ultimate or the Real as either explicitly or implicitly masculine; (b) it shows how this and other distortions have come about; and (c) it shows how, in principle, they can be overcome. Instead, then, of commenting in detail on Pentz' chapter, with most of which I am in agreement, I propose to outline a particular conception of our human religious situation.

I must start in the middle, with the large assumption that it is rational for human beings to believe in a transcendent Ultimate Reality. Let us refer to this in relatively transcultural language as the Real—*sat, al-Haq, en Soph, Tathata, shin*. Because the history of religions shows many ways of conceiving and experiencing the Real, we must suppose that the intentional object of a form of religious thought and experience is not the Real as it is in itself but the Real as perceived through the lens of some particular human conceptual system and with the training of an associated set of devotional or meditational practices—all such bodies of thought, feeling, and behavior being historically and culturally conditioned.

The epistemological clue to this situation is provided by the fundamental insight introduced into Western thought by Immanuel Kant, that the human mind is active in perception, forming and constructing in the very process of receiving. When we apply this (as Kant did not do) to religion, we can see that there must be a creative and projective element not only in sensory but also in religious experience. Kant's program was to identify the basic concepts in terms of which our perceptual experience is structured. In the epistemology of religion we have to identify the basic concepts structuring religious experience. These seem to be the concept of deity, or of the Real as personal, and the concept of the absolute, or of the Real as nonpersonal, which function as the two differently shaped and differently colored windows through which human beings are conscious of the Real. We do not, however, experience deity in general or the absolute in general but always as *schematized* (to use Kant's term) in more concrete forms. These schematizations constitute the *personae* (Yahweh, the Heavenly Father, Allah, Shiva, Durga, Kali) and the *impersonae* (Brahman, the Tao, the Dharmakaya, sunyata) of the Real. They come into existence at the interface between the Real and the various historical forms of human consciousness. As such, they are manifestations of the Real and at the same time human projections, reflecting our distorting human limitations and cultural biases. The relation between the Real and its manifestations to human consciousness is that (in Kantian language again) between noumenon and phenomena.

This general theory makes intelligible from a religious point of view the plurality of religious traditions, which so obviously embody aspects of human culture. It also makes intelligible the fact that religion has never been unambiguously good but on the contrary has always involved a human contribution, reflecting evil and error as well as virtue and insight. Intelligible also is a special case of this human contribution: how it is that the vast gender distortion of male dominance on earth is projected in male images of the Ultimate, which then validate a human male superiority complex.

Because our conceptual and linguistic machinery has been developed in relation to the phenomenal or experienced world, we cannot speak literally about the Real *an sich*. We cannot apply to it the categories of one or many, substance or process, personal or impersonal, male or female, evil or good. We can say only that the Real is the necessary postulate of the religious life when the religious life is acknowledged to be inherently plural in form.

One difference between the divine *personae* and the metaphysical *impersonae* of the Real is that the former are much more vulnerable than the latter to the distortion of male dominance. Although at the human level this distortion has been as firmly entrenched in Eastern as in Western societies and is indeed today probably more so, the Hindu and Buddhist *impersonae*—the transcendent Brahman and Dharmakaya and the immanent sunyata—are immune to sexist projections. Further, in Hinduism and in popular Buddhism the *impersonae* leave room at another level for a plurality of deities who are, in Hinduism, believed to personify different aspects of the ultimate One in relation to human life. These deities are both male and female, with the goddesses as much worshipped by men as by women; and it is recognized that it is proper to choose the deity on whom to focus one's devotional life.

Thus far it might seem that Westerners would do well to turn from the more rigidly male conception of the divine in Judaism, Christianity, and Islam to the more fluid and varied personifying that occurs within Hinduism; indeed, a number of people have done this. But the situation is not as simple as that. Although the Hindu philosophy of Advaita Vedanta has a transcultural appeal, the multitude of Hindu gods and goddesses, and the rich matrix of mythology that joins them in a common religious universe of discourse, are distinctively Indian. Shiva and Kali inhabit a different mythic space from that in which our Western souls have been formed. There is therefore much wisdom in the view that it is generally best to live within the religious tradition into which we were born and that has in so many ways created us in its own image.

Most of us thus find ourselves thrown back upon the resources of the Christian tradition. The founder of this tradition was male. (He was, to be sure, only the unwitting founder since he evidently expected the end of the age within a very few years and could have had no conception that he was launching a movement that was to continue for two thousand years). Because Jesus is a historical figure about whom there is a certain amount of evidence, I see no point in blurring the fact that he was a man and little in trying to soften it by suggesting that he was the feminine *Sophia*, or Wisdom, incarnate. In an impressive number of indications in the Gosepls, however, Jesus was not a male chauvinist but was on the contrary one who, had he lived today, might well have been a male feminist. In his own time, as throughout the ancient world, the dominant cultures allowed only male prophets, gurus, and messiahs; thus, it is not surprising that all the founders of the existing great world traditions were men. But if we accept that the Real is always and necessarily perceived by human beings through human cultural lenses, we should not reject these great spirits because they were men or reject their insights because they were often expressed in male terms. We should respond to them from within our own world, a world in which patriarchy is at least beginning to give way to a postpatriarchal—I owe this phrase to Nancy Howell—age. In doing so, Christians will be developing their tradition in a new way, although in reality that tradition has always been a process of change—and of very rapid change during the past two centuries. A development away from male to inclusive ways in rethinking the Christian gospel might now be no more traumatic than the theological revolution caused by the acceptance of modern science and the scientific study of the Scriptures or the current growing acceptance of the place of Christianity in a religiously plural world. Indeed, now that the more educated strata of the Christian mind have been acclimatized to change and women are increasingly entering the priesthood and ministries of the churches, a fairly rapid transition no longer seems unlikely, though probably only in part of the Christian world, to a postpatriarchal stage. In this transition Christians seeking to establish dialogue with other religions will be natural allies of Christian feminists, for many important insights within the other great world faiths can help Christians at this point. My main positive suggestion to Pentz is, then, that she too should open her mind in this direction.

Critique by Stephen T. Davis

Rebecca Pentz' essay rings with authenticity. Clearly, as a woman and as a theologian she has struggled with these issues and has reached conclusions that are satisfactory to her. It would be odd if I, a man, were to dispute what she says, nor do I want to do so. I am happy to confess that on most points she has entirely convinced me. The few criticisms I have of her christological essay I will mention in passing. What I prefer to do is make some comments of my own on the issues she discusses.

There is no doubt that Christianity is a religion that is amazingly flexible and adaptive. The great variety of historical, cultural, and intellectual settings in which it thrives is perhaps one of its great strengths. One of the factors that drives the evolution of the Christian faith is that each generation of Christians reads the Scriptures and does theology anew in the light of the problems and opportunities it faces. For example, in the past two hundred years, Christians have come to recognize the ways in which various groups of people have been treated unfairly. And it has become painfully clear that Christians, as well as the corporate institution we call the church, have been deeply involved in discrimination and injustice. Christians today are acutely aware, for example, of the legitimate grievances of blacks, of the poor, and of women. Christianity *has* oppressed such people and, in various ways, that oppression continues. (In my opinion, however, Christian discrimination against these people has had little to do with Christology.) Doubtless, future

Christians will discover new injustices of which the church and Christians must repent. Currently, though, as Pentz' essay symbolizes, the church is going through a painful period of adjustment in the light of the legitimate complaints of women. I take it as a strength that the church is able to recognize the need for such adjustment.

Let me now comment on three of the points Pentz makes in her essay.

(1) The fact that Jesus was male is clearly troubling to some feminists. It is odd, however, that anyone even takes seriously Mary Daly's argument: "Since 'God' is male, the male is God." To me this argument is on a par with "Since Jesus was right-handed, then right-handers are God." Other feminists seem to argue: "Since Jesus was male, then God is male." But that argument too fails and is about as convincing as "Since Jesus was right-handed, then God is right-handed." As Pentz correctly points out, Christian tradition virtually unanimously teaches that God transcends human sexual categories. Even if this were not true, i.e., even if human sexual categories applied to God, the argument would not follow. The fact that Jesus was male does seem to me to have been historically and culturally useful—it would have been more difficult for God's purposes in the incarnation to have been accomplished had Jesus been female. Sadly, even fewer would have listened to her message. But I consider Jesus' maleness theologically or metaphysically unnecessary and nonessential.

Finally, it seems to me that the argument that women are excluded by Jesus' maleness works best against minimalist Christologies. If Jesus Christ was entirely human and if his atoning work was entirely subjective (i.e., if what he did for us was primarily to set a lofty example and provide an ideal model of human existence), women may well be excluded. A male example or model may seem irrelevant to their needs; as Pentz correctly says, women need female models. Thus a maximalist Christology, combined as such notions usually are with some sort of "objective" understanding of atonement, seems far more applicable to women. (Shall we dub this "the feminist argument against minimalism in Christology"?)

(2) Pentz' distinction between power *over* and power *for* is incisive and helpful. In distinguishing between them, I think that the real question has to do with who decides whether X is going to have power over (or power for) Y. For X's power for Y (i.e., power exercised consciously by X for the benefit of Y) can be perverse and oppressive if Y does not agree to it (as Pentz recognizes). Thus, it is significant that God gives us freedom to say yes or no to God, to love God or hate God, to obey God or disobey God. Such freedom (combined with God's benevolence and compassion for us) ensures that God's power *over* us is also power *for* us. But we pay a price for this gift (as Pentz also recognizes)—freedom is a dangerous thing if misused. Sadly, we humans misuse it daily.

At one point, however, I think things are slightly more complicated than Pentz lets on. Even in clear instances of power *for*, e.g., a good coach training an athlete, a good parent raising a child, there are inevitable points of tension between the desires of the two. Surely Karolyi didn't always get his way; surely Retton had not agreed that he should; surely Retton too had a degree of decision-making power in the training process. The point is that this subtlety does not seem to apply well to the Christian notion of God. God does allow us decision-making power, of course—we can, if we want, refuse to do the will of God. But that is not the Christian ideal. Christians are to submit *entirely* to the command of God. We are to submit, so to speak, without question. It is still power for, however, both because God's decisions are made for our benefit and because those who submit to the will of God do so because they have chosen to do so.

(3) Pentz argues convincingly that Jesus, a male Savior, can save women. As she points out, however, God's redemptive purposes in Christ might be thwarted if female sins were more redemptively intractable, so to speak, than male sins. My only minor corrective here is that Pentz implies that we can be sure that God's redemptive purpose will not be thwarted, because of divine omnipotence. I think it is not quite that simple; because human freedom is involved, redemption is not merely a matter of divine *power*. Perhaps the sins of women make them more spiritually stubborn and resistant to the voice of God than men are.

The fact is, I think, that just the reverse is true. In Western cultures, for example, women surely seem more *open* to the voice of God than men are. In most Christian churches on most Sundays in Europe and the Americas, for example, there are more women than men. The plain fact is that women, in these cultures, are more religious than men. Why? Perhaps it has something to do with pride and self-sacrifice. In most Western cultures, men are trained to be omnipotent providers. We can handle any problem with no assistance; we take care of the needs of our women and children; we never cry and rarely submit to or ask for help. Women, on the other hand (at least until recently), were trained to submit (to the will of fathers and husbands, usually); they were taught to ask for help when needed and to cry whenever appropriate. Perhaps, then, it is harder for us men, trained in autonomy as we were, to abandon pride, submit to God, and accept God's grace. Perhaps it is easier for women, trained in submission as they were, to submit to God.

These conjectures, which of course are horseback sociology, may be worthless. If they are worth anything, however, they may have rather startling implications. From the point of view of religion, the reorienting of sexual roles that our society is now undergoing ought to be moving, at least at one point, not in the direction of women being more like men but in the direction of men being more like women. I am of the opinion that the main thing that keeps people from God is not the problem of evil or the lack of proof but pride. We want to be autonomous. Perhaps if all people were taught to submit and to accept help whenever appropriate, more of us would be able to turn to God.

Critique by James M. Robinson

Although I am much less familiar with feminist literature than is the author, I am, perhaps uncritically for that very reason, sympathetic with the positive answer she gives to the question she poses (or, more precisely, finds posed with such acuteness by more left-wing feminists), as to whether Jesus can save women. But I am not as content with the way she goes about it.

The presuppositions of her presentation are those of traditional Christianity. She writes in defense of "an orthodox Christology," having in view "an orthodox Christian woman," presenting a position that "is consistent with the more traditional view of Christ the Savior."

I suspect that persons who share this presupposition are not really troubled by the question whether Jesus can save them. They begin where Pentz begins, with her closing cinch-the-argument statement: "Jesus has saved me." Thus, the careful logic, arguing that it is possible for Jesus to do what one knows that he in fact has done, seems like a battering ram used to force one's way through open doors. On the other hand, the persons who have first raised that question usually do not share those traditional assumptions and therefore cannot be swayed by arguments that to them seem to beg the question. Those who share the traditional presuppositions will of course be pleased to see their side of the discussion presented in language with which they identify, but they will no doubt also sense that the argument is overdone. To believe that women are saved, does an orthodox Christian really need to be reminded that at the end one woman will be taken and the other, working beside her, will be left?

My own problem in this regard has to do with Pentz' thinking in terms of "the Jesus of orthodox Christianity." We are reminded again and again that he was male (though God is not). Much sounds as if Pentz is talking about the Galilean Jew of the first century of the common era. Yet, much sounds as if she is not. Does she really think the Galilean girl Mary composed the Magnificat? Even modern critical Roman Catholic scholarship has given up its historicity in this sense. Similarly Pentz sounds as if she takes as historical fact the three temptations, the foot washing, and the Johannine theology put on Jesus' tongue in the story of the woman at the well.

The following sounds as if Jesus has read and kept fresh in mind, as has Pentz, Valerie Saiving's interesting article: "Jesus realizes that women may find it easy to be self-sacrificing and therefore do not need to be nudged in that direction," but "calls women from particularly feminine sins." "But Jesus realizes that hearing and keeping God's word requires effort in different areas for women that it does for men. And Jesus encourages women in the areas in which they need encouragement." "Jesus rejects this attempt to exalt Mary for being a baby bearer and child nurturer." Was Jesus really so with-it?

One of the leading spokespersons for the social gospel the first time around was Friedrich Naumann, a German socialist politician and pastor. But he was basically disillusioned by visiting Palestine and seeing that the Arab *fellahin*, whom he assumed, probably rightly, were more in Jesus' cultural situation than was he, knew nothing about the things alive in German politics that he had been claiming Jesus was "for" or "against." Albert Schweitzer demonstrated how, generation after generation, we have made the historical Jesus into our own image. We need to be methodologically explicit and sophisticated if we today seek to "claim" Jesus for this or that.

In places, of course, *Jesus* does not seem to refer to the Galilean peasant Jesus of Nazareth but to a heavenly body, in that the statements most appealing to a feminist occur after his death. (In the early church, it was the Gnostics who claimed that the resurrected Jesus had a higher message than the Jesus of the public ministry, against which trend the Gospels may well have been written.) "Jesus continues to nurture us like a mother," "feeds us," "lets us make mistakes . . . just as a wise mother does. . ." "He is a mother who gives us birth." (Shades of Nicodemus!) Apparently we are being asked to think of the resurrected as still a man (*he*), but transfigured into a woman's personality.

I must admit confusion about the applicability of sexuality to the resurrected, if the language is meant literally rather than metaphorically. As God, the resurrected should have no sex (though presumably this restriction should be applied only to the divine nature, if one is still able to sort all that out), or, as resurrected human, it (?) should be like the angels, who neither marry nor are given in marriage. Yet such speculation is the kind that modern people find hard to relate to. But precisely the kind of people who find difficulty with Jesus' maleness are the kind who are concerned with understanding clearly what Pentz is talking about and what they are being invited to take seriously.

The idea of God's having control over us in the sense of being for us is a good definition of paternalism. The parent knows best, even when the child thinks what is being ordered or advised is not what the child needs, and the child simply has to accept. Such an idealized version of an Ancient Near Eastern despot is what traditional ideas of God have usually amounted to. (Actually, one of the problems with the historical Jesus seems to be that he was unoriginal with regard to the doctrine of God, in comparison with contemporary Judaism, so that talk of "his revelation of who God the Father is" can lead one to expect more than he in fact delivered in this regard.) This God has been the role model on which the ecclesiastic hierarchy has been built (in spite of certain sayings ascribed to Jesus against such a hierarchy). "In Christ's community there will be no hierarchies in which one male lords it over all others." What Christian confession or denomination does Pentz have in mind? "Because God sits at the top of the hierarchy, no human patriarch who may be tempted to oppress may aspire to this position." What about the patriarch of Antioch, of Alexandria? Just saying the way it ought to be does not make it so. In these latter days the church should not be naïve. Two millennia of talk of an ideal heavenly hierarchy have not eradicated human hierarchies, and we should not act as if such talk now is going to do what it manifestly has failed to do. The ideal that Jesus set before him and us (the kingdom of God) should not be presented in abstraction from the reality in which we live; rather, it should be put in the dialectic relationship of judgment and grace to that reality.

Pentz' Response to Critiques

I want to thank my colleagues for their thoughtful comments. I am always impressed by John Hick's inclusive, pluralistic spirit, and Davis', Cobb's, and Robinson's critiques have helped me to clarify my thinking in several areas. Davis has rightly pointed out another disanalogy in the relationship between a human mentor and his or her pupil and between God and his creatures. I note in my essay that God's goodness and knowledge far exceed any human mentor's. Davis observes correctly that pupils participate more in decision making with their human mentors than we do with God, though I might add that God is remarkably responsive to our prayers (see, e.g., Matt. 7:7–11).

Cobb rightly emphasizes the importance of using feminine language for God and although I use feminine pronouns in my critiques, I do not in my essay. In English the generic pronoun is also the masculine pronoun; when we use it generically, it frequently speaks to us in its masculine capacity. To counterbalance this effect, we need at least at times to refer to God as *she*. Of course, as all of us agree, whether we use *she*, the masculine *he*, or the generic *he*, we use these pronouns analogically. God is not a female person, not a male person, not a human person.

Because our language about God is of necessity analogical, I find it hard to understand Robinson's inference that the resurrected Jesus must be a man (I think Robinson means "male human") because he is referred to as a *he*. On the other hand, I do appreciate Robinson's methodological reminder that we do not have direct access to the historical Jesus. Of course we cannot quote some biblical passage and assume that Jesus or Mary said just those words. Nor can we pretend that the Johannine texts—nor for that matter the Markan, Matthean, or Lukan texts—are free from interpretation. Certainly we must be aware of the danger so aptly identified by Schweitzer—the danger of projecting ourselves into the historical data, of seeing ourselves rather than Jesus through the glass darkly.

Given all this interpretive overlay, what are we to use as our guide as to who Jesus was and is? We can, like Hick, "imagine" what Jesus was like, or we can search for the "remarkable" Jesus hidden behind "the proto-orthodox facade of the New Testament," which Robinson refers to in his critique of Davis' essay, or we can use the portrayal given us in the canonical texts. I for one do not care to follow an imagined Lord. And it is not clear to me that Robinson's search for the hidden Jesus can escape the pitfall identified by Schweitzer. Interpretive biases even affect what is taken to be the true historical kernel. My hunch is that we are not going to be able to find some uninterpreted fact about Jesus and that even if we can, it will be devoid of meaning. My method has been, therefore, to take the canonical texts, as full of interpretation as they are, and to investigate the picture of Jesus portrayed in them. Robinson notwithstanding, this Jesus is incredibly with-it. Other feminist studies of the Old and New Testaments that I greatly respect, such as Trible's and Fiorenza's, make full use of the historical-critical method. They too reveal a God who is remarkably with-it once the patriarchal blinders that the church has worn for so many years are taken off. Both the canonical Jesus and the Jesus revealed by the historical-critical method are with-it.

To the main point—Robinson has rightly perceived that my essay is an apologia for orthodox Christianity for feminists. In fact, one might think of my essay as an attempt to answer the question, *what aspects of orthodox Christianity are compatible with feminism?* My apologia would not be very effective if I were to give up orthodoxy in order to communicate more effectively with other feminists. Nor do I think it is necessary to do so. I think Robinson would be surprised to find how many of my sisters within the orthodox tradition are asking searching questions. Both women and men are asking whether patriarchal practices are integral to Christianity and whether the beliefs and practices that are integral contradict feminist values. Likewise, my experience tells me that my sisters outside the tradition will be more receptive to my apologia than Robinson predicts. What I have found is that these sisters are glad to discover that an orthodox Christian can with integrity fully affirm and fight for feminist values.

Because a complete apologia for orthodox Christianity is beyond the scope of this project, I have let the feminist literature dictate my concerns: Jesus' revelation of God as a transcendent Father, Jesus as a model human, and Jesus as our Savior. I was surprised to see that the critiques focus almost exclusively on my first section—Jesus' revelation of a transcendent Father—with a special concentration on my understanding of God's power. Cobb is most concerned with my defense of divine omnipotence, calling it "incongruous for a feminist" and personally disturbing. James Robinson thinks that my concept of God's power being over us but for us is merely a definition of paternalism, and as I mentioned, Davis thinks the distinction needs further refining. Because this is the common theme, I shall focus on it.

Are the concepts of *omnipotence* and *power over* inherently offensive to feminists? Before we can answer that question, we need to be clearer about what these concepts mean. *Omnipotence* refers to God's maxi-ability; it is usually defined as God's ability to do anything that it is logically possible to do. On the face of it, I do not see why having such maxi-ability should be offensive to feminists. Certainly if God has the ability to do anything that it is logically possible to do, he has the ability to demean women, to support and even instigate patriarchal systems of oppression, to control every action of his creatures, male and female. But the fact that an omnipotent God has these abilities tells us absolutely nothing about which abilities he chooses to exercise. I think one of the reasons omnipotence may seem offensive is that it is assumed that if God has an ability he will exercise it. This is of course absurd. All of us have abilities we do not exercise. I have the ability to destroy my word processor, but I certainly do not intend to exercise it. God has the ability to prevent my drinking coffee, but I sincerely doubt that he will ever exercise it. Even though God has the ability to control all of his creatures, he has chosen not to exercise it. Instead, he has chosen to exercise a different ability, his ability to endow his creatures with free will.

A second important point about omnipotence stems from this gift of free will. If an omnipotent being can do only that which it is logically possible to do, there is a sense in which God cannot do some things. If I freely choose to drink this coffee, he can prevent me from drinking, but he cannot prevent me and at the same time respect my freedom. In this instance he cannot choose both to keep my freedom intact and to overpower me. That is not logically possible. So if God does choose to respect our freedom as he does in so many cases, he cannot at the same time exercise his power over us. That is logically impossible to do; not even an omnipotent being can do it. The mere fact that God is omnipotent entails absolutely nothing about whether or not he is an oppressive patriarch and in fact gives us no information at all about which abilities he chooses to exercise. I can sense nothing here offensive to women.

In *God, Power, and Evil: A Process Theodicy* David Griffin suggested (following Charles Hartshorne) another critique of omnipotence. He argued that if God is omnipotent, he has all the power and his creatures have none. Nelson Pike, in his article "Process Theodicy and the Concept of Power," has effectively discredited that notion. I have the power to lift my coffee cup, but so does my two-year-old daughter. My having a power does not entail that you lack that power; God's having all power does not entail that we lack all power. Griffin's concern cannot be a stumbling block for feminists. In fact, Griffin has the situation exactly backward. Because our God makes his power available to us, our power is enhanced by his omnipotence.

Cobb offers another criticism. He claims that omnipotence is an Old Testament concept, whereas in the New Testament, except in the book of Revelation, "God's power is neither revealed as omnipotent nor spoken of in those terms." I am a little surprised that Cobb is concerned with the biblical testimony because he tells us specifically in his critique that biblical images are not satisfactory and that we must look to the future, not the past. I am concerned with the biblical testimony because I think it records God's unique revelation to us. In a postscript I examine in some detail the biblical source of the doctrine of omnipotence.

The notion that God has power over us does not fare as well as that of omnipotence. Christians who claim that God has power over us are making a claim about how God exercises his abilities. They are claiming that God not only has the ability to rule over us, he in fact does rule over us. This rulership can be construed as offensive; however, it is important to be clear about where the offense lies. Often the critique by process theology is that God's power as portrayed by orthodox Christianity is coercive, whereas loving power is persuasive. What is at issue here is God's style of rule, the process theologians claiming that in the orthodox view it is oppressive. But Cobb admits that my view of God's power does not entail coercion. (Certainly omnipotence entails the ability to coerce. But, as I have argued, having an ability does not entail the exercise of that ability.) Lewis Ford, a noted process theologian, suggested in an unpublished essay entitled "The Rhetoric of Divine Power" that the process polemics against the coerciveness of the classical view of God are in fact "unconvincing and probably unfair." The Christian God is not coercive. Nor does he dominate us. He is the Father who gives the prodigal his share of the inheritance and then waits for his return. He is the one who waits for our knock so that he can open the door. When he sends his Son to save us, he shuns the use of all force and becomes the suffering servant. If in fact the God revealed by Jesus refuses to use coercion, what is it that is offensive about God's power over us?

I guess in the end what is troublesome both for Cobb and for Robinson is the mere fact that someone has authority over us, however benevolent that authority may be. We humans have come of age. We can take care of ourselves, and certainly we can rule ourselves. If there are other beings in the universe, we are their partners, not their subjects. Somehow the thought that someone superior might rule over us is demeaning. As Robinson says, it is paternalistic. Or as Cobb says rather pointedly: "it is important to go from the status of slaves to that of friends." At least part of what is at issue here is our freedom. My critics seem to be suggesting that if there is a hierarchy with God the Father at the top, we are not free enough. We are slaves; we are not free. What my own experience tells me and what I read in the biblical testimony are that the only way we can be free is in relationship to God—that those who are autonomous and "doing their own thing" are the least free.

Of course making this notion of Christian freedom clear is extremely difficult. How can you be most free when you are "subjugated"? My notion of God's power over us but for us seems to aggravate this problem. Therefore, even though I as yet find nothing demeaning in the notion that God nurtures us as a mentor nurtures a pupil, I would like to examine two Pauline metaphors that perhaps better illuminate the notion of Christian freedom.

Cobb's dichotomy between slaves and friends omits a third possibility—that we are neither. Paul tells us specifically that we are not slaves (Gal. 4:7). Insofar as *friend* implies *peer*, we are not (contra Cobb) friends with God. It is the height of human arrogance to think that we are peers with the Creator and Ruler of the whole universe. The Indians used to worship Mount Rainier—*Tahoma*, they called it. Today the people who climb Mount Rainier are fully aware that it is wise to have a healthy respect for the mountain. The mountain can kill us if we are careless and disrespectful of it. Its power dwarfs us. If a mountain that is merely a small part of God's creation can dwarf us, how much more does God's power dwarf us? Even Jesus, when he called us his friends in John 15:14, prefaced his remark with the caveat that we must obey his commands. "You are my friends if you do what I command you." Abraham became the "friend of God" only by his willingness to obey the most terrible command—to kill his son Isaac. We are not God's buddies.

If we are not God's slaves and not her friends, what are we? Paul has an interesting answer. We are members of Christ's body. Christ is the head, and we are the arms, the legs, the fingers, the toes, the eyes, the ears. We are part of an organic whole with God. This Pauline metaphor speaks powerfully to me of Christian freedom. Certainly my leg is under the "control" of my brain. But think what would happen if it were "set free." It would be a nonfunctioning lump of flesh, with no freedom of movement at all. Or think of the cerebral palsy victim whose body is deprived of control by the brain. The uncontrolled movements of those arms and legs are a parody of freedom. True freedom is found when the brain is in control. I do not want to push this one metaphor too far. Paul and Jesus also call us children of God, a decidedly hierarchical notion, but the emphasis is on our being set free as children so that we are no longer slaves to sin. In both these metaphors our relationship to God is an intimate one; we are part of her body—he is our *Abba*, daddy. In both it is the relationship that enables us to be free. It is the intimate relationship itself that sets us free from all heteronomous controls.

These truths are certainly ones we women can affirm. True freedom is not found in isolation. True freedom is found in relationship. We women know how it is possible to bloom in a relationship, to become most ourselves, not in isolation from but in connection with another. As paradoxical as it sounds, I am freer now as a mother and wife than I ever was as a single woman. I am freer to love and to be loved, to give and to be given to. I am freer to let all my little idiosyncrasies show. I am freer to be bold in any undertaking I choose, be it teaching or writing or talking with women about feminism.

Of course our relationship with God is quite different from our human relationships. It is not a relationship between equals. Yet I think that for this reason it is more freeing. God created us: she knows intimately what we can be when we are freely expressing ourselves. God's interests are not divided; she is not struggling to find her own identity while we struggle to find ours. Nor, as I have mentioned, is she limited in knowledge or goodwill or power. She has the power and the knowledge to free us from whatever would enslave us. Furthermore, Paul's "head" metaphor implies a sense in which we are in a much more intimate relationship with God than we are with any human. We are part of her body. All these considerations shed light on the unique Christian experience of finding freedom by subjecting oneself to God's will. What is our status as humans? Are we slaves? We need not be. Are we friends? We dare not be. Are we free? We can be.

What are the dangers for women, then, in the notion that God has power over us and that we are dependent on her? I suppose there is a danger for women if we think that all fulfillment is found "through the male" and we do not develop a self-identity. There is a danger if we have a psychological fixation on maleness and never feel at home with our femaleness. And there is a danger if we sacrifice ourselves before we have a self to sacrifice. But as I argue in my essay, Jesus called women away from these real dangers for women to self-identity, to wholeness, to excellence as women. He did not call us to independence from God the Father. Nor do I see any danger in acknowledging dependence on the being who created us, sustains us, loves us, who is both our Father and our "head." I have no need to make some such macho statement of independence.

I fully and painfully realize, as Robinson reminds us once again, that Jesus' revelation of a "heavenly hierarchy" has been followed by two centuries of oppression by patriarchies. But must we women give up our faith because men have misused it? It seems to me that we should not allow ourselves to be so bullied. At the same time I empathize with feminists who have felt they needed to reject orthodox Christianity. It is these sisters I appeal to. Our feminist movement is an inbreaking of Jesus' kingdom here and now on earth. Within the church we are making strides in the right direction, though our pace is slow and our steps are small. We no longer say with Paul that slaves should obey their masters. Nor do all denominations have an exclusively male clergy. Nor am I as a woman prevented from doing and teaching philosophical theology.

Beyond these encouraging signs Christianity has much to offer feminists. Because we Christians affirm Jesus as God, we know that God abhors oppression because Jesus abhors it, that she values a "discipleship of equals" because Jesus values a "discipleship of equals," that the poor (who are most frequently elderly women and women with dependent children) have a special place in God's kingdom, and that everyone is accountable for how such people are treated. And we know that since God created them male and female, we too are in the image of God, that our bodies too are the temples of the Holy Spirit and should not be raped, battered, or used. More than just knowing, we experience God's power as we fight for the realization of these truths. We are not alone. The God who created the universe assures us that these truths will triumph.

In sum, what aspects of traditional Christianity must feminists give up? We must give up patriarchal accretions such as the exclusion of women from leadership, the identification of women with sin, the use of exclusively male language to describe the deity, the identification of a woman's relationship to God with her sexual relationship to men, e.g., virgin-mother. We must not passively accept the male models proffered us but must be aggressive in our biblical and historical study, searching out the mothers of the church to honor and emulate. Nor can we passively accept the male-oriented roles for women—self-demeaning sacrifice and involuntary servitude—but must hear and respond to Jesus' call to wholeness, self-esteem, and excellence. Must we give up the traditional notion of God's power when we repudiate the way men have tried to appropriate this power? Must we give up our dependence on God when we give up our dependence on men? Must we give up Jesus as our Savior when we refuse to let men be our saviors? No. Once again, I conclude, feminists can be orthodox Christians.

Postscript

The issue of whether or not God is spoken of as omnipotent in the Bible is complicated by an oddity of translation. The English word *omnipotence* is used to translate words that do not refer to God's abilities at all. They refer to God's position as Ruler of the universe. Let me explain. In Scripture, God is revealed to have two kinds of power—ruling power and ability power. These two are not the same. When we say that a ruler has certain powers, we are referring to her rights, not to her abilities. For example, a ruler may have the power to condemn her subjects to death. This does not mean that in a life-and-death battle she has the strength to win. Rather, it means that she has the authority, the right, to condemn subjects to death. A ruler may also have the power to conscript into military service. This does not mean that she has the strength to force recalcitrant draftees into military service. Rather, it means that she has the right to conscript. The powers of a ruler are the rights to perform certain functions.

Usually of course a ruler not only has rights, she has the ability to exercise her rights. Thus, it makes sense to speak of a powerful ruler, that is, one with the ability to wield effectively the normative powers given to her. God is such a powerful ruler. That one individual can have both types of power does not entail that those types are the same. Certainly rulers may have rights but no ability; just as certainly, very able persons may never be in a position to rule.

Omnipotence does not refer to ruling powers; it refers to God's abilities. Once again, from the fact that God is omnipotent we can conclude only that God has the ability to rule heaven and earth, not that she exercises this ability.

What is interesting in the English translations of the Bible is that both the English word *almighty* and the English word *omnipotent* refer to God's ruling power, not to her omnipotence. Both words are used to translate the Greek word *pantokrator*. Yet *pantokrator* means "ruler over all" and thus refers to God's position as ruler. *Almighty* is also used to translate the Hebrew title *El Shaddai*. *El* is the head god of the Canaanite pantheon, and *Shaddai* literally means "the strong one of the mountain." So *El Shaddai* is the supreme leader with numinous strength, a powerful ruler. Somewhat surprisingly, therefore, the best biblical support for God's omnipotence is not found in the passages in which God is called omnipotent and almighty, for these refer primarily to God's ruling power.

I do not mean that there is no biblical support for the doctrine of omnipotence. Job claims, "I know that thou canst do all things, and that no purpose of thine can be thwarted" (Job 42:2); the psalmist tells us,

"Whatever the Lord pleases he does, in heaven and on earth, and in the seas and all deeps" (Ps. 135:6). The best support for the doctrine of omnipotence is found in the Gospels. On two occasions Jesus teaches that God is able to do everything that it is possible to do. When the disciples hear that it is easier for a camel to go through the eye of a needle than for a rich man to enter the kingdom of God, they cry out, "Then who can be saved?" Jesus replies, "With men it is impossible, but not with God; for all things are possible with God" (Mark 10:27). Second, according to the Gospel of Mark, Jesus prays in Gethsemane, "Abba, Father, all things are possible to thee; remove this cup from me; yet not what I will, but what thou wilt" (Mark 14:36). The most straightforward understanding of these texts is that God is not only able to save whomsoever she wishes, including Jesus, but that God is able to do everything which it is possible to do; i.e., God is omnipotent. So the best support for the doctrine of omnipotence is not found in the passages in the Old Testament and the book of Revelation, where God is called almighty and omnipotent, but in the Gospels.

As the process theologians admit, there are also philosophical reasons for attributing omnipotence to God. Alfred North Whitehead claimed in *Process and Reality* that God is the chief exemplification of all metaphysical principles. Lewis Ford took this to mean that God's power cannot be limited. David Griffin argued in *God, Power and Evil* that we can worship only a being who is perfect and in whom any limitation of power is an imperfection; Charles Hartshorne, for much the same reason, argued that God's power must be "absolutely maximal." The idea these process theologians are espousing is the traditional one. God is the greatest possible being, and she would not count as God if she had less than maximal power.

4 Very Goddess and Very Man: Jesus' Better Self[1]
JAMES M. ROBINSON

> as a hen gathers her brood under her wings
> —Q 13:34 (Chapter and verse numbers of Q follow Luke)

Masculine terminology overwhelms Christology. Jesus himself was male. The Jewish idea of the Messiah is built on the model of David and his male successors as kings of Judah. Masculine endings bind *Christos* and *Kyrios* to the male realm. *Son of God* and *Son of man* do the same. Even the *Word of God* produces masculine overtones (Logos). The one christological title that is an exception is also the one that failed to make it: Wisdom (Sophia). In this essay I seek to investigate this aborted feminine Christology.

I

First it needs to be said that all due honor could have been done to Jesus without Christology. Like Jesus, John the Baptist gave his life for the cause and was believed to have been divinely vindicated: "John the baptizer has been raised from the dead" (Mark 6:14). Jesus' own praise for John is unsurpassable: "more than a prophet. . . . Among those born of women none is greater than John. . . . From the days of John until now the kingdom of God has suffered violence" (Q 7:26, 28; 16:16). Yet John was not deified as was Jesus. Nor did the New Testament elevate Jesus' successor Peter beyond the status of Rock.

Jesus did not need to be deified to receive the high honor he deserves. Probably he would have preferred that we deify the cause: the kingdom of God. "Why do you call me good? No one is good but God alone. You know the commandments" (Mark 10:18–19). But to the extent that we in our day seek to develop a Christology, as did our predecessors, we must assume responsibility for what we say and do, as did they, and not just parrot their language. If they did the best they could, given their conditions, we must do the best we can, in our changed conditions. One is that we do not live in their mythopoeic world; another is that we live in the world of modern biblical scholarship; another is that we live in a not unchallenged patriarchal society.

Jesus, no more than John or Peter, was born doing his thing. He came to it only near the end of his life. The early tradition, going back to Jesus himself, was quite aware of this and indeed of its theological significance. The inception of the time of salvation was originally not marked by the birth of Jesus but by the ministry of John: "From the days of John the Baptist on" (Matt. 11:12 from Q). This whence of Jesus had its impact on the earliest efforts to produce a Gospel: all three of the oldest attempts to decide where to begin the Gospels agree, independently of each other, to begin with John: Q, Mark, and John.

Luke may have respected this venerable tradition in composing his Gospel as well. He appealed to it in defining the kind of person who would be eligible to become one of the Twelve: someone who was "beginning from the baptism of John" (Acts 1:22). And the apostolic preaching according to Acts begins its fulfillment of the Old Testament prophecy with John. The impressive synchronized dating of the beginning of the story as well as Jesus' genealogy occur at John's baptism of Jesus in Luke 3. So the Gospel of Luke may well have begun there, as the now-largely-discredited proto-Lukan theory had it. More recently Joseph Fitzmyer, in his Anchor Bible Commentary on Luke, suggested that Luke, after composing both Luke and Acts, may have added, as a sort of belated prologue, Luke 1–2. In any case Luke was so sophisticated he was able to write an infancy narrative that, like the beginning of the public ministry, began with John, thus combining the old tradition that the story begins with John at Jesus' baptism with the new tradition that the story begins with Jesus' birth.

Jesus' activity could have been adequately conceptualized in the thought world of that day as a person possessed by God, in a way formally comparable to the unfortunates possessed by a demon. According to that thought world the human self-consciousness could be replaced either by an evil or by a holy spirit. Such a divine spirit was portrayed as having come upon Jesus "like a dove" (Mark 1:10) at his baptism by John. This spirit should not be intellectualized as some kind of Hegelian Mind; rather, it was intended as the kind of animistic spirit-world force that Hermann Gunkel introduced into New Testament scholarship from the Old Testament and the Ancient Near East, a history-of-religion corrective for that all-too-spiritual mental spirit. If Luke described the Spirit as "in bodily form" (3:22), Mark described it very animistically as driving him out into the wilderness (1:12).

As the one whom God chose to possess at the time of his baptism, Jesus is described by a heavenly voice: "Thou art my beloved Son" (Mark 1:11).

This was not originally intended just as an announcement of an inner-trinitarian relationship that has prevailed from all eternity but was meant as a Father-Son relationship that was first set up on this occasion. A common patristic reformulation of the Lukan parallel (3:22) reflects the event-character of the voice, in adding from Psalm 2:7: "today I have begotten you." That is to say, the early interpretation of who Jesus was, in terms of his baptism in John's public ministry, does not presuppose his antecedent or perennial divine Sonship, such as is reflected already in Paul and probably in Mark 1:1: "The beginning of the gospel of Jesus Christ, the Son of God" (if the last phrase was originally in Mark—the manuscript evidence and hence scholarly opinion are rather evenly split). This reading back of divine Sonship is carried much further, e.g., by Luke at the annunciation: "the child to be born will be called holy, the Son of God" (1:35), or in his genealogy, "the son of Adam, the son of God" (3:38). Thus the baptismal voice has already been rendered anticlimactic. It is difficult for us to get out of the mind-set thereby imposed on all subsequent theology.

Perhaps a *pendant* interpretation of the end of Mark from patristic times will help one to catch sight of this primitive way of thinking (heretical though it came to be regarded): "My God, my God, why hast thou forsaken me?" (Mark 15:34) became (in the *Gospel of Peter*) "My Power, my Power, you have abandoned me" at the moment when the possessing divine, and hence immortal, spirit left the Galilean mortal to die. This possession by divine spirit and the resultant transcient adoptionism fit much better the functional (rather than metaphysical) context of a Jewish understanding of God's relation to the human he chooses to use (or, to put it in our more familiar, hence bland and inoffensive, language, to inspire). For this possessing spirit is originally neither the divine nature of the Second Person of the Trinity nor the Third Person of the Trinity but a hypostasis of the divine, popular at a time in Judaism when the fear of taking God's name in vain led to not taking it at all, preferring many surrogates (such as "kingdom of heaven"), in the broader context of a polytheistic world where spirits and demons abounded.

This part that God took in Jesus, in possessing him so as to become his functional self, did not remain within such alternatives as spirit possession and demon possession but modulated into various male-oriented christo-logical titles. A clear subordination was retained ("God" for the Father, "Lord" for Jesus; giving glory to God, Christianized not as giving glory to Jesus but as giving glory to God *through* Jesus). Christological titles nonetheless headed in the direction of Chalcedon and the traditional deification of Jesus. This was at first dated from the resurrection: "God has made him both Lord and Christ, this Jesus whom you crucified," (Acts 2:36); "obedient unto death. . . . Therefore God has highly exalted him and bestowed on him the name . . . that Jesus Christ is Lord" (Phil. 2:8–9, 11). Thus the looser, more functional relationship of Jesus and the Divine Spirit gradually sedimented into two distinct parts in a tripartite deity that blossomed under Neoplatonic tutelage into the Nicene Trinity, with the Holy Spirit as the Third Person, then into the Chalcedonian two natures of the Second Person.

II

The connection between the titles and the sex of God becomes more apparent when we recall that the gender of nouns was often taken as indicating the sex of the subject to whom the noun referred. The Hebrew word for Spirit, *ruach*, is usually feminine (though at times it is used masculinely). Thus, in a Semitic world of thought the tripartite deity could reflect the core family of father, mother, and child. But the Greek word for Spirit, *pneuma*, is neuter, so that the question became relevant as to whether the Third Person (the Spirit's position when no longer the mother in the core family) is actually a person at all. Because the Latin word for Spirit, *spiritus*, is masculine, the personality of the Spirit was thereby assured . . . as was the all-male trinity. Even though a theologian-linguist such as Jerome (in his commentary on Isa. 40:9-11) could point out that the three diverging genders of the noun for Spirit show that God has no sex, the metaphorical suggestiveness of the gender of the nouns dominated classical theology.

To see the Semitic branch of Christianity[2] at work on the femininity of the Spirit, one need merely turn to the Syriac *Odes of Solomon*, dated contemporary with the New Testament (24:1–2; 28:1–2):

> The dove fluttered over the head of our Lord Messiah, because he was her head. And she sang over him, and her voice was heard.

> As the wings of doves over their nestlings, and the mouths of their nestlings toward their mouths, so also are the wings of the Spirit over my heart. My heart continually refreshes itself and leaps for joy, like the babe who leaps for joy in his mother's womb.

This female dove, the "incarnation" of the Spirit, is Jesus' mother (36:1–3):

> [The Spirit] brought me forth before the Lord's face. And because I was the Son of man, I was named the Light, the Son of God.

This is also reflected in the apocryphal *Gospel of the Hebrews*, with the Semitic overtones that this title suggests (cited in Jerome's commentary on Isa. 11:2):

> But it came to pass when the Lord had come up out of the water the whole font of the Holy Spirit descended upon him and rested on him and said to him: My Son, in all the prophets I was waiting for you that you should come and I might rest on you. For you are my rest. You are my first-begotten Son that reigns forever.

Here the parenting of Jesus as Son has nothing to do with his birth or with Mary but takes place at his baptism. He is not directly the Son of God but is parented by the Holy Spirit, which is an integral part of the baptism story. The feminine Spirit as Jesus' mother becomes explicit in another fragment of the *Gospel of the Hebrews* quoted both by Origen and Jerome:

> Then my mother, the Holy Spirit, took me by one hair of my head and carried me away to the great mountain, Tabor.

Here a mythological episode about the mother of the Savior has been borrowed from a tradition attested in the *Apocalypse of Adam* (Nag Hammadi Codex V, Tractate 5) and in Revelation 12.

Once Jesus' divine investment was shifted from his baptism to his conception by Mary, the idea of a divine mother could hardly be rescued (*The Gospel of Philip*, Nag Hammadi Codex II, Tractate 55, lines 23–28):

> Some say, "Mary conceived by the Holy Spirit." They are in error. They do not know what they are saying. When did a woman ever conceive by a woman?

Thus, when the Semitic feminine spirit was not replaced by the Greek neuter or Latin masculine Spirit, it was replaced by the human Mary.

A parallel development may have been even more significant at the beginning but less well known today because the protagonist, unlike the Spirit, has faded from the theological aristocracy: Wisdom. Here again the Hebrew word, *hochmah*, is feminine, as are the Greek *sophia* and the Latin *sapientia*. Thus the survival of *Wisdom* in the top echelon of deity would have assured a female part at the top (which may be part of the reason *Wisdom* was dropped). *Wisdom* was fading fast by the time the New Testament itself was written. It may be no coincidence that within the canon the strongest attestation for it (and not very strong at that) is early, two texts that are from the central third of the first century rather than from the last third, from which the bulk of the New Testament comes: 1 Corinthians 1–4, among the authentic Pauline letters dated approximately A.D. 50 and Q, probably equally old, at least in its first draft, and clearly older than Matthew and Luke, which incorporate more recent versions of most of it.

One of the problems that used to beset New Testament scholarship is how Christology could have developed so rapidly, from a holy man of A.D. 30 to the high Christology of such a text as the pre-Pauline hymn of Philippians 2:6–11. But this has to do with the hymnic setting of most of the earliest high Christology and with Wisdom Christology of the hymns. Christology seems to have grown most rapidly in the exuberance (inspiration) of hymnic ecstasy and in this ecstasy to have flown on the wings of Wisdom mythology.

The standard outline of a Jewish prayer of the day was an opening blessing or thanksgiving to God, for having done this and that (in *parallelismus membrorum*). This was followed by the body of the prayer, typically recounting in more detail God's mighty works, often oriented toward anticipation of the third part, in which God was petitioned to do again the kinds of things he had just been praised for having done for others in the past. This Jewish prayer outline could be Christianized by referring to Jesus in connection with the thanksgiving to God, as in Colossians 1:12, 14 ("giving thanks to the Father . . . transferred us to the kingdom of his beloved Son"); the central section could be christological, in hymnic style, beginning with the masculine relative pronoun *who*. This would explain this otherwise inexplicable beginning word in the christological hymns Philippians 2:6–11, Colossians 1:15–20, and 1 Timothy 3:16. In 1 Timothy 3:16 the problem is especially difficult because the apparent antecedent of the masculine pronoun *who* is the neuter noun *mystery*. This led to the misreading of *who* (OS) as *God* (THEOS, abbreviated to THS), as in the King James Bible. Though the comparable christological hymn embedded in the prologue to the Gospel of John does not begin with the masculine relative pronoun but with an analogy to Genesis 1:1, the introduction of the masculine noun *Logos* provides the equivalent male orientation. Thus the high Christology of these hymns, upon which all subsequent high Christologies have been built, became male oriented.

This high Christology, taking place within a generation of Jesus' death, was able to arise so rapidly because the intellectual apparatus it needed had been formed within Judaism. It only needed to be transferred to Jesus (as was done in other christological concepts such as Christ and Son of man) in order for this quasi-divine hypostasis of Jewish Wisdom speculation to become perhaps the highest Christology within primitive Christianity. But this first approximation to the divine nature of the Second Person of the Trinity was feminine: Wisdom.

III

One of the relevant dimensions of this Wisdom speculation is that, like the title "Prophet" (which also did not prevail as a christological title), it is not exclusively applicable to Jesus. Most christological titles were "divine" enough to share in the exclusivity of monotheism, in that *only* Jesus is Lord (1 Cor. 8:5–6), Son of man, Son of God (Q 10:22), Savior (although of course giving Jesus such quasi-divine titles alongside the Father as also God was not pure monotheism, as our Jewish colleagues like to remind us; see again 1 Cor. 8:5–6). But through the ages Wisdom has spoken through various spokespersons whom she has inspired, according to the Jewish Wisdom tradition (Wisdom of Solomon 7:27):

> Though she is but one, she can do all things, and while remaining in herself, she renews all things; in every generation she passes into holy souls and makes them friends of God, and prophets.

This approach continued in Jewish-Christian (that is to say, primitive Christian) Wisdom Christology. "Yet Wisdom is vindicated by her children" (Q 7:35). This refers to the repudiation of John and Jesus by "this generation" in the preceding context. Rather than saying "they" (or "John" and "the Son of man," as they had just been designated), the punch line speaks only of "Wisdom," as if what was at stake were not the bearers of Wisdom as human individuals but the divine Wisdom they bore, and as if it were *her* children, not designated as *them* or *their* disciples, who vindicate her.

The nonexclusivity of the Wisdom Christology may be suggested in another Q text, where a saying is ascribed not to Jesus, but to Sophia (as Luke faithfully reports Q, though Matthew shifts to the first-person singular, thus making Jesus the speaker):

> Therefore also the Wisdom of God said, I will send them prophets and apostles, some of whom they will kill and persecute, that the blood of all the prophets, shed from the foundation of the world, may be required of this generation, from the blood of Abel to the blood of Zechariah, who perished between the altar and the sanctuary. Yes, I tell you, it shall be required of this generation. (Q 11:49–51)

The saying in Q apparently continued in what follows in Matthew, although Luke put the continuation elsewhere:

> O Jerusalem, Jerusalem, killing the prophets and stoning those who are sent to you! How often would I have gathered your children together as a hen gathers her brood under her wings, and you would not! Behold, your house is forsaken. And I tell you, you will not see me until you say, "Blessed is he who comes in the name of the Lord." (Q 13:34–35)

The extent to which this saying refers more appropriately to Wisdom than to Jesus can be illustrated by the following anecdote from the history of scholarship. One of the traditional debates in the quest of the historical Jesus had to do with the minimum amount of time that must be conjectured for Jesus' public ministry. It was assumed this could be calculated in terms of how many annual Jewish festivals Jesus is said to have attended in Jerusalem during his ministry. Such speculation led to the choice between a minimal one-year public ministry in the Synoptic Gospels and a minimal three-year public ministry in the Gospel of John. Because the Synoptic Gospels became the basis of the quest of the historical Jesus and the Gospel of John was relegated to the role of the "spiritual" Gospel and an honored top billing in New Testament theology (and Christian theology in general), Jesus' ministry has been assumed to be one year. But advocates of the Johannine timetable have pointed to this Q passage in the Synoptic Gospels to argue in favor of the Gospel of John, maintaining that during his public ministry Jesus went to Jerusalem more than once ("how often"). Again, though, this is one of the places in Wisdom Christology where the emphasis is on the person of Wisdom, not the human who bears Wisdom. She has sent "prophets and apostles" (or, in Matthew, "prophets and sages and scribes"), a stream of martyrs "from the blood of Abel to the blood of Zechariah," without any explicit reference to John and Jesus (in Matthew "kill and persecute" becomes "kill and crucify"; "killing the prophets and stoning those who are sent to you" remains unaltered). Thus it is she, rather than John (who was beheaded) or Jesus (who was crucified), who has repeatedly called on the Jerusalemites to gather under her wings. The female metaphor of the hen and her biddies is introduced in full harmony with the feminine noun *Wisdom* and the resultant female hypostasis or personification Wisdom.

It may be part of the Wisdom Christology's nonexclusivity that the followers of Jesus are seen as carrying on his mission and message (just as he had carried on John's): "The kingdom of God has come near" (Q 10:11) (the message of the disciples); "He who receives you receives me, and he who receives me receives him who sent me" (Q 10:16). In Q, this is without the rupture of crucifixion plus the reestablishment of the disciples through Easter experiences and Pentecost (just as Jesus had carried on, John's death not suspending their shared message and John's resurrection not becoming a saving event needed to relaunch the mission and its message). These two tragic deaths, like those of the prophets before and since, cannot stop Wisdom—the mission and its message go on. To be sure, she can withdraw her presence as an anticipation of judgment (she "found no dwelling-place" and so "returned to her place . . . among the angels" [Enoch 42:1–2]), as shaking the dust off the disciples' feet symbolizes, but she will be there at the day of judgment to be vindicated and to save (Q 13:35). The finality of the abandonment of "this generation" to its fate seems to have taken place, according to Q, neither with the murder of John nor with that of Jesus but only with the final repudiation of the Jewish mission, at which time a Gentile mission is nonetheless envisaged.

Perhaps such a Wisdom Christology, precisely because of the nonexclusivity of its beginnings, would be useful in our society today, when leaving a male deity at the top of our value structuring often seems more like the deification of the omnipotent despot of the Ancient Near East than an honoring of God, more a perpetuation of patriarchalism than a liberation of women (and men—the feminist movement has of course produced insights that are also liberating to men). It is good news that we, like Jesus, can be inspired by the feminine aspect of God.

IV

In this connection I wish to speak to the question of the "Easter faith" of the Q community, which had no Passion narrative or Easter story, and thus of the Easter faith implicit in much of the original Wisdom Christology. Modern concepts of the resurrection of Christ tend toward a monolithic cast that is quite different from that of the first generation. Probably the first resurrection appearances were not experienced as they have been recorded in Matthew, Luke, and John, upon which our modern assumptions about the resurrection are primarily based. Rather, these texts, from the last third of the first century, tend to be apologetic tendentious correctives of dangers perceived as latent (or perhaps already rampant) in the original perception of the resurrection a generation earlier.

Jesus' resurrection seems to have been experienced at the time quite differently from the visualization with which we are familiar, in that Jesus appeared as a blinding light rather than as a human body mistakable for a gardener or a tourist on the Emmaus road. The only New Testament texts written by persons who had actually had a resurrection experience described it as luminosity—Paul (1 Cor. 15:42–53 and Phil. 3:21) and the seer of Revelation (1:12–16). A luminous appearance could perhaps be discounted as just an apparition and was in fact the kind of appearance the Gnostic sources favored. Hence, the concern of emergent orthodoxy to prove the physical resurrection of Jesus, an apologetic already discernible in the resurrection stories at the end of the canonical Gospels, led readily to a replacement of the luminous visualization with a very human visualization.

This replacement may explain a series of odd and not unrelated facts. It was generally agreed (1 Cor. 15:5; Luke 24:34) that the first appearance was to Peter. Yet the narration of that appearance is completely missing from the ends of the canonical Gospels. The apocryphal Gospel of Peter does record it, though with some details that might seem to us (and them) excessive and with some details that seem presupposed in some of the canonical narratives, such as a role at the resurrection itself for the two mysterious figures at the tomb in Luke 24:4. The Gospel of Mark, surprisingly enough, contains no resurrection appearances—only the empty tomb and the promise of Galilean appearances. Remember the bad press that Peter received in Mark (8:33: "Get behind me, Satan! For you are not on the side of God, but of men"). Mark did record a luminous appearance primarily to Peter (though also to the other two of the inner circle), but it is not at the end of the Gospel as a resurrection story; it is in the middle, as a confirmation of Peter's confession. It is the story that we traditionally distinguish from resurrection appearances by calling it the transfiguration. One may wonder whether Mark has not blunted the dangerous implications of the luminous resurrection story, with all its disembodied suggestiveness, by putting it before the crucifixion, in the middle of the public ministry, when Jesus' physicality was obvious.

Perhaps the left wing of bifurcating primitive Christianity had been using the luminous resurrection appearances to place importance on what Jesus said after the resurrection, when he was no longer shackled by a body of flesh and had recently been to heaven to learn firsthand the ultimate, as the Gnostics would put it. This would in effect play down the authority of what Jesus said during the public ministry. It may be no mere coincidence that Mark planted this authority-bestowing (9:7: "This is my beloved Son; listen to him!") luminous appearance in the middle of the public ministry. For Mark was the first to write a Gospel narrating the public ministry, thereby both playing down the relative importance of Jesus' sayings in comparison to his miracles and placing the sayings in Jesus' lifetime rather than acknowledging the validity of those people who claimed they were still hearing from the resurrected Christ. (According to Acts, God continued after the first forty days to communicate through the Holy Spirit rather than through resurrection appearances.) That is to say, Mark may have clipped the wings of the trajectory that is visible in the sayings tradition as we move from Q to the Gnostic Gospel of Thomas.

This way of handling the story of the resurrection appearance to Peter may be analogous to the way the story of the resurrection appearance to Paul is narrated (three times) in Acts. Luke told the story as a luminous visualization. But he placed it outside the forty-day span of resurrection appearances. Furthermore, for Paul, apostleship was defined by being an eyewitness of the resurrection; Acts 1:22 adds to that definition being an eyewitness of the public ministry, which would exclude Paul. And Acts does not concede to Paul the kind of apostleship that he was so eager to maintain for himself (Gal. 1:1), using only the temporary and rather unimportant meaning of *apostolos*, a delegate of the church of Antioch on the first missionary journey.

If the resurrection of Jesus during the first generation was experienced in such a luminous visualization, such appearances could well be more characterized by auditions than by actions, such as eating fish or having one's wounds touched. The blinding light spoke only to Paul (Acts 9:4–6). The itinerant preachers that transmitted the Q tradition before it was

written down and then incorporated it in Matthew and Luke kept Jesus'
sayings alive by reproclaiming them, not as their words but as his, that is to
say, as Wisdom's. In the process they not only reproclaimed what he had
said before his crucifixion, they also ascribed to him—her—new sayings,
which continued to emerge throughout that generation. It was the cause for
which he stood, his message, that was still valid, just as John's cause had still
been valid for Jesus after John's death. That is to say, the substantive,
theologically relevant aliveness of Jesus after his crucifixion was that of his
cause, God's reign. In terms of Wisdom Christology, Wisdom lived on in the
ongoing message, much as John's message—i.e., Wisdom's message—had
survived in Jesus'. And Wisdom would continue as the authority figure until
the day of judgment, when her guidance would be vindicated as the criterion
determining human destiny. Rudolf Bultmann's dictum that Jesus rose into
the kerygma could thus be adapted to Wisdom Christology by saying that
Jesus rose into the life of Wisdom's ongoing proclamation.

V

This Sophia Christology, precisely because it did not come to fruition in
Western Christianity but shared in the Western neglect of Eastern
Christianity, is less a recording of a traceable strand of Christian history than
a nostalgic reminiscence of what might have been. Because the mythical
world in which Christianity began is for us dead, this stillborn Christology
may be forever lost.

Though we have seen through myths, in recognizing their nonliteral
and purely symbolic meaning (e.g., in demythologization), they may as
symbols have a new lease on life. If Gnosticism could engender artificially its
mythology out of the myths of the Ancient Near East, or Plato could create
the myth of the cave to portray his idealism or Freud could appeal to Greek
mythology to interpret the Oedipus complex, it is not inconceivable that this
Sophia Christology could have an appeal in our day.

In this connection we should not ignore the problem that besets the
usual christological language with which we are quite familiar. Most of
Christian myth is weighed down with the all-too-familiar, all-too-literal
context in which we are accustomed to hearing it. It is easier for enlightened
people today to free themselves of the pre-Enlightenment idea that Jesus is a
God, however that may have been languaged through the centuries, than to
ask how that might still address us today. To embrace that meaning would
seem all too much like a reversion to a premodern worldview to which we
have no inclination to return. But to turn to Jesus inspired by Wisdom could
have a freshness that would make it possible to listen for meaning rather
than simply to flee from obscurantism.

The Wisdom that inspired Jesus is like the reign of God that Jesus proclaimed. The basic difference may be that Wisdom was portrayed as the personal Spirit that possessed him, whereas God's reign was what he, under the sway of her possession, envisioned. Wisdom would thus seem to be internal, christological; God's reign would be external, eschatological. If mythologically that reign was located at the end of time, it would be Wisdom that, like the Son of man, would return for vindication. Conversely, God's reign, like Wisdom, was mythologically experienced as somehow present in Jesus, as was Wisdom: Jesus' exorcisms, effected by the finger of God (which is interpreted in Matthew 12:28 as the Spirit of God), were already the coming of God's reign upon the demon possessed (Q 11:20). Much more important, one must come to grips with what these symbols mean nonmythologically. It is only pseudo-theology to seek to reconcile into some harmonious doctrinal system the various *mythologoumena* with which meaning came to expression.

The shared trait, that one has to do with the Wisdom *of God* and the kingdom *of God*, may provide a relevant lead. Jesus' insight is not the crowning achievement of some Periclean, Augustan, or Elizabethan age, any more than his vision is that of a purification of the kingdoms of this world into a Christian establishment (Christendom as the kingdom of God). What went into Jesus and came out of Jesus is not of this world. *Of God* means it is transcendent. Not of course in a literal sense: just as Wisdom did not fly down onto Jesus like a bird, the kingdom is not some other place or here in some other time. God's reign is the utopian goal, the ultimate, just as Wisdom is the purity of intention, the commitment. Jesus' whole life was caught up in the cause of humanity, which possessed him with a consuming passion and came to expression through his radical vision. Those who are caught on fire by him are possessed by the same Wisdom and proclaim the same utopian reign.

Critiques

Critique by Rebecca D. Pentz

Good news for feminists—another Sophia Christology. Or is it good news? I shall consider this question, first by sketching what I take to be Robinson's Christology and second by outlining three reasons why Robinson's Christology may not be good news for feminists.

If I understand Robinson's essay correctly, and I shall be glad for any clarification my remarks prompt him to give, he is presenting a Sophialogy, not a Sophia Christology. His emphasis is on Sophia and her prophets rather than on Christ. In fact there is no Christ, no Second Person of the Trinity, in Robinson's presentation. Jesus is merely one of Sophia's prophets, as are Solomon, Jonah, Abel, Zechariah, and John the Baptist. The Spirit of Sophia possesses her prophets one after the other and enables them to speak her wisdom. Jesus was so possessed at his baptism. After his crucifixion Sophia's message is communicated temporarily through luminous visualizations, traditionally called the resurrection appearances, but Jesus' disciples carry on her message as well. In fact, part of the "good news" of Robinson's Sophialogy is "that we, like Jesus, can be inspired by the feminine aspect of God." We too can be prophets.

The first feature in Robinson's account that I find troubling is that he strips both Jesus and Sophia of their personhood. He makes the usual points of a Sophialogy—that Sophia is primary and the prophets secondary; that the prophet Jesus is an "otherwise irrelevant man," as he put it in another essay; and that there is a nonexclusivity about the prophets because they are so numerous. But in this essay he seems to go further in that neither Sophia nor Jesus live on as personal beings. Jesus returns after his death as luminous visualizations and lives on only in the sense that the message he preached lives on. When Robinson speaks from within the Sophia myth, what seems to be important about Sophia is her "ongoing message." When Robinson demythologizes Sophia, she is reduced to a set of psychological abstractions. She is not a personal being; she is "the purity of intention, the commitment."

I, for one, do not find this depersonalization good news for women. I agree that Sophia is mythological and that the myth in all its details need not be taken as literal fact. God does not stand on street corners calling out to men (Prov. 8:2–3) any more than she is such a beautiful woman that young men long to win her for their brides (Wisdom 8:2). But I fail to see what basis Robinson has for his interpretation that Wisdom is "purity of intention, the commitment," and I fail to see why women should find his way of demythologizing helpful. Women have no need to strip the heavens of a personal God, replacing her with psychological abstractions.

Second and more important, it is decidedly bad news for women if Sophia is not literally transcendent. And this is just what Robinson claims. Robinson tells us at the end of his essay that the Wisdom of God is transcendent but "not of course in a literal sense." Literally, Wisdom is a psychological abstraction. But if Sophia is not literally transcendent, she is not literally powerful either. And yet, one of the things I find most attractive about Sophialogy is that Sophia is such a powerful figure. She is God's delight at the creation, and "she decides for him what he shall do" (Wisdom

8:5). She has sway over the waves of the sea, the whole earth, and over every people and nation (Sirach 24:6). Through her, kings are sovereign, and princes act like princes (Prov. 8:15–16). Whether we image the transcendent God as a woman or as a man, God is powerful.

Women sometimes shy away from power. Sophia did not. Nor should we. Nor should we just model Sophia's behavior. We should make use of the biblical promise that her power is available to us. She will use her power, just as she used it in the past for Israel (Wisdom 10), to guard us and keep us safe (Prov. 4:6). But, of course, if Sophia is not literally transcendent, none of her transcendent power is available to women. If she is not transcendent but is only the commitment, the consuming passion for the cause of humanity, she is only as powerful as a human with this commitment. A human, even with a consuming passion, cannot decide how to create the universe or have sway over the whole earth or keep us safe. The biblical promise of the transcendent power is lost to us. But we women need it. We need the power of the transcendent God of the universe when we fight against succumbing to our particularly feminine sins. We need the power of the transcendent God of the universe when we fight against particularly masculine oppressions. We don't need to be *inspired* by wise sayings; we need to be *empowered* by a wise God. A nontranscendent Sophia is not good news.

Third, a recurring problem in Sophialogy is that often there is no place for Christ. Sophia, speaking through her prophets, is thought to be sufficient. We see this in Robinson's account, but we also see it in feminist accounts. Elisabeth Schüssler Fiorenza develops a Sophialogy in *In Memory of Her* in which Jesus is the supreme prophet of Sophia. Fiorenza does speak of "Jesus-Sophia," but she is clear that Jesus died a prophet's death. I cannot follow her or Robinson in this. What Jesus accomplished on the cross was not just martyrdom. He birthed us. He labored that we might live. He fought our battle against oppression in the world on a cosmic scale, confronting and defeating evil. This is indeed good news for women. Women do not need any more martyrs. We do not need to know that selfless, inclusive love leads to suffering and death. But we do need to know that God fights our inner and outer battles and that God in Christ has won.

In sum, a Sophia Christology is good news for women—if it is the biblical Christology, the one given in late Q, Matthew, and Paul. The good news is that Jesus simply *is* the transcendent personal Sophia. Jesus is "the wisdom of God" (1 Cor. 1:24).

Critique by John B. Cobb, Jr.

Robinson writes with his usual original insight and scholarly authority. That it is used here to bring alive the ancient Wisdom Christology is for me a reason for rejoicing. I can only express appreciation for the encouragement it gives me to pursue this Christology and the hope it gives me that during the decades ahead Wisdom Christology may again achieve wide visibility and convincing power. He also shows how greatly theological ideas are informed by the gender of the key nouns that are used to name God.

My task here, however, is not to praise but to raise critical questions. In reading the essay I was aware of discomfort at two points. First, Robinson writes as if the early church proceeded rapidly to a deification of Jesus and as if this deification were quite unqualifiedly expressed by Chalcedon. This view sets the early church and Christian orthodoxy generally at a greater remove from the Wisdom Christology he describes than I believe to be warranted. I cannot express my objection fully, both because my space is limited and because I lack the historical erudition for an adequate argument. Nevertheless, I will outline a different reading of the history culminating in Chalcedon and going beyond.

Robinson notes a parallel between Wisdom Christology and Logos Christology. Yet he seems to suggest not only that the shift from Sophia to Logos moved from female to male imagery (which is clearly correct) but also that it moved from an inclusive to an exclusive Christology. This, I think, is incorrect. Whether it was the Wisdom of God or the Logos of God that was present in Jesus does not make much difference on this question. The Logos was not more limited to the historical Jesus than was the Wisdom. Many of the early church fathers appreciated this, and Logos Christology remains to this day a check on exclusivist claims.

The debate that culminated, but did not end, in Chalcedon was not whether the Logos could be found elsewhere than in Jesus, but whether its presence in Jesus, unlike its presence elsewhere, replaced some human element, in short, whether Jesus was fully human. Robinson's language about the mode of Wisdom's presence in Jesus raises the same question. He speaks of Jesus' being "possessed" by Wisdom. I believe this rhetoric is unfortunate insofar as it could suggest that in some respect Jesus' human faculties were displaced or rendered ineffective through the possessing by divine Wisdom. Very few passages in Scripture seem to me to support this. Even Mark's account of the Spirit's driving Jesus into the wilderness does not. The temptations in the wilderness do not. The temptations in the wilderness are not of the possessing Spirit but of a very human Jesus.

It is true that in the Alexandrian school there were strong tendencies toward a deification of Jesus, that is, toward a view that looked upon the center of Jesus' being as purely divine. But the Antiochene school resisted these tendencies, and they were defeated at several councils. At Chalcedon the church again reaffirmed the full humanity of Jesus, this time in terms of a full, and fully, human nature. Later, when those who wanted to deify Jesus argued that Jesus' will was God's will and that only, the church again declared for the full humanity of Jesus, this time by insisting that Jesus possessed a human will. As far as I know, no subsequent council of the church has agreed to a denial of Jesus' full humanity.

I agree with Robinson that in spite of the official church position, especially in the West, full humanity was denied, and Jesus was deified by the doctrine of the impersonal humanity of Jesus. The wide acceptance of this doctrine seems to me a catastrophe that has seriously distorted Christain faith and teaching, leaving a heritage of confusion. No doubt it even led some to think of Jesus as "a God," as Robinson indicates. But I object to Robinson's leaving the impression that this was ever a part of standard Christian teaching. The doctrine of the impersonal humanity could justify the declaration that Jesus was God. It could not support the view that he was "a God."

My objections here may seem petty, but they reflect a quite different sense of the appropriate relationship of contemporary Christians to Christian tradition. I rejoice that the bishops assembled at Chalcedon refused to deny the full humanity of Jesus. They insisted that the incarnation of God in Jesus in no way reduced or modifed Jesus' full humanness. I take that to be Christian orthodoxy. I claim to be orthodox myself, at least on this central point. In the name of Chalcedon I oppose the false deification of Jesus and its accompanying exclusivism. I object to the implication that Chalcedon supports the very teachings that I oppose.

Of course the church taught also the full deity of Jesus, and the language could easily be understood to mean the deification of Jesus. The issue at Nicea, however, was not the relation of the divine and human in Jesus but the nature of that supermundane reality that became human in Jesus. That issue can be raised in terms of Wisdom. Is the Wisdom of God another reality than God? Is it a creature of God? Perhaps in the mythological imagination it was. But the church rejected that mythology and insisted that what became incarnate in Jesus was truly God. I too affirm that the Wisdom of God that possessed Jesus, or, I prefer to say, was present or incarnate in him, was truly God. No doubt this involves some demythologizing, but I do not see that it cuts us off from a rich appreciation of the Wisdom Christology of the earliest tradition. Why should God be thought of as separable from God's Wisdom?

The second point at which I find myself in some tension with Robinson can be stated very briefly. It is the other side of the first point. For me, talk of God's presence or incarnation in creatures is not problematic but at the heart of my understanding of reality. Hence, at least some of what Robinson finds dead in the mythical world in which Christianity began is for me very much alive. This does not mean that I have any objection to what Robinson says positively in his conclusions. It does mean that much of the tradition that he seems to dismiss as pre-enlightened is very precious to me.

Critique by John Hick

I agree with James Robinson's basic contention that in seeking to understand, properly to honor, and appropriately to respond to Jesus of Nazareth we do not need what has come to be called Christology. There is ample scope for discussion about how Jesus thought of himself and of his relationship to God, what he meant by the "Son of man" phrase, whether he was the expected Messiah; and we could (but I hope shall not) label this nest of questions Jesuology or Nazarology. In distinction the term *Christology* properly refers to the systematic study of the Jewish topic of Messiahship. In fact, however, the term has come in Christian discourse to refer to the body of rival theories supporting the deification of Jesus. Accordingly Christians who seek to follow Jesus as their Lord but who believe that he would have regarded the church's deification of him as profoundly mistaken are described as having a low or reduced or defective or minimal or heretical Christology. This is like saying that those who do not subscribe to the theory of demon possession have a low, defective demonology. Such a strategy mistakes a problem for its solution. What is primarily at issue in our response to Jesus is not which theoretical apparatus we shall employ to deify him, but whether deification, relatively commonplace in the ancient world, is in our postmythic world meaningful and appropriate. Now that modern biblical scholarship has concluded that in all probability the historical Jesus did not think of himself as God, his deification requires reconsideration on its merits.

The realistic response to these issues today, in my view, is to recognize that although in theory we do not need Christology, in fact we have it; thus, we must consider how the church may continue to benefit from that which is of value in it while gradually discarding its harmful aspects. What is valuable is above all the beautiful poetry of the Christmas story—the idea of God's Son coming down from heaven to earth, the baby in the manger, the blessed mother and the holy family, the star and the Wise Men from the East, the shepherds and the choir of angels. All this forms a hauntingly beautiful mosaic of myth and legend whose mythic truth lies in the fact that through Jesus of Nazareth God still speaks to us. On the other hand, what is harmful in the one-world of today is the elevation of Christianity as uniquely superior to the other great religious traditions of the earth. The deification of Jesus implies that Christianity alone was founded by God in person and that its gospel is accordingly the divinely guaranteed truth, which judges all other gospels. In their attempts to retain this claim to ultimate superiority while,

however, making it sound less arrogant, contemporary theologians have
developed a multitude of epicycles of theory—implicit faith, anonymous
Christians, eschatological conversion. But all these are vain attempts to
square a circle. The solution, it seems to me, is to retain the traditional
language, recognizing its metaphorical character and using it liturgically and
poetically rather than quasi-scientifically. To *sing* of Jesus as the divine Son
who came down from heaven is to use a poetic image to focus thought upon
Jesus' message of God's gracious and demanding love without, however,
setting up negative implications concerning our non-Christian neighbors'
relationship to God.

Robinson is very clear that christological language, properly understood, is mythological in character, and he recommends, tentatively at least,
the revival of a mythic theme that was lost in an early phase of Christian
history. Instead of speaking of the Son, or the (linguistically masculine)
Logos, why not speak of the (linguistically feminine) Sophia, identified as
the Wisdom of God? As long as this proposal is a proposal for myth-revision
I can see it as potentially useful; and since it is proposed in response to the
work of contemporary feminist theologians it seems appropriate to await
their reaction. Further clarification may, however, help them to react. What
is the relationship between Robinson's and Cobb's suggestions, both of
which use the Sophia symbol? It seems as though Cobb is identifying Sophia
with God understood as a unity of three Persons and that Robinson's
proposal is rather different, but perhaps this is not really so. At any rate it
might be helpful if Robinson and Cobb could clarify the relationship
between their proposals.

Robinson is conscious that a Sophia Christology would lead us back
into a mythic world that we have long since lost. This appears to be its chief
drawback. To say that Jesus was inspired or engraced by God seems to me
intelligible. But to talk of a "Jesus inspired by Wisdom" sounds archaic. If
the only reason for such talk is that the Greek *sophia*, the Hebrew *hochma*,
and the Latin *sapientia* are feminine nouns, is not this rather an abstruse
reason? Must modern Christianity endorse the ancient superstition that the
gender of a noun signifies gender in its referent? The value of mythic
language is that it resonates in the popular consciousness. But can the myth
of Lady Wisdom's appearing on earth as a man be more than a philologist's
learned conceit, more persuasive in the academy than in the pulpit, the pew,
or the marketplace?

An awkward question remains. How far and how rapidly can such
christological reidentifications go before they begin to look like facile
concessions to surrounding pressures? Having decided, in response to the
feminist challenge, that Jesus was the incarnation of the feminine Sophia,
should we then add, in response to the gay liberation movement, a doctrine

of the lesbian nature of Sophia, and in response to the movement for black liberation, the further doctrine that Sophia is black? Could such easy adaptations have any real value? I do not raise these ironic questions out of any lack of sympathy with the many-sided demands for human liberation. On the contrary I ask them as a way of pointing to the deeper question whether strategies such as the switch to a Sophia Christology take these demands seriously enough. Or does such a theological method only play with symbols while the human situation remains unchanged?

Critique by Stephen T. Davis

As Robinson admits, no full-blown Wisdom Christology was ever developed in the early church. Thus, my initial reaction to his essay is to wonder whether there is enough material in the New Testament or in the tradition as a whole to build a Christology on, especially a Christology sufficiently spelled out to be of use to the Christian community. Nevertheless, I am willing to let the notion of a Wisdom Christology be tried, and surely Paul holds that Christ is "the wisdom of God" (1 Cor. 1:24).

Robinson sees three values in Wisdom Christology: first, it is nonmasculine and is thus much more congruent than orthodox Christologies with our contemporary consciousness of the needs and rights of women; second, it is nonmythological and thus is much more congruent than orthodox Christologies with our enlightened "thought world"; and third, it is nonexclusive (i.e., it does not single out Jesus as the *only* this or that) and thus is much more congruent than orthodox Christologies with our awareness of religious pluralism. I can endorse the first point but am suspicious of the second and the third, as I will explain.

I have three main criticisms of Robinson's essay. The first concerns the source New Testament scholars call Q. In discussions of Q, scholarly standards of evidence and verification seem amazingly flexible and intuitive; hypothesis and speculation abound. We need to be reminded that we do not know for certain that such a document existed (though I am inclined to suppose it did) or that there was a community that used it, or that that community's Christology was fully expressed in that document. As a collection of sayings of Jesus, Q does not, I suspect, exhaust what Christians want to say about Jesus (though naturally it has implications for Christology). The same is true of the resurrection—for obvious reasons Q says little or nothing about the resurrection, but it would be absurd to conclude from that fact that the Q community considered the resurrection unimportant.

My second criticism concerns Robinson's Wisdom Christology itself. I want to argue that it is far too low, or minimalist, a view of Jesus. I am not even sure we should call it a Christology—the term *theology of Wisdom* might be more appropriate. Notice that Robinson says little about why Jesus is important, let alone supremely important, let alone supremely important to us. Jesus does deserve high honor, Robinson says—like others (e.g., John the Baptist), he was used by God, gave his life for the cause, and was divinely vindicated. But what is important is not the person Jesus but the divine Wisdom that possessed him. Other people have been so possessed; perhaps (Robinson hints in his concluding sentence) we can be too. Because Jesus was possessed by divine Wisdom, a kind of loose, functional relationship existed between Jesus and the divine Spirit, but Robinson makes it clear that this relationship has nothing to do with the precritical, mythological, eternal, divine Sonship of orthodox Christology. Robinson explicitly points out the adoptionist and subordinationist implications of his Christology. Jesus was, readers of Robinson's essay conclude, a mere human being who was chosen, inspired, possessed, and used by God.

Robinson seems committed to the methodological principle that as far as the New Testament and Christian theology are concerned, *earlier is better*. That is, the earlier the text or the idea, the more valuable or believable it is. I resist this notion—theology must begin with those texts the church has accepted as Scripture, not with their hypothesized literary ancestors. Also, we do not know (despite Robinson's assumption that we do) that the Wisdom Christology he finds hints of in various places is earlier than the more orthodox notions he rejects as mythological. If we knew that a Q community existed, and if we knew that it was pre-Pauline, and if we knew precisely what Q contained, and if we knew that Q exhausted the community's Christology, then Robinson might be on firm ground. But we know precisely *none* of these things. Thus I strongly doubt that Robinson's Christology is earlier, and (as my own christological essay implicitly argues) I strongly deny that it is better. (Incidentally, I find grotesque Robinson's suggestion that the early emergence of high christological notions was due to hymnic ecstasy. Does the fact that some of the earliest texts containing high christological notions seem to be in poetic or hymnic form mean that the statements contained there were not taken seriously or believed as true?)

My third criticism concerns Robinson's fascinating hypothesis that Jesus' resurrection appearances were luminous, i.e., were in the form of a bright light rather than a body. As I noted earlier, a great deal of speculation seems to be involved in Robinson's attempt to establish this thesis. The main point I wish to make emerges from a distinction between the following two questions:

(1) If we assume that the original resurrection appearances of Jesus

were luminous, can we explain the relevant New Testament texts on the basis of that assumption?

(2) Do the relevant New Testament texts themselves convincingly lead us to the conclusion that the original resurrection appearances of Jesus were luminous?

The answer to the first question may well be yes. Indeed, I believe it is often possible to rationalize an eccentric interpretation of the Bible first by looking carefully for confirming hints here and there and then by arguing that all the disconfirming texts were intentionally placed there by writers or redactors who aimed to rule out the eccentric interpretation in question. Thus, if one holds, as did the second-century Gnostics, that Jesus appeared in luminous form, as Robinson seems to do, it does seem possible to suggest a way of looking at the New Testament that allows for this interpretation.

But the answer to the second question is surely no. The case Robinson makes in favor of an affirmative answer is tenuous. For one thing, we need to distinguish between two sorts of luminosity. The first is a (disembodied) bright light, and the second is a glowing or glorious (embodied) humanlike figure. Robinson seems to conflate the two; thus, he can argue (in his full essay on the topic; see note 1) that Luke's three accounts of Paul's conversion in Acts (where Paul encounters Jesus as a bright light) captures Paul's notion of the resurrection in his own writings. But the only kind of luminosity we can find any *possible* support for in Paul's writings is the second, i.e., that of a glorious figure or body—not a disembodied bright light.

Should we agree that the resurrection appearances of Jesus were luminous even in the second sense? I think not. It is true that Paul believed that our resurrection bodies will be like Christ's and that Christ's resurrection body is "glorious" (1 Cor. 15:42–53; Phil. 3:21). But does the term *glorious* here mean *luminous*? Not necessarily. Paul's use of the term *dóxa* seems as rich and varied as is the Bible's as a whole and does not always connote glowingness. The words from Philippians that the RSV translates "his glorious body" seem to mean not "his luminous body" but "the body he now has in his exalted state."

Why should we believe that Mark's account of what has traditionally been called the transfiguration is a misplaced resurrection account? It is true that Peter is a central figure in this event, so if we knew that the resurrection appearances were luminous we might argue that this is an account of the otherwise missing but twice-mentioned (Luke 24:34; 1 Cor. 15:5) resurrection appearance to Peter. But James and John were witnesses to the transfiguration too—so this was not an appearance to Peter only (which is the strong impression we gain from Luke 24:34 and 1 Cor. 15:5).

Furthermore, to those who are not predisposed to accept Robinson's luminosity thesis, the fact that the Markan transfiguration account includes an aspect of luminosity may well argue *against* its being taken as a resurrection account.

All things considered, it seems to me much more sensible to hold that Jesus appeared after the resurrection in bodily form. The luminous experiences of Jesus recorded in Acts and in Revelation (1:12–16) and used by Robinson were later *visions* of Jesus (of the sort that may still continue to this day) rather than resurrection *appearances* of Jesus.

Robinson's Response to Critiques

Rebecca Pentz builds her critique around the idea that a Sophia Christology—or what she prefers to expose as a reductionist Sophialogy—is not good news, i.e., is not the gospel that saves. Her formulation is new in that it is a response to my essay, but the idea is of course not new. It is merely an updated instance of the debate recurrent throughout this century over the so-called social gospel and the so-called old-fashioned gospel.

The efforts that have been made to transcend this dichotomy by the tradition of dialectic theology (in which I stand) have been unfortunately ignored. Rather than posing an awkward choice, "either Jesus or Paul," as the liberalism of the opening of the century put it, the Bultmannian tradition of midcentury talked about an indirect or implicit Christology in Jesus' Word, which became direct or explicit after Easter. And the summary of Bultmann's position that he subsequently accepted—that Jesus rose into the kerygma—did not refer to psychological abstractions, as Pentz alleges, but to the continuity of what she would prefer to call the deity of Christ.

I do not suggest that reference to this hermeneutical tradition solves our problems. I do suggest that the unexamined assumption that my essay is just another instance of the kind of classical liberalism against which one has long since closed one's mind is not the best point of departure for interpreting my essay.

Part of the problem I find in going along with Pentz' critique comes to the surface in her formulation (which she puts on my tongue) of "no Christ, no Second Person of the Trinity." If in her Christology there is "no Christ" unless one takes that to mean "no Second Person of the Trinity," then Jesus, the Apostles, and most of early Christianity had no "good news for feminists" (or for anyone else). One must face squarely the problem of whether one is willing to believe in a person who refused the compliment "good" on the grounds that there is no one good except God and who did not claim for himself the title "Christ" (much less imagined the Trinity or himself as its Second Person). Pentz, in all consistency, would have to reject Jesus as having "no place for Christ." It is only an evasive tactic to reject modern biblical criticism or my presentation based on it. I find the hermeneutical patterns "implicit-explicit" or "indirect-direct" Christology historically, theologically, and existentially preferable as a point of departure.

One cannot overcome this basic problem with the anachronism of reading into New Testament texts the later creedal codifications and intellectual innovations of them such as the doctrine of the Trinity. For example, the Apostles' Creed was not known to the Apostles but developed as the baptismal creed of second-century Rome.

Persons who do not know or do not accept the critical reconstruction of early Christianity are in this sense simply not modern people and should not so strongly criticize those who would like to stand at the growing edge of their disciplines—as modern Christians. One has to make an effort to be a bit old-fashioned to go along with Pentz, and this is a "work" that should not, any more than circumcision in Paul's world, be a prerequisite to being a Christian.

Pentz does not want "to strip the heavens of a personal God" and thinks it would be bad news "if Sophia is not literally transcendent." Perhaps my opposition to literal transcendence is too literal (or perhaps Pentz's transcendence is too literal). Just as Bultmann would not accept the "reductionism" of "psychological abstractions" as a valid interpretation of what he meant by Jesus' rising into the kerygma, I would not accept such a reductionism as what I mean. What *God* means transcends your and my psychological experience, in the sense that it is not exhaustively intelligible in terms of the psychological. There is (or should be) a reality intended in God talk that goes beyond the psychological. But that reality is not therefore to be identified with the doctrine of God of traditional theology.

Literally, *transcend* comes from *trans-* plus *scandere*, "to climb," and hence is a spatial metaphor. Its literalism is emphasized primarily by its critics, to make fun of literalists. When I was studying under Bultmann, I lived in the home of an old-fashioned liberal theologian, Emil Balla, professor of Old Testament at the University of Marburg. Balla ridiculed the doctrine of the assumption of the Virgin Mary, which was elevated to dogma at that time (just before space travel!), saying that in the cold of space the frozen-stiff Mary rotates and that from time to time she passes her ascended and equally frozen son. The person the Soviet Union sent first into space returned to announce that he had found no God out there, thus reaffirming the ideology of atheism. Is Pentz really talking in this kind of literalism when she says she does not want "to strip the heavens of a personal God"? I do not want to ascribe that kind of literalism to her, lest it seem a cheap shot, a caricature. I think that traditional Christian language is not really heard literally by Pentz or other traditional Christians but that it functions for most Christians as our myth, our story. There is a familiar *de-literalizing*, when put in terms of scholarly hermeneutics, even by those who advocate taking the Bible "literally."

Pentz shifts her critique to the dimension of power (which I did not discuss but which is important in feminist discussion), in that women should not "shy away from power." She infers that "not literally transcendent" requires the inference "not literally powerful either." "If Sophia is not literally transcendent, none of her transcendent power is available to women." Is this a theological rationale for divine star wars? If we shoot from outer space, is God on our side (since we, from outside, are on his side)? I do not suggest that Pentz means this kind of literalism. I think rather that she is hermeneutically fuzzy about the nonliteralness of her theology and that her fuzziness may surface most clearly in her concession: "I agree that Sophia is mythological." How does she then proceed to interpret this mythological Sophia? By eliminating "details" of the myth that are literally improbable, such as God standing on street corners! What kind of hermeneutic is this, in which myths, cleaned up of such details, are then to be taken literally? If she assumes one must take cleaned-up myths literally or not at all, she is hermeneutically naïve.

As to power, the pen is more powerful than the sword: Aristotle taught Alexander the Great, but Aristotelianism has demonstrated more staying power than Alexander's military force. Again, I assume that Pentz agrees with such edifying thoughts, hence that her criticism lies elsewhere.

Her interpretation of my presentation does seem to me to have the shortcoming of reductionism. I "merely" mean that I have "reduced to a set of psychological abstractions," by placing importance on Sophia's ongoing message, from which Pentz infers that "neither Sophia nor Jesus live on as personal beings." Her reformulation of my position is thus that "she is not transcendent but is only the commitment, the consuming passion for the cause of humanity." It is, I think, a basic misunderstanding of the interpretation of metaphorical language, such as that of transcendence, to saddle it with an accusatory "merely" or "only." A biblical statement, translated out of its hoary and comfortable traditional language, language that no one can understand literally but that seems to ring true, does seem reductionist when translated into a specific intelligible point, because of its specificity. Sooner or later, the richness of the biblical language must take on focus to gain intelligibility and speak to the concrete situation. That does not mean that other things latent in the language are rejected—they just do not seem at the moment to speak to the point.

There is in metaphorical language a *sensus plenior*, more in the language than its literalistic statement and more than any and every translation into a concrete and specific and limited point. The dangerous task in preaching the word is to risk such concreteness, such specificity, not on the assumption that the text is "merely" or "only" this, but that it is "at least" and "surely" this, not some vague, sentimental platitude that lulls to sleep but helps no one.

Stephen Davis' critique presents much the same problem as Pentz' critique; hence, what I have already said can be presupposed in my response to Davis. Much of Davis' critique is simply misunderstanding, lack of familiarity with modern biblical criticism and the hermeneutical tradition in which I stand, which is the main hermeneutical tradition of this century. The use of descriptive, history-of-religions language rather than the language of Zion is for him apparently alienating.

The existence of Q is of course a scholarly postulate. It was made a century ago and now dominates critical New Testament scholarship, although of course there is, and presumably will continue to be, a minority of the scholarly community that challenges that postulate. However, it is the task of New Testament theology to seek to build on the critical reconstruction of primitive Christianity and its literature, trying to decide what can be said about the thinking of the first century of Christianity. Such a critical theology, which is inevitably based on ongoing critical historical and philological research, is never absolutely proven. But it is nearer what actually went on and was thought in the first century of Christianity than are traditional theologies that insist on being called biblical, apostolic. Perhaps the "fragility" of a theology of Q is "safer," precisely because it is so exposed, than are the "solid" theologies of the establishment, which are ultimately based not so much on primitive Christianity as on the overlay of tradition from the intervening centuries. One must choose between the uncritical tradition and the critical reconstruction. The critical scholar should listen to the tradition of interpretation and respect it for what it is but should not substitute it for the reconstruction called for by the current level of critical scholarship.

It was common in the Q research of an earlier generation to assume that Q presupposed what it did not expressly state, such as the kerygma of cross and resurrection. It was assumed that Q was the *didache*, the catechetical instruction or ethical application, for the converts to the kerygma. The current generation of scholarship assumes that Q presents the general view of its community and is not limited to hortatory inferences from an unexpressed gospel. Rather than embedding Q's Christology or its view of the resurrection into that of other primitive Christian communities (e.g., the Christologies of Paul or the Gospel of Mark) or later communities (e.g., that of Matthew and Luke), Q scholarship has made real progress in drawing attention to this previously neglected primitive Christian theology represented by Q.

Davis questions whether a Q community existed. Actually, the existence of a Q community is not completely dependent on the existence of Q. The existence of bearers of the Synoptic tradition cannot be doubted. In studying that tradition, one must note the divergence of its theology from that of a Pauline congregation. Somebody transmitted the sayings ascribed to Jesus for a generation or two before they were incorporated in the canonical Gospels. Not all the Galileans whom Jesus helped left Galilee; some remained there and believed in and witnessed to Jesus. The absence of adequate source material for Galilean Christianity should not lead us to lose sight of that community or of the main written source material that may have survived from it—Q. To come to the point: the theological problem posed by Q is not its hypothetical nature, but the content of the sayings. The content must be faced because Q consists almost exclusively of sayings; they cannot be bypassed in favor of preferred Markan or Johannine contexts. For example, the Sermon on the Mount, the centerpiece of Q, is such a hot potato that no one wants to touch it with a ten-foot pole—claiming all the while, of course, to be believers in Jesus.

Davis' second criticism has to do with the Christology presented in my essay. That a "loose, functional relationship existed between Jesus and the divine Spirit" has, as he reads my paper, "nothing to do with the precritical, mythological, eternal, divine Sonship of orthodox Christology." Again, my hermeneutical understanding of the task is simply ignored. I have sought to put into modern words my effort to understand how a Jewish sect of the first century could have experienced and languaged God's overpowering presence in Jesus' ministry as a first step in the history of Christology, whose later stages we know much better. Rather than having "nothing to do" with each other, they have everything to do with each other. But the early stages should not be assumed anachronistically to be cast-backs of the later formulations.

I do not assume that "earlier is better." I specialize in early Christianity (the only one of the contributors to do so) and was included in part so that at least one presentation in the volume would have a New Testament focus. The Sophia Christology is not earlier than some other early Christologies, which were moving through trajectories that were sometimes in interaction, sometimes separate. I present it not because it is earlier but because it has been more neglected and yet is more relevant to current feminist interest.

Nor do I "reject as mythological" "the more orthodox notions." Sophia Christology is also mythological but is not for that reason to be rejected. To identify the mythical with the false is to misunderstand. Because a message is coded does not mean it is to be rejected. The very fact that it is coded probably means that its contents are important, for which reason no expense should be spared in breaking the code. Demythologizing is not to be confused with eliminating the mythical (separating the eternal from the temporal, the kernel from the husk), which characterized classical liberalism. Bultmann began the essay in which he proposed demythologizing by distinguishing between demythologizing and eliminating. Those who wish to talk about the mythical in this context should at least acknowledge the intent to make the distinction.

Davis finds the common scholarly view that the high christological notions came to expression in hymnic ecstasy "grotesque," since then "the statements contained there were not taken seriously or believed as true." This is simply a misunderstanding. Such ecstasy was interpreted in the primitive church as a gift of the Spirit, i.e., divinely inspired. Is it grotesque in Davis' theology to refer to New Testament texts and their high Christology as divinely inspired? Obviously he believes in the inspiration of Holy Scripture, but as a theological abstraction that he has never tried to think of in history-of-religion terms. What Davis really finds grotesque is that I do not use traditional language in theology. But serious theology does not consist in the repetition of familiar phrases. Incidentally, John Hick's critique rejects a literal interpretation of christological titles but affirms that we are "to *sing* of Jesus as the divine Son who came down from heaven." Is Hick's theology grotesque?

Davis' concrete description of the procedure he ascribes to me in my analysis of the resurrection of Jesus does not help. I do not have an "eccentric interpretation" I am seeking to "rationalize" by looking for "confirming hints" and then ascribing "disconfirming texts" to secondary layers. Critical biblical scholars seek as best we can for objectivity from our own theology and assume that new insights will be learned from inductive study of the text, such as the originally luminous visualizations of the resurrected. I do not just hold, "as did the second-century Gnostics, that Jesus appeared in luminous form," but also with the only New Testament authors who claim to have seen the resurrected—Paul and the John who wrote the book of Revelation. Does Davis want me to disagree with these eyewitnesses?

Davis avoids this dilemma by introducing a distinction between "a (disembodied) bright light" and "a glowing or glorious (embodied) humanlike figure." Paul was able to use the term *body* for the luminosity that was later characterized (e.g., by Gnostics) in contrast to bodily existence. I do not know (hence, do not make an assumption) whether Paul experienced the luminous resurrected Lord as a human body with arms, legs, feet, or as a heavenly body such as the sun or moon. Only Revelation 1 gives a lurid description of such a luminous resurrection appearance. I do not assume that Paul would have used the same language. Of course I do assume, in contrast to Davis, that *glorious* meant luminous, as is true of the glory of God in the Old Testament and as is typical of epiphanies. In the narrations of Acts, Paul's eyes were blinded by what he saw. What appeared to John in Revelation 1 was luminous, as was the transfiguration, which I take to be a resurrection appearance. Davis in fact concedes that all three of these appearances were luminous.

What Paul saw was clearly different from what was described in the resurrection stories at the ends of the canonical Gospels, in which Jesus could be mistaken for a gardener or a tourist going to Emmaus. This distinction, rather than the one Davis proposes, is the distinction that the texts themselves call to attention and that as such calls for explanation. Davis bypasses this distinction in the texts; I propose an explanation of it.

To reduce Revelation 1 and Paul's Damascus road experience narrated in Acts to *visions* rather than *appearances* is in a sense primitive Christian—similar to the view of Paul's opponents, who contested his apostolicity, which he defended in Galatians 1 precisely on the grounds that his was not just a vision (which he would not think worth mentioning—2 Cor. 12:1–6) but a resurrection appearance.

John Cobb expresses concerns that are in large part quite congenial to me, to the extent that I did not realize I was giving rise to the problems he senses. The problems are largely a matter of my inadequate formulations and/or his reading of things I had not intended.

I do not mean to deny any inclusive potentialities latent in christological titles other than "Sophia." Even "Messiah" goes back to a dynasty of anointed kings of Judah, and Qumran seems to speak of two Messiahs. If the Logos hymn that was reused as the prologue of the Gospel of John was originally used by the Baptist sect with regard to their founder John (as the corrective prosaic interpolations in the prologue have led scholars to assume), that would itself be an inclusive trait, from a historian's point of view, even if, for the Evangelist, the Word was not John but Jesus.

I do not suggest that a Sophia Christology excludes the full humanity of Jesus. I use the rhetoric of *possession* as a history-of-religion corrective for the modernization of the concept of the Holy Spirit as self-consciousness or the like, which dominates modern theology. It is not fully clear to me to what extent Jesus experienced ecstasy or rapture or other such trancelike phenomena (e.g., seeing Satan fall like lightning from heaven). One of the dimensions about which we can speak very little, in view of the problem of getting back to the historical Jesus, has to do with his personality, or psychological state. Because the Gospel writers tended to present him in terms of their interests, I hestitate to point to the three temptations as proving his full humanity. But I also think it would be precarious to infer (e.g., from Mark's language—the Spirit's driving Jesus into the wilderness) that he was not fully human.

Wisdom as a hypostasization is of course metaphorical or mythological language of the Hellenistic-Roman world, indicative of a religious sensitivity of that time, to express God without profaning God's name or merging God too closely with the world. Thus Sophia would hardly lie on the creature side of the Creator-creature distinction and no doubt would function as "truly God," minus the liability of potentially profaning God's name. Listening to Sophia meant listening to God, and Sophia at the last judgment would function as (or for) God as Judge. Existentially (and this should mean theologically) Sophia would be fully God. The history of dogma worked this through in the Holy Spirit as fully God, though eternally generating by the Father (and the Son?).

I do not suggest that one should "dismiss as pre-enlightened" "God's presence or incarnation in creatures." The mythology alive in one culture and dormant in another can nonetheless be demythologized, which means the very reverse of being dismissed, as I have already stated. Our culture is of course a mixture of the modern and the premodern. Many people today live in more continuity with the mythopoeic past than with modernity. But I think the way to interpret theologically the language of a mythopoeic culture is to seek to hear what the whole text means in some language that we can identify with reality rather than to pick from the mythopoeic language the items that seem to us still real and embrace them literally while discarding the rest. That was, for example, the procedure with the rationalists' Lives of Christ, to remove the mythical and leave the historical—a banal biography hardly worth recording, much less believing. What God's presence meant in its mythological context of primitive Christianity is what we are to seek to understand, not God's presence cut off from (rescued out of) that "outmoded husk."

John Hick asks: "Must modern Christianity endorse the ancient superstition that the gender of a noun signifies gender in its referent?" Obviously not. In fact, I am far from sure that ancient societies always heard such associations—our Assyriological colleague Tova Meltzer suspects they did not. But such hypostasizations reflecting awareness of gender did occur in the environment of primitive Christianity and thus may well have been sensed by early Christians. Wisdom is clearly a woman in the trajectory from Proverbs 8 to Nag Hammadi Gnostic texts, between which poles primitive Christianity lies. If so, to call to our attention their sensitivity may be relevant, especially at a time when women's experience throughout Christianity is of special interest to all of us. Thus it is not "a philologist's learned conceit" but more nearly an average person's fantasy or feeling of that day, which has become in our time a recurrent theme in feminist biblical interpretation.

One need only refer a moment to feminists who think of biblical religion as hopelessly patriarchal and hence worship the Goddess, whether of a Hellenistic religion (e.g., Isis) or of a Nordic religion of the pagan Celts or the like. My focus is upon the bearer of Wisdom, the male wizard, the female witch. The word *witch* has been given negative overtones by Christian polemics to the extent of burnings, so that the cognates *wise* and *wit* have been replaced in our ears by the cognate *wicked*. If a positive identification with much maligned witches is "in" in such feminist circles, why argue that *Wisdom* is so arcane that only a dusty philologian would be interested?

Hick is concerned with "facile concessions to surrounding pressures." The reason Sophia is relevant "in response to the feminist challenge" but not to gay rights and black liberation is that the texts themselves seem to suggest that the feminine ingredient was sensed, but not the lesbian or black potential. A paper, such as that of Gilles Quispel, on the Black Madonna, might be relevant in response to the challenge of black liberation, but not to that of feminism or gay rights. My essay is not an "easy adaptation," which, as Hick suggests, would hardly have "any real value." That is to say, my appeal to Sophia Christology is more serious than a do-gooder's effort to be supportive of the feminist movement. It is a feminine dimension of primitive Christianity that must be appreciated as such.

5 Christ Beyond Creative Transformation
JOHN B. COBB, JR.

In this essay I want to summarize the Christology I have already published and then to discuss the challenges I have felt most keenly. Of these challenges, the first is from other religious traditions. I select Judaism and Buddhism as two examples.

The second challenge to which I want to respond is from Latin American liberation theology. I have not previously responded in print to what I perceive as its challenge to my Christology. Accordingly I do that somewhat more fully here.

The third challenge is from feminism. Although I have dealt with it more than once in the past, I am dissatisfied with what I have written. Hence I conclude this essay with fresh reflections on this topic.

In *Christ in a Pluralistic Age* I identified Christ as creative transformation. I continue to find it fruitful and appropriate to think of creative transformation as Christ. But I have increasingly come to the conviction that creative transformation does not exhaust the reality of Christ. Hence the title. What more I now see to be included in Christ appears chiefly in my responses to liberation theology and to feminism.

I

Any attempt to fix the meaning of *Christ* is doomed to arbitrariness and artificiality. Even in the New Testament there is fluidity in its use. In the course of Christian history this fluidity has expanded. *Christ* is a living symbol, not a proper name or a common noun.

On the other hand, the history of this symbol does not allow it to be used with unlimited freedom. It is quite legitimate to argue about its proper usage. Christians almost unanimously would protest against calling Hitler *Christ*. But this protest is not limited to the association of Christ with those whom we most condemn. To call Moses, Socrates, Gautama, or Confucius

Christ or even a *Christ-figure* seems inappropriate to the point of error, however much we may admire these towering figures. Lesser women and men, such as Mother Teresa and Martin Luther King, do evoke this symbolism. There are criteria for its use whether or not they are articulated.

Christ does not function only to refer to individual historical figures. It makes sense also to ask what Christ is doing in our world or how we can share in Christ's work in our world. Theologians can call us to be Christs to one another. We cannot simply substitute *Jesus*; yet the image of Jesus guides us in our uses of *Christ*.

I suggest that the meaning of the symbol is tied in three directions. First, *Christ* is tied to Jesus, as I have already suggested. The tie may not be to Jesus as he actually was, since we have so little reliable information about him. It may be rather to Jesus as he was remembered by believers. Second, the use of *Christ* is tied to salvation as that is understood by Christians in different times and places. *Christ* as used by believers must name that which they experience as salvific. Finally, *Christ* is tied to God. That tie was not immediately evident in the early church, but in the rejection of Arianism it was established.

There are those who would deal with this complexity by collapsing the three and turning the symbol *Christ* into a proper name. They say that *Christ* is the name of Jesus who is *the* Savior and who is God. But this will not do. The salvific work of God is attested in the Jewish Scriptures long before the birth of Jesus. It continues in the Holy Spirit, who cannot simply be identified with Jesus. The idea that Jesus is God without qualification is heresy and simply makes no sense. Orthodox teaching is that Jesus is the fully human incarnation of the everlasting Word, or the Son, who is one with the Father. *Christ* could be identified with Jesus when *Christ* meant the expected Jewish Messiah. But the expected Messiah was not to be the incarnation of God. Christians can no longer understand *Christ* primarily in terms of Jewish expectations.

The question is not, then, how to delimit or define *Christ* for all Christians at all times and places but how we today most appropriately identify *Christ*. In posing the issue in this way, I suggest that the theologian's task cannot be to speak for all Christians. The diversity is too great. On the other hand it cannot be to express merely private opinions. It must be to propose symbols and ideas that could lead toward possible consensus while recognizing that no final agreement will ever occur in history. It is to take part in the unending process of reformulation in view of the sensibilities and insights of the time.

One can begin with our current knowledge of the historical Jesus, our reconstruction of the first kerygmatic proclamation, the outcome of the christological controversies, or recent Christologies. One can also begin with the doctrine of God. However, questions of salvation are today so pressing that I prefer to begin there, recognizing that what I see and how I see it is already informed by my belief in God and my understanding of Jesus and of the church's Christology.

The whole world is now in danger of nuclear destruction. Even well-intended peaceful activities lead to pollution, ecological disruption, resource exhaustion, and climatic changes that are capable of destroying our descendants. Meanwhile tyranny grows worse in much of the world and threatens even relatively free peoples. In this context individuals find little purpose or meaning. We despair, cling to what we have, or thrash about angrily. Even neighborly responsibility and civility decline. Our need for salvation is comprehensive and urgent as never before. We should not use the symbol *Christ* for anything less than the power that works savingly in this comprehensive way. *Christ* must be the life that struggles against the death-dealing powers that threaten us and the way that leads through the chaos of personal and global life to just, participatory, and sustainable society in which personal wholeness is possible.

But are we justified in calling the way and the life that now constitute our hope for salvation *Christ*? That depends on whether that which is this way and life is truly God and on whether it is truly that which was incarnate in Jesus. To answer this is not to decide whether what we can identify as saving today is exactly the same as what the author of the fourth Gospel had in mind. But it must be an appropriate development for our time of the Christ of our heritage.

In *Christ in a Pluralistic Age* I proposed that the way we need today is the path of creative transformation. If, as I assume, continuation along the path humankind is now following can lead only to destruction, fundamental change is urgent. But there is not some clearly visible way that would resolve our problems, either personal or global. Our vision of the future is limited largely to ideas derived from the past, and these do not suffice to guide us. Yet this is not the whole story. We are not—or need not be—simply products of the past. We also hear the call of God offering us alternatives. These do not eradicate what we bring to the present from the past. On the contrary they enable us to appropriate more of what is positive in the past. But in the process of appropriating God's gifts we are transformed, creatively.

This transformation is not a once-for-all event. Dramatic instances of particular creative transformation sometimes take the form of conversions from one tradition to another. Unless, however, those who are thus changed are thereby opened to continuing sensitivity and responsiveness to God's call, the one transformation, with all its potential for good, will become an idol. Creative transformation continues, leading to unforeseeable consequences. Because it is God's work, it can be trusted. Because it is God's work, it offers hope beyond our ability to envision a hopeful scenario.

The call of God is one expression of God's grace. As grace it is not something external to us. On the contrary it functions within our experience. It is God's immanence, and it is constitutive of who we are. How effective it will be in us is finally, in part, our decision. But that decision is not whether or not to accept an externally proffered gift, for the possibility of the decision is itself part of the gift, which is the presence of the Giver. The way of creative transformation is the way of freedom. The more fully we allow ourselves to be creatively transformed, the more we participate in the gift of freedom.

Creative transformation has its clearest manifestation to us as energizing and providential grace in personal life. But as Charles Birch and I argued in *The Liberation of Life*, it is also the life in all living things. The living differs from the inanimate in that it is not a mere product of its past. Life is also always a transcending of the past. Creative transformation as the immanence of God in the world is not only the way but also life itself, the life by which all that is alive lives. Furthermore, the distinction between the living and the nonliving turns out not to be ultimate. Both are physically constituted of similar events, now conceived at the quantum level. This fact long led scientists to attempt to understand organisms in terms of configurations of inanimate matter in motion, but the evidence now supports considering the component parts of both mechanisms and organisms more as organisms than mechanisms. Creative transformation is a constitutive element in every truly individual event.

However, that does not yet justify speaking of *Christ*. The symbol *Christ* is indissolubly bound to Jesus. From what has been said already, it is clear that creative transformation was immanent in Jesus, as it was in Moses, Socrates, and Gautama, and as it is in each of us. The question is whether we are justified in seeing Jesus as not simply one more embodiment of God's working in the world, but as a special locus of that working. Since the word *incarnation* is key to Christian language, let us say that in an important sense God is incarnate in all things. Is there, then, anything about the incarnation of God in Jesus that justifies associating distinctively with him the incarnation of the power that alone can save the world?

The *locus classicus* of the doctrine of incarnation is the prologue of the fourth Gospel. There we read of the Word that was with God and was God and that is the life of all living things and the light that illumines all human beings. Clearly this is analogous to what I have said. The Gospel goes on to say that this light and life already present in the world "became flesh" in Jesus. This should never have been interpreted as a metaphysical break radically separating Jesus from all other human beings, but it does express the conviction that this life and light were embodied in him in a special way.

It does not suggest simply a fuller presence or effectiveness, a difference of degree, as is often proposed. It suggests—in some important sense—a qualitative or structural difference.

Before asking whether that belief can make sense to us, we need to ask first why the conviction of Jesus' difference from us was so prominent among early Christians and whether those reasons or others lead us to share that conviction today. I believe the reasons were that especially after the resurrection, Christians experienced new light and new life as coming to them because of Jesus, and in encountering Jesus they saw him as the source of their new light and life rather than simply as one more beneficiary. The point can be made in other New Testament language. Christians experienced themselves in a new way as children of God, and they felt this new experience to be a derivative from Jesus. Jesus' sonship did not seem derivative in the same sense. Accordingly they celebrated the living presence of God in their own lives and communities, speaking of this most often as the Holy Spirit. But in their language about Jesus they tried to express a presence of God to which they owed the gift of the Holy Spirit. Without much conceptual clarity they distinguished between the indwelling of God as Spirit in the believers and the incarnation of the Word of God in Jesus.

It is my contention that the experience of contemporary Christians leads to the same need to distinguish what we experience in ourselves from what we discern in the One to whom we owe so much. We owe to Jesus our engrafting into Israel's history with God. We owe to him also our understanding of the light and life within us as God's presence in our lives. We owe to Jesus the form of hope by which we live. We owe to him also the ability to discern God in the midst of defeat and suffering.

I do not mean that we can be sure that Jesus taught all this. Presumably he did not, or he did so only indirectly or by implication. Nevertheless, it is the life, teaching, death, and resurrection of Jesus that, along with believers' interpretation of them, so altered the course of history that our lives are profoundly affected. It is natural, if not necessary, that we attribute to the One who played a role so different from ours a status that is also distinct. And because the heart of the question for us too is our relation to God, we may appropriately ask whether it makes sense to think of Jesus' relation to God as somehow different from ours. Was the embodiment of the way and the life in him different from their presence in us?

Any answer to this question can only be faith's speculation. Tragically, having formulated an answer based on such speculation, the ancient church demanded of all who would be believers that they accept it uncritically. If faith continues to speculate today, it should not continue the desire to impose on all Christians a common answer.

My speculation begins with the belief that there is not one structure of human existence but many. In *The Structure of Christian Existence* I described some of these structures in correlation with different cultures or religious traditions. I believe many of us participate in a structure of existence that became actual in human history because of Jesus. The question is whether Jesus brought this structure into being by embodying it in himself or whether his own structure of existence differed from ours.

Very briefly, I perceive the structuring of our existence as Christians as centering on a distinction between the *I* and God. This duality tends to express itself as a tension. It is natural in this structure of existence to distinguish between my will and God's will, to speak of God's gift or demand or call, to think of human resistance or obedience or conformation. The imagery that expresses this experience may go deeper than *I and Thou* to a real sense of the indwelling Spirit. But the relation to that Spirit is not one of identity but of gratitude and expectancy, and sometimes of struggle. The work of the Spirit does not obliterate the difference between the *I* and the divine presence.

As I turn from this experience to the Gospels, I encounter something different. It is true that an author such as Kazantzakis can present Jesus in fictional form as an extreme instance of tension between the *I* and the divine Spirit. And one can support this in part from the stories of the temptation, the Gethsemane prayer, and the cry of dereliction. I do not doubt that whether or not these are historically reliable in detail they tell us something true about Jesus. It shows that he was indeed tempted as we are and that any representation of him as metaphysically different from us in his relation to God cannot do justice to the Gospel witness.

But what is more striking is the contrast between the figure of Jesus in the Gospels and that portrayed by Kazantzakis. Those sayings of Jesus of whose authenticity we are most confident do not express a torn soul struggling with an alien Spirit but an assurance that he speaks for God. This does not suggest that he is possessed by the divine Spirit so as to become a mouthpiece for its utterances, like a medium speaking in a trance. It suggests instead a unity of Jesus' *I* and the divine presence within him, which enables him to focus not on his own experience of God but on others and on the world. His perception of others and the world seems to be free from the distortion introduced by personal interests and ego defense. In most Christians the *I* as the center of perception and decision making is constituted by its inheritance from the comparable center in earlier experiences; in Jesus it was sometimes, perhaps often, coconstituted by this inheritance and the presence of God within him. For us the presence of God is felt as something other than the *I*; in Jesus it was, at times, so united with the *I* that the characteristic inner struggle of the Christian is not what most strikes us about him. Such a difference allows us to say that in him the Word that was the life of all living things and the light of all human beings "became flesh." It can also enable us to agree with much of the intention of Chalcedon. God's constitutive presence in Jesus' selfhood in no way reduced his humanity. On the contrary, it perfected it.

I believe that what I have called creative transformation is the life of all living things and the light of all human beings, that it is the activity of the Word of which the prologue speaks, that this Word was with God and was God, and that its effective presence in the world as creative transformation is our hope for salvation. I believe also that the Word became flesh in Jesus and that the result of this enfleshment has been to give a new effectiveness to the everlasting creative and redemptive work of the Word in the world. I feel, therefore, no hesitation in speaking of creative transformation as Christ.

II

I have summarized my previously developed christological ideas rather briefly so as to leave space to deal with some of the most obvious problems. One of these I treated in *Christ in a Pluralistic Age*. Can these strong claims be made about Christ without negative, even hostile, implications about other religious traditions? If Christ is the way and the life, then what can be said of those who do not speak of Christ at all or consciously reject what they hear?

In dealing with such questions, I must not categorize together all who are not Christian. People are to be viewed in terms of what they do affirm rather than in terms of what they do not affirm. I will write about two religious traditions, hoping that their differences will suggest that each of the others also needs separate treatment. When the question is posed as the relationship of Christianity to "other religions," little that is helpful can be said. I must ask instead about Confucianism, African primal religions, Jainism, and so forth. I must also ask about post-Christian humanism, scientism, and Marxism. No two traditions pose to the Christian just the same questions. For this essay I have selected Judaism and Buddhism for discussion.

What does the claim that Christ is creative transformation and that creative transformation became flesh in Jesus mean with respect to Judaism? It certainly does not mean that God's creative and transforming work has been absent from the history of Israel or is now absent from contemporary Judaism. On the contrary it is in this tradition that it has been most clearly discerned and thematized. The incarnation in Jesus had as its first consequence our engrafting into this history so that we might share in the Jewish knowledge of God's reality and work in the world. To this day most of the Christian Bible is composed of the Jewish Scriptures.

Jews, of course, do not name the creative and redemptive work of God in the world *Christ*. For them *Christ* means "Messiah," and the Messiah cannot be separated from the coming of the Messianic Age. Christians cannot disagree with Jews when they stress that that age—what Christians call the kingdom of God—is not manifest in the public life of today's world! It is only as *Christ* has been transformed in meaning from the bringer of the messianic age to the incarnation of God's Word that Christians can now assert that Christ has come. But salvation does not depend on language, important though language is. The same God whose salvific presence Christians name *Christ* works also in Judaism. In both traditions this work is recognized and attended to in worship. For both, this God alone is our hope. What both hope for is the salvation of the whole world.

Despite the extensive community of history, experience, and hope, there are real differences between us. In the Jewish Scriptures are many themes, and no one community or tradition has succeeded in giving full weight to all of them. In Judaism generally the most important is the Torah, the pattern of life and society established by God for the Jews as the elect people. They gladly accept its responsibilities and burdens because these are the mark of the covenant with God. To be a Jew is to be part of this elect community.

Christians have also known themselves as elected by God. Too often they have wrongly interpreted this election as superseding that of the Jews. Paul is less clear on this than we could wish. Nevertheless, Christians today must emphatically repudiate any such notion. The Christian claim to have displaced Jews as God's elect has played a primary role in the appalling history of Christian persecution of Jews. The repentance to which we are called must be a profound *metanoia*, a fundamental creative transformation. That Christians have a role to play in God's salvific work in no way puts an end to God's covenant with the Jews.

Christians have been called, not to observe the Torah, but to live in the freedom of the Spirit—in Christ. Christianity cannot, therefore, offer a fully structured way of life similar to that of Judaism without betraying its election. It is called to transcendence of culture, mores, ethnicity, and even gender. Of course, it does not live up to its calling. It witnesses to a way that it fails to embody. But even that unfulfilled witness is threatening to every established form and structure. It is the prophetic note of the Jewish Scriptures rather than the Torah that becomes central in Christianity.

In Romans 10, Paul severely criticized Gentile Christians for thinking themselves superior to Jews. He suggested that the true meaning of faith would become manifest only as the Jews reappropriated Jesus. This certainly implied also that the Jews who did not accept Jesus were truncated in their own Jewishness. Christians cannot cease to hope that in time Jews will reclaim Jesus—and also Paul—as their own. To some extent this is already happening. It cannot be completed without an inner transformation of Judaism, but it certainly does not require that Jews become members of Gentile Christian churches. It is the fulfillment of Judaism, not its conversion into something else, for which Paul hoped. Meanwhile, in our separation from Judaism, we Christians remain incomplete, one-sided. We need to be creatively transformed through a fresh encounter with Judaism, ideally with a Judaism that is itself transformed by the reappropriation of those whom Christians see as its two greatest sons, Jesus and Paul. To acknowledge our need to learn from Judaism in no way conflicts with the Christology I have outlined.

The relationship to Buddhism is quite a different matter. Whereas Christianity came into being as a Jewish sect, its relations with Buddhism, through most of their respective histories, have been distant. Although Buddhists have had ways of referring to what Jews and Christians know as God, Gautama turned his attention elsewhere. He found discussions about the gods, or even about God, unprofitable. The amazing genius of the Buddhist tradition has been its penetration into a different mystery. If God is the power of creative transformation that brings life and light to the world and is its only hope for salvation from personal despair and global destruction, what can this other mystery be? Astonishingly, it is the mystery of what is, of *what*, therefore, is transformed or destroyed, the mystery of being itself, or rather, as Buddhists have shown, of Nothingness, Emptiness, or Emptying. In Christian terms, Buddhists have meditated on the Nothing out of which God created and creates. For human beings truly to realize Emptying as what they are, and what all things are, is Enlightenment.

The realization of Emptying is quite different from placing faith in God's creative and transforming work. Of course, creative transformation can lead toward Enlightenment, and Enlightenment is a remarkable form of being creatively transformed. But this does not mean that these are two ways of thinking about the same type of event. To submit oneself in faith to the work of creative transformation is quite different from taking upon oneself the disciplines that lead to Enlightenment. But this difference provides no reason to disparage either. To acknowledge the beauty and nobility of Enlightenment in no way conflicts with the conviction that Christ alone is our hope for salvation from despair and destruction. Of course, to make both statements is to intitiate new reflection on the role of Christ in the process of Enlightenment and on the contribution Enlightenment can make to the salvation of the world. These are complex issues, and I have dealt with them elsewhere, especially in *Beyond Dialogue*. My purpose here is only to indicate that the deep differences of Buddhism and Christianity need not require the weakening of the truth of either as each acknowledges the truth of the other. The process in which Christianity is to be creatively transformed by Buddhist understanding is one in which we can recognize Christ.

III

To locate Christ in these terms is to adopt culture as the context of theology. In one way or another most of my christological work has done this. For this reason I have felt with special force the challenge of liberation theology (the Latin American form). Christ is located in the context of a struggle for social justice and freedom and is not identified with the creative transformation of thought, of personal experience, or of cultural forms, to which I have given primary attention, but with the poor and oppressed. To serve Christ is quite concretely to serve these people.

We do not have to seek far for the justification for this Christology. When we despiritualize our readings of the Gospel accounts of Jesus, we find it unequivocally clear that he sided with the poor. Riches were for him an insuperable obstacle to salvation. The kingdom he proclaimed was a reversal of the structures of society as they existed then and as they exist now. In the light of this I can only confess that my neglect of this basic fact about Jesus reflected my participation, along with my teachers, in a middle-class society whose interests were cultural, religious, and existential rather than socially revolutionary.

The question I confront is whether the confession of this limitation requires the abandonment of the structure of christological thought that I have sketched. I hope not. To pose the motif of liberation theology sharply against the cultural motif, as if one must choose between them, is a mistake. Latin American theologians are beginning to realize the importance of the culture of the poor, especially the Indian poor, in their own context. Class analysis alone does not suffice. The importance of culture has been manifest all along in Black theology in the United States, and cultural elements are playing an increasing role in Asian and African theology. Minjung theology in Korea is an example. The need is not for a choice but for a synthesis. The question for me, therefore, is whether a Christology of creative transformation, shaped in the context of reflection about culture, can incorporate—and be creatively transformed by—the convincing insights of liberation Christology. I hope so.

I will begin at points where the connections are easy. Years ago, when I first read Paulo Freire's *The Pedagogy of the Oppressed*, I felt an immediate sense of partnership. The conscientization he described quite concretely was the self-transcending I had identified quite abstractly as the structure of Christian existence. It was a vivid example of what I meant by creative transformation. Because I continue to believe that liberation of the oppressed cannot occur except as the oppressed become the agents of liberation, I continue to see their conscientization as central to liberation. I call this *Christ*.

In a similar way, many of us North Americans were forced by the writing of Gustavo Gutiérrez and others to reflect critically on what we had been thinking and doing. Our horizons of understanding were widened. We saw with new eyes. Here too is a paradigmatic case of creative transformation. Without such creative transformation on a wide scale there is little hope for North American support of Latin American liberation. The need has never been more urgent than today. What little has already occurred, especially in the churches, may be all that inhibits our government from still more violent ways of imposing supposed Yankee interests on those seeking liberation in Central America.

The more difficult issue arises in Christ's identification with the poor. This rhetoric is powerful and appropriate, but it is in tension with the rhetoric of creative transformation. To speak of the importance of conscientization is to imply that the poor lack understanding. To think of this conscientization as Christianization is to imply that the poor are not Christian until they are conscientized. That might be taken to mean that Christ is not present among the poor until conscientization is begun. The association of creative transformation with the transformation of thought and of culture can lead—indeed it has led—to locating Christ primarily among the cultural and intellectual elite. The poor then appear as the rearguard of God's work in the world. Thus the rhetoric of creative transformation can lead to consequences quite opposed to the idea of Christ's identification with the poor.

This identification has important advantages. To locate Christ fully in and with the poor does justice to Jesus' belief that what we do to the least we do to the Son of Man. It points out the error of our overwhelming tendency to think that the successful are those of more importance and worth. It shows that we should measure the real effectiveness of our policies by their effects upon the "least." It also teaches us to listen to the poor. It opposes our assumption that the experts (who are rich) are those who know best what the poor need. If Christ is identified with the poor, then to hear the poor is to hear the voice of Christ. They know the reality in which they live in ways the observer never does. They also know the reality in which we who are rich live, and they do not share the illusions by which we conceal that reality from ourselves.

Nevertheless, there are dangers in this rhetoric. It must not be allowed to mean that no further work of Christ is needed in, among, and for the poor. Christ is present in the vacant stare of the protein-starved girl, in that Christ suffers in her suffering and rejoices in her joys, however limited these may be. But Christ's work of life giving and healing has been thwarted by the poverty that denied her food. That Christ is already there in the faces of the poor cannot mean that we or they are content with the mode of Christ's presence.

Further, this rhetoric can be used to encourage an immediate service of human need that disparages consideration of the systemic reasons for human misery. There is nothing inevitable about such a use of the rhetoric. Most liberation theologians are deeply concerned with systemic issues. But the rhetoric has a life of its own, and at a time when so much rethinking is required, we need a christological rhetoric that will encourage rather than inhibit demanding intellectual work. Nothing can be more urgent today than articulating an alternative economic order that would not support our mad rush to self-destruction and our tyranny over the poor.

The rhetoric of creative transformation deals better with the danger of the misuse of rhetoric. The question for me is whether creative transformation can be transformed to encompass the truth that Christ identifies with the poor. I think it can, if we add to the affirmation of Christ as the way and the life (viewed together as the Johannine Word, or Logos, and as incarnate in the world as creative transformation) that Christ is also the truth, which is the way all things cohere in God. This means that Christ is not only the way God is in the world but also the way the world is in God. Christ is not only creative transformation but also the suffering of God with us and the inclusive and ultimate perspective upon all the finite and conflicting perspectives that make up the world.

Such an addition cannot be made lightly. There were reasons for limiting Christ to creative transformation as the incarnation of the Logos. I need to make the reasons explicit so that the full meaning of the change is clear.

The doctrine of the Trinity arose to express distinctions within God. Some divine activities were more appropriately attributed to one *Persona* than to another. As time passed it became clear that these distinctions were relative. Finally, it was concluded, all three *Personae* are involved in every activity of the Trinity.

One exception was made. It continued to be held that the incarnation was only of the Second Person, the Son, or the Logos. In my earlier Christology I held to that doctrine. I followed the prologue to John in holding that the Logos is the creative, life-giving, enlightening activity of God in the world and that this was incarnate in Jesus and is present wherever there is creativity, life, and understanding. I used *Christ* to name this creative-transformative work of the Logos in the world. My understanding of this work was shaped by Whitehead's influence on my thought. Specifically, I identified the Logos with what Whitehead calls the primordial nature of God.

Whitehead distinguished the primordial from the consequent nature of God. The consequent nature is the truth. In the consequent nature, God suffers with us in our suffering and rejoices with us in our joy. What we do to the least of our neighbors we do to the consequent nature of God. But I associated this aspect of God with the Holy Spirit and the kingdom of God rather than with Christ as the incarnation of the Logos. I have acknowledged the limitations that imposed upon my Christology.

I now propose that we reject the exception of the incarnation from the general unity of the Trinity in its activities *ad extra*. Let us think instead quite straightforwardly that it is God who is incarnate in Jesus and that this God is the Trinity in its totality. Then *Christ* names God in God's relation to the World without limitation.

If now we recognize that it is the Triune God who is incarnate in Jesus, we can say—must say—that the one who is incarnate is one who suffers in the suffering of the least. *Christ* names this suffering one as much as *Christ* names creative transformation. This one who suffers with all who suffer and rejoices with all who rejoice is the one in whom all things cohere, the one in whom all that is and has been is everlastingly what it is, in short, the truth. As the Word is present in all things as the way and the life, so all things are present in the truth, and the truth is present in all things. The truth is not knowledge about things but their full and everlasting realization in God. Christ is not only the way and the life but also the truth.

The emphasis that Christ is the truth enables us to do justice to the second point effectively brought out in the rhetoric of Christ's identity with the poor. This is that the poor have a grasp of truth that is obscured in the perceptions of the rich. We, the rich, have much to lose, so we devote our collective energies to preserving our status and our possessions. Because our continued luxury in the midst of destitution is without moral justification and because we are unwilling to acknowledge this truth in any serious way, our perception of right and wrong is markedly skewed. We are incapable of seeing the social reality simply as it is. Although those of us who are Christians profess to follow Jesus, we do not take at face value his teaching on wealth and poverty. We cannot, and remain rich. The poor, on the other hand, know the reality from daily experience. They have nothing to lose in accepting the truth. They may be ignorant of many things we have learned in school, but the basic truth of the human situation is perceived by them, not by us. To listen to them is to hear again the word of Jesus. This I have learned from liberation theologians.

Again, it is Christ as the truth rather than as creative transformation that fits the need. The truth is reality as it is for God, beyond all distortions of interest and perspective. To have our minds creatively transformed is to move toward that truth. Indeed, all creative transformation is directed by truth. That truth comes to us, in fragmentary ways, in the immediate enlightening of our minds by God's presence. It addresses us also from Scripture and in the proclamation of the Word. Whenever we hear it, we recognize Christ. Christ addresses us also, therefore, and especially, from the mouths of the poor.

IV

The deepest challenge to my Christology comes not from other religious traditions or even from liberation theology but from feminism. This challenge is addressed not in particular to my formulations but to the enterprise of Christology in its totality. That enterprise, most feminists think, and I agree, cannot be separated from celebration of the centrality to our faith of Jesus and of the apostolic witness to him. Feminists ask whether the truly salvific process, at least for women, is really bound up with Jesus. Their questions are searching, and many of those who pose them answer negatively.

I have spoken of the grasp that the poor have of Christ as truth. I must speak also of the truth grasped by women who have taken off the patriarchal spectacles with which society has fitted all of us. Before their gaze all the accepted customs and habits of thought of our society, the noblest as well as the basest, appear in a new and truer light, as pervaded by patriarchal interests and perspectives. These interests and perspectives in turn seem to have no more justification than the ideologies by which the rich justify their advantages.

It quickly becomes apparent that Christianity as a whole (along with Judaism) has shared in the patriarchal character of all Mediterranean and Western civilization during the past three thousand years. To many feminists it seems that seeking a nonpatriarchal core that can be reclothed in nonpatriarchal forms is hopeless. Christianity is more like an onion than an apple, and each new layer turns out, in its turn, to be patriarchal. Indeed the argument can be made that Judaism and Christianity are not religious traditions that merely conform to cultural patriarchalism but are expressions and instruments of patriarchy's struggle for dominance. In this view they are patriarchal, not incidentally, but essentially.

Against extreme views of this sort one can point out that nonpatriarchal ideas and images abound throughout the Scriptures, that in general the Scriptures are not as patriarchal as they have been made to appear by translators and interpreters, and that, especially in the dawning of Christianity, there was a break with culture that included a break with patriarchy. Jesus lived by a vision of eschatological reversal that did not leave even patriarchy intact. Elisabeth Schüssler Fiorenza has discerned behind our present New Testament texts the evidence of a very early nonpatriarchal Christian community. Although Paul made concessions to patriarchy, his basic theological vision did not support it. Women probably played leadership roles in Christianity as long as its basic institution was the house-church.

Nevertheless, whatever can be said to mitigate the charge of un-alleviated patriarchy in Jewish and Christian tradition, one must acknowledge the almost total victory of patriarchy in the church by the third century. Until recently, male hegemony was rarely questioned. The historical efficacy of the originating events of Christianity has been to mitigate tendencies to extreme misogyny but not to challenge patriarchy in general.

Can, then, a feminist be a Christian? Not if that means affirming the adequacy of any past or extant form of Christianity, even that of the community of Jesus' disciples or the pre-Pauline church. In these general terms this is not a problem for feminists alone. Surely few can seriously identify their understanding of the meaning of Christ for today's world with any past expression of Christianity. The question is not whether any form Christianity has thus far taken is adequate for the future. The question is whether we can identify a power to which Christians have witnessed that is capable of shaping new forms and worthy of our trust and devotion. This is the question also for those feminists who are concerned about their relationship to Christianity.

This question is still a very difficult one. It is possible that just as that to which Buddhists have directed their attention is different from the power that Christians trust and worship, so also that which women find salvific for themselves differs from the power to which men look. Perhaps what Christians trust and worship is the power to which men look. If so, the feminists who reject Christology are right in an important sense. Even then, from the Christian side this dualism cannot be the last word. Christians need to encompass the complementary process of salvation for women, without abandoning what has been salvific for men. Indeed it is precisely faith in Christ that will require male Christians to open themselves to the Goddess or to whatever else women orient themselves for their salvation.

If, instead, it turns out that the saving reality discovered by women is indeed that which has been named Christ, the question is whether that name can be retained. The name may be so bound up with the history of its use, especially with the male Jesus, that women who now find salvation in sisterhood with other women cannot invoke it. If so, and if this proves not to be a passing phenomenon, Christians must face a most critical problem. Can we survive without our most central symbol, without the name that names us? If this is our direction, it obviously spells the end of Christology. I do not deny that this may be our destiny, but I am not reconciled to it. I prefer to explore the possibility that *Christ* can be so creatively transformed that it can become usable by feminists.

One major problem for feminists is that the symbol *Christ* is bound up with the cross and that the cross represents to many the ultimate of suffering love and self-sacrifice. Christian men have viewed self-sacrifice as a beautiful ideal that checks self-assertion and self-aggrandizement. But when women see that they, and for the most part they alone, have been expected to embody this ideal, especially in relation to husbands and children, they see the destructiveness of this image. Their need is for self-love and self-assertion. In their experience the self they learn to love and assert is not independent of others but part of a web of interconnectedness, so that self-love is expansive, not exclusive. It is not opposed to love of others. It includes it.

My own view is that what the feminists see is needed to counterbalance the dualistic and individualistic views of the self that have been cultivated by men in a patriarchal culture. Also, it would be absurd to depict the world for which we hope in terms of the crucifixion of everyone for the sake of everyone else. Human suffering is evil even when it is accepted voluntarily for the sake of others. If Christ is our salvation, we should not identify Christ with suffering love. That can be destructive, and feminists rightly point out that it has been destructive for women.

Nevertheless, the meaning of *Christ* cannot be separated altogether from suffering love, and it is my hope that in time feminists will be able to reappropriate that idea or an analogous one. Our ideal is a world in which the self-fulfillment of each conduces to the self-fulfillment of all, and when we realize with the feminists how deeply we are bound together in the depths of ourselves, this ideal takes on new and richer meaning. We are truly members one of another. In the world, as it has long been and still is, full mutuality often requires elements of personal sacrifice. The richest relationships, whether within the family or between friends, are costly. We pay the price gladly for the sake of the promise, but the element of sacrifice remains. In the extreme instance we are called to make the sacrifice even though the good for which we sacrifice may not be one in which we participate. As an image for the general norm for life, the cross can be destructive. But as an image of the extreme possibility to which, in a hostile world, the commitment to mutuality can lead, it is not expendable for the Christian. In my view feminists will also need some such image. That the cross has been misused to oppress women is reason now for opposing the image, but it should not prove an ultimate obstacle to the feminists' appropriation of *Christ*.

In my own Christology, for reasons related to those the feminists have raised, I have avoided placing the cross as symbol of sacrificial love at the center. I have interpreted cross and resurrection as dying to the old self and rising to the new. This is paradigmatic for creative transformation. Of course there is no creative transformation without some sacrifice of the self that is to be transformed. But the focus is on the ever new self to be attained rather than on sacrifice as inherently desirable. So this aspect of the feminist critique of Christology occasions no major change in my formulation.

I have been more conscious in the past of the problem caused by the dominance of masculine language. I have proposed that Jesus, the male, pointed us toward a fulfillment, a *basileia*, that is feminine in gender and in character. The work of Christ as creative transformation is to take us toward that end. I thought women and men could share in that process without inauthenticity. But I have come to realize that my formulation still failed to incorporate in very important respects the insights of feminists.

The fundamental error was to follow the tradition of the church in speaking of that which is incarnate in Jesus and salvific for all as only Logos, or Word. The resultant limitation appeared in the section on liberation theology. The Logos correlates with creative transformation as the divine activity or agency in the world. It does not correlate well with the divine presence with the poor, suffering with them their poverty and oppression. To deal with this problem, I suggested that Jesus should be conceived as the incarnation of the entire Trinity rather than simply the Logos as the Second Persona.

Although this change allows a richer understanding of the saving power in which Christians put their trust, it still does not deal adequately with the issues posed by feminists. Traditionally all three Personae of the Trinity have been masculine. To speak of the Trinity as a whole as incarnate does little to overcome the exclusively masculine imagery and language associated with *Christ*. One approach is to reclaim *Spirit* from its masculine use and emphasize its feminine character. I continue to see merit in that move. But Christian feminists have pointed to a better way.

If we need a word to speak of the way, the truth, and the life together, I suggest *Wisdom*. *Wisdom* can name the creatively transforming Word together with truth. The connotations of *Wisdom* have the richness that is needed. Furthermore, the idea that Jesus is the incarnation of Wisdom has adequate biblical grounding, and it connects Christology to an important tradition in the Jewish Scriptures. *Wisdom* is free of the predominately masculine connotations that restrict the usefulness of *Word*. Indeed, whereas *Logos* is a masculine noun, *Sophia*, the Greek word for Wisdom, is feminine, and the feminine pronoun already appears prominently in the Jewish Scriptures in which the divine is referred to as Sophia.

I am proposing, therefore, a Christology in which *Christ* names Sophia as she embodies herself in the world and receives the world into herself. To turn to Christ is to turn away from the wisdom of this world to the wisdom of God. Jesus is the incarnation of Sophia, the divine Wisdom.

Many feminists have little interest in such proposals for the creative transformation of Christology. For their salvation they have turned away from the church and established new communities. They use a rhetoric partly formed in direct opposition to Christianity. Much of value and power has become manifest in this way.

The question is not whether it is right and appropriate for feminists to establish their identity and develop their thought and spirituality over against Christianity as a whole. That is no doubt the calling of some. The question is whether Christians will harden themselves against the new insights and perceptions or will allow themselves to be creatively transformed by them. Surely the latter is the choice that is faithful to Christ, as the effective presence of Wisdom in all things.

Critiques

Critique by John Hick

This updating of John Cobb's Christology is an important extension of his theology. I find it particularly interesting from the point of view of theological method. How is Cobb using language? In what kind of exercise is he engaged?

I see him as creating what he calls a rhetoric—he speaks of "a Christological rhetoric," "the rhetoric of creative transformation"—or, as one could equally well say, a myth. The value of such a rhetoric lies in its effect upon human motivation and behavior. It was because the rhetoric of creative transformation was not adequate to guide behavior in the ways called for by contemporary liberation and feminist concerns that he has amended it.

It is both the strength and the weakness of rhetorical theology that it proliferates in ambiguities. One ambiguity that can, however, perhaps be resolved concerns the relationship among Cobb's three christological equations:

(1) Christ = Logos = creative transformation = primordial nature of
    God

(2) Christ = conscientization = the poor = the truth = the Trinity
(3) Christ = Wisdom (*Sophia*, f.)

Is the first now superseded by a conflation of the other two: Christ =
conscientization = the poor = the truth = the Trinity = Wisdom? Or are
(2) and (3) alternatives? Or are all three now included in the comprehensive
equation Christ = Logos = creative transformation = primordial nature of
God = conscientization = the poor = the truth = the Trinity = Wisdom?

The creative transformation rhetoric arose from the fact that in a world
threatened by nuclear and other forms of destruction we need a salvation
consisting of the creation of a "just, participatory, and sustainable society in
which personal wholeness is possible." Fortunately we are aware of the lure
of ethical ideals and a tendency for life to produce change for the better, a
force of "creative transformation." This is evident whenever, starting in the
human heart, movement occurs in the direction of peace, justice, sanity,
freedom. Cobb's original proposal was to identify this force of creative
transformation, or of change for the better, as Christ—not the historical
Jesus of Nazareth but the Christ or the Logos that became incarnate in him.

That constructive forces, factors, tendencies, make for a saner and
juster world is, happily, not controversial. Nor need anyone object if some
find it helpful to think of these factors under some unifying symbol. It can
sometimes be convenient, and imaginatively satisfying, to simplify and
hypostatize a range of complex factors in this way, speaking, for example, of
progress, democracy, or the dialectical process. Why not hypostatize the
forces that make for human betterment as life or as creative transformation?
If, further, Christians want to call this hypostatization *Christ*, why should
they not? Thus far, *Christ* can be accepted as a Christian way of symbolizing
something for which other traditions will naturally prefer to use their own
symbols.

The Christ symbol is, however, inherently ambiguous in that as well as
being capable of being used to refer to various abstractions (such as creative
transformation) it is also traditionally a title given to Jesus of Nazareth. In
this traditional meaning Christ is not a principle but a person. This
ambiguity surfaces in Cobb's essay when, speaking of a protein-starved girl,
he says, "Christ suffers in her suffering and rejoices in her joys"—something
that can be said only of a personal consciousness.

This ambiguity is perhaps continuous with a larger ambiguity.
Although it is an optional rhetoric for Christians to give the name *Christ* to
the transforming power in life, it would be highly contentious for us to claim
that this transforming power has been fully revealed, manifested,
incarnated, only in Jesus of Nazareth. Christians would then stand in a
special relationship to that power, as those who have responded to its

uniquely full manifestation in human history. This would be the traditional Christian doctrine of the incarnation, though expressed in a novel way. It would not entail exclusivism, claiming that salvation—the creative transformation of human life—operates only within Christians. It would, however, seem to entail Christian inclusivism, claiming that although this creative transformation occurs throughout the world, its source and nature are fully revealed only in its incarnation in Jesus of Nazareth.

I do not find it easy to be sure that Cobb is making this inclusivist claim. He is emphatic that the creative transformation that he identifies as Christ has been at work throughout the world and throughout history: "it is clear that creative transformation was immanent in Jesus as it was in Moses, Socrates, and Gautama, and it is in each of us. . . . in an important sense God is incarnate in all things." At the same time, however, he seems to be arguing for "associating distinctively with [Jesus] the incarnation of the power that alone can save the world." He claims that the experience of contemporary Christians leads to the same need that the early Christians experienced to distinguish the power of transformation in ourselves from that in Jesus. The latter was not "simply a fuller presence or effectiveness, a difference of degree," but "a qualitative or structural difference"—yet, on the other hand, not "a metaphysical break radically separating Jesus from all other human beings." I find this conjunction of statements hard to interpret. Cobb seems to be claiming that although creative transformation = Christ = Logos = the primordial nature of God is incarnate in varying degrees in all life, in Jesus it was incarnate not merely to a greater degree but in a qualitatively different way, one that constitutes Jesus as the incarnation of God in a unique sense. It seems to follow (a) that Christianity is based upon the one supreme and unequaled revelation of God's nature, and (b) that Christians, insofar as we live in response to this revelation, have greater religious privileges and responsibilities than do the rest of humankind. So, over against Buddhism, whose ultimate goal he identifies with the nothingness out of which God created the world, Cobb affirms that "Christ alone is our hope for salvation from despair and destruction."

Can Cobb's tendency toward an inclusivist affirmation of the superiority of Christianity avoid being intensified by his move, in response to the challenge of liberation theology, from the thought that one Person of the Trinity, the Logos or Son, became incarnate in Jesus to the thought that the entire Trinity became incarnate in him? Cobb says, "Let us think quite straightforwardly that it is God who is incarnate in Jesus and that this God is the Trinity in its totality." Will this support the traditional Christian totalitarian claim on behalf of Jesus and his church?

There is no space here to argue (as I have argued elsewhere) that Christian inclusivism, although an advance on exclusivism, is nevertheless not fully adequate and that we have to move beyond it to a pluralism that recognizes the equal value of the other great world faiths as different but independently valid spheres of revelation and salvation, enlightenment and liberation. Thus although some may well believe that Cobb has already departed too far from Chalcedon, I believe, on the contrary, that he has not departed from it far enough.

Cobb faces this possibility when he turns to the contemporary feminist challenge to Christology. "Feminists ask whether the truly salvific process, at least for women, is really bound up with Jesus." Since women constitute half the human race, this is a large challenge! Cobb's solution is his third equation, Christ = Wisdom, Wisdom being named in Greek by the feminine noun *Sophia*. "Jesus is the incarnation of *Sophia*, the divine Wisdom." I have space left only to ask five questions:

(1) Is it any less sexist to identify Christ as *Sophia* (feminine) than as *Logos* (masculine)?

(2) A few pages earlier Cobb says that "quite straightforwardly . . . it is God who is incarnate in Jesus." Now he proposes that "Jesus is the incarnation of *Sophia*." Are God and *Sophia* identical? Or is God a Quaternity, consisting of Father, Son, Spirit, and *Sophia*? Or is *Sophia* to be identified with the Second Person? Is the Son then really the Daughter? And would not this still leave a two-to-one male majority in the Trinity?

(3) Should we take so seriously the ancient superstition that feminine and masculine nouns reveal the feminine or masculine character of their referents?

(4) Are all these problems avoided by reiterating that what is being offered is a "Christological rhetoric"? Perhaps rhetoric can legitimately thrive on inconsistencies that "snarling logicality" would reject.

(5) Would it not be better to acknowledge, more radically, that salvation is *not* bound up, in any exclusive sense, with Jesus but that God's salvific activity occurs in many ways? Freed from the totalitarian claim implicit in traditional Christology, women (and also men) will then be able to discriminate and to receive from Christianity such salvific truth and value as we are able to find there.

Critique by Stephen T. Davis

John Cobb's essay is a fascinating study on many levels, not the least of which is that in it the reader finds a first-rate theologian and a sensitive human being rethinking his christological conclusions. In my view, a profound tension is evident in the essay. On the one hand Cobb recognizes that Christian use of the term *Christ* ought to be tied to the person of Jesus Christ and that the *Christ* of any Christian generation must be an "appropriate development" of the *Christ* of the tradition. On the other hand *Christ* is for Cobb not primarily a person but a kind of *principle* or *symbol*—one that seems so broad at times as virtually to amount to anything salvific or even good in the world.

Cobb seems to see the task of Christology as that of *locating* or *identifying* or *naming* Christ. It is almost as if what we must do is look about us and discover who or where Christ is in the world. Theologians once saw it as part of their task to explain the person and work of Jesus Christ—perhaps even to get people to believe in Christ. Now it is apparently a matter of helping people to look about them and find who or what is Christ. Thus, I say, Cobb finds himself pulled in the direction of *Christ* as a kind of vague symbol or principle. I think Karl Barth's perceptive comment is apt: "When we pronounce the name of Jesus Christ, we are not speaking of an idea. The name Jesus Christ is not a transparent shell, through which we glimpse something higher" (*Dogmatics in Outline*, p. 67).

Cobb once identified Christ with creative transformation. He now thinks that Christ is more than just this, but it is clear that Cobb still thinks the old identification is basically correct. This naturally leads us to wonder precisely what creative transformation is. The truth seems to be that this concept is used by Cobb in an amazingly broad and generous way. Creative transformation is repentance and conversion, grace in one's personal life, the life in all living things, the way and the life, a constitutive element in every individual event, the conscientization spoken of by liberation theologians, and the activity of God or the Logos in the world.

Despite Cobb's caveats that the symbol *Christ* must be tied to the person of Christ, that the image of Jesus guides Christians in their use of *Christ*, Christ virtually comes to be identified by Cobb with whatever is good in the world. Now I believe Cobb means to be taken seriously when he insists that the concept of *Christ* must be tied to Jesus, to the work of God, and to salvation. Even if you agree with Cobb on those points, *Christ* can still become for you the "transparent shell" Barth speaks of if you also think (as Cobb seems to think) that whatever is good in the world is the work of God or Christ. Thus, I say, despite his earlier warnings, *Christ* becomes for Cobb an almost infinitely broad symbol rather than a particular person. My criticism, then, is that Cobb's use of *Christ* is so far removed from the person of Jesus and from what christologists (even fairly liberal ones) have traditionally talked about as to be virtually unrecognizable. *Christ* ends up having remarkably little to do with Jesus or even with Christianity.

A minor point: how odd it is to find Cobb criticizing orthodox Christologies on the grounds that God worked salvifically in Old Testament times, i.e., before Jesus lived, and that God works in the world today not through Jesus but through the Holy Spirit. Would Athanasius or Augustine or Aquinas or Luther or Calvin or Barth have denied that? I am one of those who think *Christ* is primarily a proper name rather than a symbol; to dissuade me from that view, Cobb will have to come up with stronger arguments than this one.

On the other hand I would like to endorse most of what Cobb says in his section on liberation theology. The only important exception is his interesting suggestion about the Trinity. The problem there, as I see it, is that if *Christ* simply names God's relations to the world, then there is no Holy Spirit and thus no Trinity. Or at least, that is a danger in Cobb's notion. Despite this point, what Cobb says about the poor, about Christ's relation to the poor, and about the truth, which the poor uniquely know, seem to me to be illuminating and true.

I also agree with much of what Cobb says in his section on feminist theology. It is interesting, however, that Cobb's methodology seems to signal a profound change in the sorts of things that cause theologians to respond. Until recently, changes in theology were typically brought about by *theological criticisms* or by the existence of *competing theologies*. These criticisms were sometimes raised by fellow theologians, sometimes by religious people in the same tradition who were judged to be heretical, sometimes by people from another religious tradition, sometimes by people of no religion at all. Now, however, Christian theologians seem to be responding not to criticisms or competing theologies but to *grievances* brought against Christianity by people who blame their problems on certain theological positions standardly taken by Christians.

I raise no objection to Cobb's Christology at this point. I myself hold that the grievances raised by various oppressed people—blacks, women, the poor—are legitimate grievances that ought to be redressed. I also agree that the Christian church has not done nearly as much as it should have done to bring about justice. Finally, I agree that lamentable historical realities sometimes have hidden theological causes and that Christian theologians must courageously look for them. My only negative comment is that some theologians seem to me all too prone to blame almost anything unjust in the world on Christianity or on traditional Christian formulations. Such people are apt to say things such as "Christianity is essentially patriarchical" or "Orthodox Christologies are inherently anti-Semitic" or "The church is always on the side of the rich and powerful." My fond wish is that theologians think long and hard before jumping to such conclusions. Not everyone who rejects Christianity does so for a reason that ought to cause theologians to rewrite theology.

In the current context Cobb is a difficult person to categorize, let alone criticize. Knowing him as I do, I feel there is a side of Cobb that is orthodox, in terms of the Christian faith that he believes and especially in terms of the

Christian faith that he practices. But there is also another side to Cobb—a side in which he is almost as theologically iconoclastic as Hick. Unfortunately (at least it is unfortunate from my viewpoint), it seems to me the iconoclastic side usually wins. Certainly in his Christology it does.

Finally, let me say a word to Hick and Robinson as well as Cobb. It is obvious that these three scholars propose in this book Christologies that amount to radical revisions of traditional notions. It ought to be clear that I find these revisions far too radical. All three, in my opinion, end up with an entirely human Jesus or with one who is divine in only a weak or metaphorical sense. Scholars, it seems to me, ought to be free to follow their thoughts wherever they lead, and those who are theologically untrained or who are theologically more orthodox ought to be tolerant of such scholars. We need not (and I certainly do not) question the sincerity of such thinkers as Cobb, Hick, and Robinson, or the depth of their Christian commitment. But I do want to be quite clear that I think these thinkers have departed too far from the central traditions of the church in Christology.

Critique by James M. Robinson

Perhaps the most appealing thing about Cobb's Christology of creative transformation is that the Christology itself is in his essay undergoing creative transformation. This of course should mean, in terms of this theology, that it is inspired, or, since the Holy Spirit has largely been replaced by the symbol *Christ*, it is the ongoing word of the resurrected.

As a biblical scholar I find an interesting strain of biblicism in Cobb's Whiteheadian Christology, for example in its explicit Johannine orientation to the verse memorized in Sunday school, "I am the way, the truth and the life, no man cometh unto the father but by me." Thus Cobb's Logos Christology of creative transformation had affirmed that Christ was the way and the life, but not the truth. "My understanding of this work [i.e., of the Logos in the world] was shaped by Whitehead's influence on my thought. Specifically, I identified the Logos with what Whitehead calls the primordial nature of God. Whitehead distinguished the primordial from the consequent nature of God. The consequent nature is the truth. In the consequent nature, God suffers with us. . . . But I associated this aspect of God with the Holy Spirit. . . . I have acknowledged the limitations that imposed upon my Christology."

But now Christ is, by an extension of Cobb's Christology, also the truth, that is to say, the consequent nature of God. This part of Johannine Christology Cobb has learned from liberation theology. Cobb thinks that "creative transformation can be transformed to encompass also the truth that Christ identifies with the poor . . . if we add to the affirmation of Christ as the way and the life (viewed together as the Johannine Word, or Logos, and as incarnate in the world as creative transformation) that Christ is also the truth, which is the way all things cohere in God." Thus the biblicism of a Johannine Christology had been inhibited by Whiteheadian metaphysics. It also, though perhaps more peripherally, had dogmatic limitations: "The doctrine of the Trinity arose to express distinctions within God. . . . Finally, it was concluded, all three *personae* were involved in every activity of the Trinity. One exception was made. It continued to be held that the incarnation was only of the Second Person, the Son, or the Logos. In my earlier Christology I held to that doctrine. . . . I now propose that we reject the exception of the incarnation from the general unity of the Trinity in its activities *ad extra*." Thus the whole question of potentially competing authorities—Scripture, dogma, philosophy, and experience—seem caught up in this creative transformation.

The challenge of liberation theology leads Cobb to question his practice of adopting "culture as the context of theology." According to liberation theology, "Christ is not identified with the creative transformation of thought, of personal experience, or of cultural forms, to which I have given primary attention, but with the poor and oppressed." To be sure, Cobb would like to avoid an either-or choice and so points to ideational dimensions of liberation theology, such as "conscientization" and liberation theology's insistence that the problem is "systemic." Yet Cobb concedes: "When we despiritualize our readings of the Gospel accounts of Jesus, we find it unequivocally clear that he sided with the poor."

Of course on first glance no one would want to "despiritualize our readings of the Gospel accounts of Jesus." But perhaps all of us should, once we recognize what "spiritualizing" has meant. There was a basic "spiritualizing" misunderstanding of the New Testament until Hermann Gunkel's famous essay on the effects of the Spirit at the opening of the century put the biblical Spirit into the context of the Ancient Near East and the Hellenistic world and took it out of the "God-conscious" orientation of German Idealism's *Geist* that has characterized philosophical theology since Schleiermacher.

The Spirit that descended on Jesus like a dove "drove" him into the wilderness to be tempted, according to the oldest Gospel Mark (a crudity that later Gospels clean up). Jesus' most concrete actions for the needy are his exorcisms, which he performed "by the finger of God," according to Q, which Matthew theologizes as the "Spirit of God." This "animistic" meaning of Spirit does not need to be "despiritualized" to be where the poor are but functions in terms of their need. I of course do not mean to propose that we resort to such primitive or pre-Enlightenment doctrines. But we should demythologize them, that is to say, bring to expression what they in their way brought to expression, rather than "spiritualizing" them in the way we traditionally have, that is to say, using the biblical language but meaning by it something quite distinct, namely, what those words mean in our language.

Cobb confesses: "In the light of this I can only confess that my neglect of this basic fact about Jesus reflected my participation, along with my teachers, in a middle-class society whose interests were cultural, religious, and existential rather than socially revolutionary." This is in a sense a recognition of the same problem that was recognized in Germany after World War I, when its culture collapsed. The more revolutionary theologians in that situation criticized the inadequacies of contemporary theology, as what they called *Kulturprotestantismus*, and ascribed it to the philosophical theology of modern times rooted in Hegel. As Rudolf Bultmann expressed that criticism:

> The attaching of the *existential* subject to history does not take place at all—at least if the existence of humanity lies not in the general, as reason, but rather in the individual element, in the concrete moments of here and now. Precisely for this reason the idealistic observer sees nothing in history which makes a claim on him, specifically in the sense that here something new would be said to him which he does not potentially already have, over which he does not already have control by means of his participation in general rationality. He finds nothing that encounters him as authority, he finds in history always only himself, in that the content of history is reduced to the movement of ideas for which the groundwork is laid in the reason of mankind. So he has control from the very beginning over all possibilities of historical occurrence. (*The Beginnings of Dialectic Theology*, ed. James M. Robinson [Richmond, Va.: John Knox Press, 1968], 1:239)

This call for taking history seriously, not just as a generalization, as a philosophy of history, or theologized as *Heilsgeschichte*, but as the concrete, specific history of one's poverty, of one's sex, of one's encounters that produce things important enough to call for basic commitment, has traditionally been part of the problem of the particularism of Christianity (and Judaism and Islam), in making Moses' or Jesus' or Muhammad's history indispensable. Other religions are less "historic" in their theological cast (though their religious history may be as old or older) and in that sense are more open theologically to dialogue. But we are told that "the deep differences of Buddhism and Christianity need not require the weakening of the truth of either as each acknowledges the truth of the other." One of the criticisms of Hegelian theology was that it replaced what it called "the Christ person" with "the Christ principle." For Cobb "the symbol *Christ* is indissolubly bound to Jesus," but the necessity for such a link is less clear in his presentation, perhaps because of this philosophical theology heritage.

Of course in a converse sense it is precisely the taking seriously of the particular history of each religion that makes such an interreligious dialogue serious. The other religion would have every right to be mistrustful of an approach from Christianity to the effect that the differences between Oriental and Western religion are "just" different ways of saying or doing the same thing and can hence be reduced to a least common denominator. It is sometimes said that the philosophy of history is a "Christian" addition to the history of Western philosophy (such as in Augustine), but if it is a valid addition, then it would underline the history of Oriental religion as well as the history of the dominant Western religion. To take Oriental religion seriously, we would have to assume that we can learn or experience something that the West cannot derive from the West.

Critique by Rebecca D. Pentz

In the fourth section of his essay John Cobb modifies his Christology in response to feminist concerns. Many of the concerns he raises are the very concerns I raise in "Can Jesus Save Women?" and I am in complete sympathy with them. Certainly we women must reject the accretions of patriarchy on Christianity. Certainly we women should be self-loving and self-asserting. Certainly destructive suffering love should not be any Christian's goal (though servanthood made possible by ego strength should be). But I find the change Cobb makes in his original Christology inadequate.

In *Christ in a Pluralistic Age* Cobb identified Christ as the incarnate Logos and went on to identify it as "masculine in connotation," being "order, novelty, call, demand, agent, transformer, and principle of restlessness" (pp. 263–64). Cobb now repents of this masculine portrayal and in his newest Christology *Christ* is the symbol for the incarnate feminine Sophia.

We need to be clear about this change and the resulting advantages. I can identify at least three advantages to a Sophia Christology. First, a Sophia Christology emphasizes the characteristics of Christ that are "feminine in connotation." Sophia is caring and nurturing. Read the Wisdom of Solomon, in which Sophia counsels those in prosperity, comforts those in anxiety and grief, "ranges in search of those who are worthy of her," saves Adam after the fall, guides Noah, strengthens Abraham, empowers Moses, and leads the Jews through the wilderness, becoming "a covering for them by day and blaze of stars by night" (Wisdom 6, 8, and 10). Or read Proverbs 4, in which Sophia guards us and keeps us safe, or Proverbs 9, in which she invites us to her house so that we can grow in understanding. Second, a Sophia Christology makes it clear that women have access to the divine, that the so-called "masculine characteristics" of the divine, such as power, do not stand between women and God. In fact Sophia is not just nurturing. She works powerfully now from her place beside God's throne, deciding for God what he shall do, filling his prophets, overcoming evil, and ordering all things well (Wisdom 7–9). She is God's mediator at the creation (Prov. 8:22–31), and she is the law (Sirach 24:23). Third, a Sophia Christology does not have the tendency of a Logos Christology to turn Christ into an abstraction. Sophia herself is personal, not abstract. She is the law, but as the law she personally keeps people from going astray (Sirach 24:22). She is present at creation but not as a blueprint; she is God's darling, present at his side (Prov. 8:30). Logos in the Old Testament is also personal, being God's word. But in Stoic philosophy, Logos is the abstract principle of reason, and some Logos Christologies (e.g., see the second-century apologists) make heavy use of the Greek rather than the Hebraic Logos.

Given these positive aspects of a Sophia Christology, two things concern me about Cobb's new Christology. First it is not at all clear that Cobb's Sophia Christology is any more than window dressing. Cobb now calls Christ "the incarnate Sophia," but has he made any change in the substance of his Christology to reflect the advantages of a Sophia Christology? Does his Christ have the feminine characteristics of Christ, the caring and nurturing characteristics? In response to liberation theology, Cobb now sees his Christ not just as order, novelty, call, demand, agent, transformer, and principle of restlessness but as one who suffers with our suffering and rejoices with our joy. Does this caring lead to nurture, so that Cobb's Christ, like Sophia, guides us, instructs us, strengthens us, and keeps us safe? Second, does Cobb's Christ reflect the feminine power of Sophia, her position as God's helpmate and our Savior? Sophia saves us by giving us the strength to master all things and by preserving us from sin (Wisdom 10). Can creative transformation do that? Finally, is Cobb's Christ personal like Sophia or abstract like the Stoics' Logos? Cobb's *Christ* is a living symbol, not a proper name. Is a living symbol personal? In short my first concern is that I do not see how Cobb has changed the *substance* of his Christology when he changed its name.

Second, when Cobb adopts a Sophia Christology, even though he applauds it as having "adequate biblical grounding," he does not make his Christology any more biblical. In fact, in his methodology he is not concerned with being biblical. He calls Christ "the way, the truth, and the life," but he doesn't see this as reflecting the content of John 14:6. Cobb tells us specifically that he is not trying to identify what the author of the fourth Gospel had in mind. So how does he get his content? In *Christ in a Pluralistic Age* he gets it by examining art, theology, history, nature, personal experience, and the philosophy of Alfred North Whitehead. In this essay he takes part "in the unending process of reformulation in view of the sensibilities and insights *of the time*" (italics mine). This in my view is Cobb's mistake. Rather than starting with God's revelation in the biblical account of Jesus, Cobb starts with the human sensibilities and the human insights of the twentieth century.

You can see the straits Cobb's approach gets him into in his response to liberation theology. The liberation theologians remind us that Jesus told us in no uncertain terms to care for the poor. Cobb's original Christology takes no account of this. Nor is this surprising, given his method. He was not at first concerned with what Jesus had to say. Now, to take account of what Jesus did say, Cobb has to rework his Christology. He expands what the symbol *Christ* stands for so that it represents not only the primordial nature of God but the consequent nature as well. It now represents not only the process of creative transformation but the way in which the world affects God and "the inclusive and ultimate perspective upon all the finite and conflicting perspectives that make up the world." In short, *Christ* now represents everything and anything about how God and the world interact. All this because Jesus told us that neglecting the poor is tantamount to neglecting him and because the liberation theologians have pointed out that taking these words seriously has grave societal consequences.

Models such as Sophia are useful if they help us to understand what God is doing and who he is. But they must be true to who he is. The best way to ensure this is to start with his revelation, not with our human symbols.

Cobb's Response to Critiques

All the criticisms of my essay are thoughtful and incisive. Some of them simply express disagreements. Others, however, indicate that I have not communicated my thought clearly or that there are confusions and inconsistencies within it that I would like to overcome. I appreciate this chance to try to state more exactly what I mean.

Davis and Pentz criticize me for separating Christ too far from Jesus. Hick criticizes me for tying Christ too closely to Jesus. I do not expect to satisfy any of them. I want to assert strongly that Christ is not limited to the historical figure of Jesus. I also want to say equally strongly that it is irresponsible to speak of Christ without the connection to Jesus. To that extent I will simply reaffirm my Christology against theirs. But both Hick and Davis find my position confusing and inconsistent. Because I like to be clear and explicit about my beliefs, I will try again to say just how I hold the two emphases together.

I begin with a concern to use *Christ* in a way that takes account of its use in the piety and liturgy of the church. That concern has led me to the conviction that no single definition suffices. Sometimes *Christ* refers directly to Jesus. Sometimes *Christ* refers to the Logos, the everlasting Word, the Second Person of the Trinity, that is, to God. The doctrine of the incarnation brings these two uses close together but does not identify them. The Logos is that which is incarnate in Jesus. Jesus is the fully human being in whom the Logos is incarnate.

I do not question that *Christ* has functioned as a proper name for Jesus and sometimes also for the Logos. As I see it this has been a source of confusion and even of error in the church's teaching. I strongly recommend that *Christ* be used as a name for both Jesus and the Logos, but not as a proper name. To call Jesus or the Logos *Christ* is, or should be, to speak of them in such a way as to highlight certain aspects or roles rather than others. To call Jesus *Christ* highlights the way God or the Logos was incarnate in him. To call the Logos *Christ* is to highlight the claim that the Logos was incarnate in Jesus. It is confusing to substitute *Christ* for *Logos* when we are reflecting on the relationships among the three members of the Trinity, and that has rarely been done. To me it seems confusing when disbelievers call Jesus *Christ*. The name *Christ* belongs with the confession of faith. But I acknowledge that as a result of Christian use of *Christ* as a proper name for Jesus, this empty usage has become widespread. I am consciously opposing it.

In this essay I have focused on *Christ* as the presence and activity in the world of that which was incarnate in Jesus rather than on Jesus as the fully human being in whom God was incarnate. I did so because it was this feature of my earlier work that I wanted to revise. For the moment I am prepared to let stand what I have written in *Christ in a Pluralistic Age* about the two natures of Jesus and the relation of Jesus' person to his work as well as what that work is. Davis correctly points out the absence of that discussion here and the resulting one-sidedness of my statement. It is far from a complete Christology! But I believe that what I have discussed here complements a basically Chalcedonian view of Jesus' person and a basically Pauline view of Jesus' work as I have developed them elsewhere. And I think this side of the discussion is also important.

In different ways Hick and Davis are somewhat bothered by the comprehensiveness I attribute to the work of Christ, viewed here as the working of God in the world. Davis rightly points out that my inclusive use of *Christ* raises questions about the work of the Holy Spirit. I will return to this trinitarian question later. But if we do understand that *Christ* names God as creatively and redemptively working in the world, that is, as present and active therein, then I assume that the fact that I find Christ everywhere is faithful to both Scripture and tradition. As far as I can see, this is continuous with the Logos Christology of the early church and with the prologue to John's Gospel, which played so important a role in shaping the church's thought.

Hick thinks that in speaking of Christ I am hypostatizing a range of complex factors. I understand myself, instead, to be discerning where the one God is present and active in the world. Because I believe that God is present and active in every event whatsoever, my concern is to see where the activity is most effective and significant. I am guided in that by what I learn in the New Testament of the working of God in life, light, newness, grace, freedom. I have proposed that one way of understanding the unity of all of this is through a contemporary phrase, "creative transformation," and I tried, in *Christ in a Pluralistic Age*, to provide a careful analysis of what is involved. I hope that this is not vague or confused.

The complaint of vagueness and confusion is especially focused on the question of whether Christ is a person. When *Christ* names Jesus, there is no question that Christ is a person. When *Christ* names God, the question is more difficult. Traditionally God is spoken of as three persons, and in this language my argument that the whole Trinity is involved in all God's acts *ad extra* implies that Christ is tripersonal. But I think that both Hick and Davis raise the question more in terms of the modern use of *person*, which I associate with the oneness rather than the threeness of God. In this sense, insofar as the term *person* can be freed of its anthropomorphic and temporalistic connotations, I do affirm that God is Person. Hence in this respect also what *Christ* names is *Person*, or in Hick's terms *personal consciousness*.

I will turn now to the issues raised more distinctively by each critic, beginning with Hick. I hope that what I have already said will enable me to make brief answers that are nevertheless clear.

Hick notes that I write frequently of the rhetoric I am using and speaks of my theology as a rhetorical theology. He associates my use of *rhetoric* with *myth*. I myself would use the term *myth* in a more limited way and would not describe most of the rhetoric I recommend as mythical.

It is my belief that the language we use to speak of God is very important. It is important, first, that it not mislead with respect to truth. But it is also important that it bring to attention those features of the divine reality that are most relevant to our current situation and needs. And it is important that it direct imagery and reflection in ways that will lead to appropriate forms of action. Not every true statement about God is theologically appropriate in every situation. And of two equally true ways of speaking about God, one may be much better than another under certain circumstances. All these are questions of rhetoric.

A very important rhetorical question today is that of the pronouns used to refer to God. Some continue to use masculine pronouns. Some shift to the feminine or the neuter. Some avoid pronouns altogether. It would be hard to argue that one of these choices is closer to the conceptual truth than the others. But this does not render the choosing unimportant. The language has consequences for images, emotions, and actions. The rhetorical question is theologically important. Feminine language about God considered in abstraction from our historical situation is just as sexist as masculine language, but concretely it may help to rectify age-old errors.

The question of how to name the divine reality that is incarnate in Jesus and present and active everywhere in the world is also a rhetorical question. The question is not the existence of separate and distinct entities—Sophia, Logos, and Pneuma—and a necessity that we engage in an empirical inquiry as to which one factually became incarnate. That *would* be mythical thinking! I believe it to be true to say that Logos was incarnate in Jesus. I believe it is also true that Pneuma was incarnate in Jesus. And I believe it is true to say that Sophia was incarnate in Jesus. These statements do not contradict one another. But their meanings are not identical. Each has been shaped by a history of use. A theologian cannot simply redefine them to suit her or his purposes.

I found, for example, that my focus on Logos as that which is incarnate in Jesus prevented me from speaking of Christ's suffering with those who suffer and rejoicing with those who rejoice. I do strongly believe that God suffers and rejoices with us. The aspects of God's reality brought to focus in *Logos* were different. On the other hand, when I think of *Sophia* as incarnate in Jesus, I can include in *Christ* what I previously understood under the name *Logos* and also this further important aspect. Because of the language of the New Testament and of the tradition and because compassion is so central to the character of Jesus, this has seemed to me a significant weakness in my earlier Christology and a strong reason for adopting a Sophia Christology. It is because of the shift to a more inclusive meaning of *Christ* that I am able to say that Christ suffers with the protein-starved girl.

Hick lists three sets of equations he finds in my essay with respect to Christ. I prefer to alter them a little. Conscientization appears to me a particularly clear example of creative transformation. But the special association of Christ with the poor and with truth requires the extension from Logos (creative transformation) of which I have been speaking. It is Sophia that seems to embrace adequately what before I had kept separate.

Hick is puzzled by my view that God was distinctly present or incarnate in Jesus but that this distinctiveness is not metaphysical. In *The Structure of Christian Existence* I identified a variety of structures of human existence. Each structure is different from the others, not as a matter of degree, but as a matter of kind. The mode of being of primal peoples differs from the mode of being of a Jewish prophet, not by having more or less of some property exhibited by the latter, but by being structured differently. The prophet's existence similarly differs from that of the enlightened Gautama, not by having more or less of some property exhibited by the latter, but by being structured differently. The differences of structure are extremely important. But all people belong to one species, *Homo sapiens*. It makes no sense to me to think that metaphysical differences exist among the members of a single species, even though the role and effectiveness of God's presence in these diverse structures also differ. That God is present and active in all is a point of metaphysical commonality, but the role God's presence and activity plays in each is not determined by metaphysics.

I have explained elsewhere that I believe the structure of Jesus' existence to have been different from any of the above. Indeed I believe that we have no evidence that anyone else has participated in the same structure of existence as Jesus. A very important part of the difference between Jesus and others is the role that God played in him. But that in no way means that Jesus was more or less a member of the human species than anyone else. Certainly no metaphysical differences exist between him and us. The qualitative and structural differences are important. As far as we know, the way in which God was present and active in Jesus was unique to him. But this uniqueness does not make him metaphysically different from the rest of us. I hope that these views are not confused or ambiguous.

Hick thinks that because I believe that the incarnation of God in Jesus was distinctive, I should therefore hold "(a) that Christianity is based upon the one supreme and unequaled revelation of God's nature and (b) that Christians, insofar as they live in response to this revelation, have greater religious privileges and responsibilities than do the rest of mankind." This line of argument, which of course is not in any of my writings, follows in part from Hick's shift from my rhetoric of incarnation to his rhetoric of revelation. I find it very unfortunate that the language of revelation has assumed such prominence in modern theology. It is peripheral in the Bible, and in the early church my language of incarnation was far more prominent. The shift to revelation in the modern church reflects the equally deplorable shift in philosophy from the primacy of ontology and cosmology to the primacy of epistemology. I simply do not think of Moses and Amos and Confucius and Socrates and Gautama and Mohammed as various revealers of God, who are either to be declared equal or ranked in terms of excellence. For me, each of them belongs to a different category, and each is a shining example within the category. But as far as I know, none of them claimed that his primary function was to reveal God. That was not the claim of the historical Jesus either, as far as I know, or, until recent times, the major claim that the church made about him. It is, at any rate, not the claim I am most interested in making.

I do not mean by this, however, to dismiss Hick's question. If I reflect on what I think I know of God, Jesus is extremely important to that knowledge. It was through Jesus that I could be engrafted into Israel's knowledge of God. Also through Jesus' life, teaching, death, and resurrection, those who followed him modified and developed Israel's previous understanding, placing the emphasis differently. And it is true that what happened among early believers shapes extensively my own thinking about God.

Do I then believe that Christians have a knowledge of God that is supreme and unequaled? That is difficult for me to answer. I do believe that features of the Christian understanding of God are true and that they have potential contributions to make to all of us. I want to affirm them strongly, and this leads me, as a theologian, to Christocentrism. I am also aware, as I encounter Jews and Muslims, some seriously one-sided elements in the Christian view of God need correction through our learning from them. It is difficult to say whether what we have to teach is more important than what we have to learn. I, for one, see little to be gained either by asserting equality or by ranking.

When I turn from the biblical family of religions to the East, I find the question of degrees of excellence in revealing God even more distorting. Certainly God has been at work in all, but what is distinctive and important about Gautama was not that he revealed this God. On the contrary, he realized Emptiness. That is, as far as I can see, something quite different and quite wonderful. But its role and contribution in the world will not be the same as the creative and redemptive working of God as Christ. Any notion of ranking along a single scale is precluded.

Davis perceives in my work a tension between orthodoxy and iconoclasm. He sees the iconoclasm as dominant in my Christology. My defense consists in vehement denial that orthodoxy and iconoclasm are opposites. I believe, on the contrary, that true orthodoxy calls us again and again to iconoclasm.

The original *iconoclasts* were those who saw in the use of icons by the Greek church a tendency to idolatry. To what extent they were correct is not my concern here. But I understand that as we generalize the meaning of iconoclasm in Christian theology, we are referring to the opposition at any time and place to whatever, at that time and place, threatens to become an idol, that is, to claim for any creature what belongs truly to God alone. As a theologian of the church, I affirm iconoclasm as an important part of my vocation.

Davis and I may understand *orthodoxy* differently. Perhaps Davis understands it as the beliefs that have been most commonly held and insisted upon by the greatest number of respected past thinkers of the church. I understand it in the sense of right doctrine. That does not mean that I would casually toss aside any consensus to be found in our tradition. On the contrary, I own all that as my tradition. But that tradition contains elements of which I believe the church must repent if it is to be faithful to its calling today. Some elements at some times and places, including our own, have misled many Christians into idolatries. The Bible, the creeds, the church, the Pope, Christianity, faith, even and especially Jesus—all have been presented at times in ways that encourage us to accord them the attributes that belong rightly only to God. That is not right teaching. It is not our task to criticize the great teachers of the past. It is our task to warn against idolatry and to find formulations that reduce the risk of idolatry. And the idolatries to which we should be most sensitive are those that arise within the church and from the church's own teaching.

Our ability to criticize past theologies is closely related in my mind with evangelical freedom. The gospel sets us free. But if the church teaches that faithfulness to the gospel binds us to dubious beliefs that we must accept on threat of rejection by the Christian community, a very severe tension arises. To me it seems important not to bind with doctrines those whom the Spirit has set free. That does not make doctrine unimportant. Quite the contrary. Doctrine is essential in the service of evangelical freedom.

Iconoclasm may have taken on negative connotations because some seem to enjoy smashing things simply for the sake of upsetting believers or displaying their personal "liberation." To whatever extent I am guilty of this, I can only repent. But of iconoclasm in the service of the Spirit, of the good news, of faith, and of evangelical freedom, I do not repent. If in particular instances it has led me to teachings that hinder the faithful worship and action for the Christian community, I hope to be shown my error, and I trust that I will change. But I do not propose to reduce my vigilance in opposition to idolatry and to the letter that binds.

In defending my claim to be a responsible theologian of the church I have fallen into the rhetoric of Spirit. I am comfortable with that rhetoric, and in many contexts I use it in preference to *Christ*. But Davis is correct that in my essay I have left little, if any, distinctive role to the Holy Spirit. At this point I need help. I do believe that at certain times and places one word is more appropriate than others, so a distinction is in order. Thus far my efforts to formulate that distinction have done more harm than good. Paul's assertion that the Lord is the Spirit indicates how very closely Christ and Spirit are associated in his thought. The fact that, with the one exception I noted, the church has taught that all persons of the Trinity are active in every act of the Trinity *ad extra* indicates that I am not the first to see this difficulty. But Davis' criticism is correct, and it is a reminder to me of unfinished business in my own theology.

Some of Rebecca Pentz' criticisms are sufficiently similar to those of

Davis that I will not respond to them again. But she raises two points to which I do need to reply.

First, she points out that simply appropriating the name *Sophia* for the divine that was incarnate in Jesus does not ensure that the theology itself overcomes its masculine bias. She is certainly correct. I seem to have greater concern about masculine and feminine language than she does, but certainly other matters are more important. I am grateful to Elizabeth Schüssler Fiorenza and also to Pentz for beginning to teach me the fuller meaning of *Sophia*. I know I have a long way to go.

The second, and main, criticism is methodological. One should, Pentz believes, begin with "God's revelation in the biblical account of Jesus." She thinks that I begin with "the human sensibilities and the human insights of the twentieth century." I cannot accept this antithesis. On the one hand, if I really *began* with the sensibilities and insights of the twentieth century, unaffected by the Bible and by Christian tradition, it is exceedingly unlikely that I would be dealing with Christology at all! On the other hand, if Pentz were not affected by the sensibilities and insights of very recent developments in the feminist tradition, she would not have found in God's revelation in the biblical account of Jesus what she has found. Surely all of us who are theologically concerned begin with Scripture and tradition and contemporary insights and sensibilities.

There are indeed differences among us, but they must be nuanced more carefully. None of us intend simply to repeat the words of Scripture or tradition. But some aim at reaffirming it, or some core of it, changing only the rhetoric to make it plain to contemporary people. Others see the history of the transmission of traditions in which they take part as one of continuous reworking of what is inherited, so that in effective transmission what is received from the Christian heritage is creatively synthesized with ideas and insights that have arisen partly outside the Christian community. I belong to the group who understand the vocation of the theologian in the latter way. I think Pentz leans to the former, although her essay includes elements of the latter.

Those of us who seek to reform and enrich the tradition as we transmit it depend heavily upon the work of those who seek patiently and open-mindedly to discern again what was meant in earlier stages of the tradition, especially in those expressed in Scripture. From our point of view these tasks are complementary. I regret that they seem not to appear so to Pentz.

I have said nothing yet in reply to Robinson. His comments are critical in a more oblique way, so they do not elicit direct rejoinders. He knows and rightly notes that I am not a biblical scholar, so there is much of lay piety, which he calls biblicism, in my use of the Bible. I think I have been influenced by the work of biblical scholars more than he notices, but he is correct in his criticism. Indeed, my awareness of my weakness here often leads me in my writing to make less direct reference to Scripture than would otherwise be natural to me.

I mention this because it reflects a serious problem in the theological community, at least in this country—that of our division into disciplines. Many biblical scholars limit themselves largely to history, leaving many contemporary questions of belief unanswered. They do not welcome participation in the interpretation of the Scriptures by those who have not earned the right to interpret through immersion in the scholarship. Many systematic theologians are intimidated by the detail and complexity of biblical scholarship and so operate at a level of considerable generality with respect to biblical teaching or else limit their discussion of Scripture to small portions in which they have become competent. Robinson himself has overcome this dichotomy by qualifying himself fully to participate in both disciplines. Unfortunately, few others are doubly qualified.

Perhaps a comment is in order concerning Robinson's tendency to view developments in North American theology in terms of their similarities to earlier events in central Europe. His astute comparisons never fail to illumine. This way of viewing North American theology was standard practice in Germany until recently. Now, however, a number of German observers have become more interested in the indigenous and distinctive features of North American theology. There is much to commend this approach as well.

At one point, it seems to me, Robinson's interpretation of my essay in the light of earlier German developments led him to misunderstand me. He sees the reason for despiritualizing in the crudity of the notion of the Spirit, which demanded demythologizing. However, I am not referring to this problem. My reference is to the more recent German theology known as political theology and especially to Latin American liberation theology. The meaning of despiritualizing associated with this theology is best understood in relation to Matthew's addition of "in spirit" to Luke's "Blessed are the poor"! This changed the meaning in such a way that the concrete social and economic impact of the teaching was lost. To despiritualize is to return to Luke's form.

Dorothee Soelle has argued that emphasizing the concrete social and economic impact of the teaching is to carry Bultmann's demythologizing program to its logical outcome. Few of Bultmann's followers have followed her lead. The meaning of *demythologizing,* therefore, remains "existential interpretation." My use of *despiritualize* has to do with what is called *political hermeneutics* rather than existential interpretation.

Whether my efforts to clarify my meaning will help much I do not know.

The attainment of mutual understanding takes a long time! But I am grateful to be able within the confines of one book to become aware of the confusion caused by my christological formulations and to have the chance to explain myself. The relevant and perceptive criticisms of my colleagues have been very helpful.

A Jewish Postscript
MICHAEL WYSCHOGROD

I

Because Christology is the most intractable issue separating Judaism from Christianity, it was not easy for me to accept the invitation to contribute a Jewish response to *Encountering Jesus*. Although the Christian contributors to this volume disagree about many things (their contentiousness is, however, very Jewish: the debates of the Talmud are a model for the format of this book), all of them can subscribe to John Hick's remark, highlighted by John Roth, that "the figure of Jesus has profoundly affected us by meeting our own spiritual needs." A Jew cannot make that statement, at least not without serious qualifications. The cross has been for Jews not a source of comfort but of fear. It was the symbol of that "teaching of contempt" for Judaism that has infected Christianity almost since its beginning and that has been reflected in Judaism's evaluation of Christianity.

To some extent, this teaching has begun to change. Since the Holocaust, significant elements of Christianity have been determined to purge themselves of the anti-Judaism that was for centuries an essential tenet of the faith. This process is reflected in *Encountering Jesus* at various points. When John Cobb wishes to enumerate what contemporary Christians owe Jesus, he starts by noting that "we owe to Jesus our engrafting into Israel's history with God." Lest this be interpreted as implying the familiar doctrine that the church has superseded Israel and is indeed the new Israel, Cobb writes: "Too often they [Christians] have wrongly interpreted this election as superseding that of the Jews. . . . Christians today must emphatically repudiate any such notion. The Christian claim to have displaced Jews as God's elect has played a major role in the appalling history of Christian persecution of Jews."

On the Jewish side, a certain reassessment of the personality and teaching of Jesus has also been visible. Joseph Klausner[1] and David Flusser[2] are two names, among others, that come to mind, though neither is mentioned by any of the contributors to this volume. They and other Jewish scholars have begun to examine the New Testament and early Christianity in a far less polemical spirit than has been customary for Jewish writers of the past. In the process and aided by Christian scholars versed in Second Temple Judaism, the Jewish background of the New Testament has become increasingly clear so that a grounding in Second Temple Judaism and in rabbinic literature (most of which is later than the New Testament but reflects currents of first-century Judaism) is now almost indispensable for New Testament scholars.

But all this deals with "the Jesus of history" or with "Christology from below," to use expressions invoked in the Introduction to this volume. Classical Christology as formulated at the Council of Chalcedon in A.D. 451 represented a profound break with the Jewish roots of Christianity. To Jewish sensibility, with its long schooling in the prophetic struggle against idolatry, the deification of any human being is simply unthinkable. It must be recognized that the Messiah as understood in prophetic and rabbinic literature is a human descendant of David who was chosen by God to be King of Israel and who will usher in the peaceable kingdom. This anointed one (in Hebrew, *Messiah*) will be no more divine than the other great figures in Judaism, such as Abraham, Moses, or David, all of whom did the work of God and were inspired by his Spirit without thereby becoming divine in addition to being human.

I take note of John Cobb's claim that "the idea that Jesus is God without qualification is heresy and simply makes no sense." The classical Christology of Chalcedon, alive and well in Davis' essay, is more nuanced than the simple claim that Jesus was God. The claim is that Jesus has two natures, one human and one divine, and that the divine nature incarnated in Jesus is that of the Second Person of the Trinity, not of the other two. Whether this doctrine can be stated coherently has been debated over the centuries, and much of that debate is reflected in *Encountering Jesus*. In medieval Jewish-Christian polemics the Jewish side usually argued that trinitarianism and incarnation should be rejected because either no clear meaning can be attached to these concepts or they are self-contradictory. I have never been overly impressed by these arguments because they seem to lay down a self-certifying logic to which theological utterances must conform. But God is not only the Creator of the world but also of the logic or logics to be found or invented in it. It is not sound theology that must conform to a preordained logic but logic that must conform to sound theology.

The fact is that Christianity has never given up the claim to be a monotheistic religion. The bulk of Jewish medieval opinion opted against classifying Christianity as simple idolatry and invented the term *shittuf* (Hebrew, "association" or "partnership") to describe Christian trinitarianism.[3] Christians, it was believed, "associated" the person of Jesus with God to a degree unacceptable to Judaism. But in so doing, they did not totally undermine their belief in the one God, Ruler of heaven and earth. Christianity was accepted by many Jewish authorities as a flawed monotheism, but a monotheism nevertheless.

Since a flawed monotheism is inferior to a perfect one, it follows that Judaism should have fewer problems with Islam than with Christianity. Moslem monotheism is so uncompromising that its rejection of trinitarianism and incarnation is, if anything, more absolute than that of Judaism. And yet, curiously enough, when it comes to the question of teaching Torah to Moslems or Christians, Maimonides prohibited the former and permitted the latter.[4] Christians, he argued, accept the divine origin of the Hebrew Bible but interpret it wrongly. Teaching them Torah might correct their mistakes. But Moslems consider the Hebrew Bible a Jewish distortion that falsifies God's revelation in crucial respects. Jewish teaching cannot possibly benefit them because they would reject the source from which all Jewish teaching emanates—the Hebrew Bible.

Maimonides thus understood that the great bond that connects Christianity with Judaism is the reverence in which both hold the Hebrew Bible. And it is this dimension that I find underrepresented in *Encountering Jesus.*

The volume comes down to a debate between those who find it possible and necessary to adhere to the Christology of Chalcedon (Davis and Pentz, though Pentz is so interested in the feminist issue that she says almost nothing about classical Christology; in her response to Davis, however, she raises issues that do not seem to indicate any basic disagreement with Davis' defense of classical Christology) and the others who, in varying degrees, find it necessary to modify Chalcedon.

I would be less than honest if I pretended that my sympathies do not lie with the revisionists. I followed Davis' logical acrobatics with great interest but, at the end, Hick seems to me to get the better of it. If Jesus had some properties *as* God that are incompatible with other properties he had *as* a human being, then we do not have one Jesus but two. When forced to choose, Davis, in his reply to Hick, opts for a Jesus with one consciousness and a human one at that. Although he still seems to think that a Jesus who does not know that he is also fully God can still be fully God, it is significant that the consciousness he chooses for Jesus is the human one. The reason for this, I suspect, is that although a human consciousness can be said to be ignorant of significant aspects of the self, a divine consciousness, being by definition omniscient, cannot be ignorant of anything. But if the person is defined, in the broad sense, by his consciousness and if Jesus did not know that he was also God, then in what sense is the divinity of Jesus a real property of the one person Jesus? It is highly probable that if Jesus did not know that he was also God, then this thought would probably have outraged him (Luke 18:20: "Why do you call me good? No one is good except God alone"). We thus have arrived at the absurd possibility that Davis would insist on the full divinity of Jesus even in the presence of Jesus, who would protest vehemently against this interpretation. Davis would simply dismiss Jesus' protestations as emanating from the Jesus *as* human being who is ignorant of the truth about himself *as* God.

II

But I am not completely at ease in the world of the revisionists either. Fundamentally, what is it that motivates Hick and Cobb (Robinson is in a separate category)? Although Hick sees serious logical difficulties with orthodox Christology, I do not think that such logical considerations are at the root of his difficulty with the old Christology. Rather, it is his conviction that "traditional absolutist Christology . . . now hinders an unqualified acceptance of what is today, within God's providence, the reality of our human situation. In claiming that the life of Jesus was the one and only point in history at which God has been fully self-revealed it implicitly sets Christians apart from the rest of humanity." He quotes Emil Brunner, who wrote: "Only at one place, only in one event, has God revealed himself truly and completely—there, namely, where He became man."

Hick cannot accept traditional Christology because the reality of the religiously pluralistic world of his title has too deeply influenced him. And the same is true of Cobb, whose *Christ in a Pluralistic Age* expresses the same insight. Speaking of traditional Christology, he asks: "Can these strong claims be made about Christ without negative and even hostile implications about other religious traditions?" Because both Hick and Cobb answer this question in the negative, they find it necessary to develop less absolutist and therefore less exclusivist Christologies.

Now I do not wish to deny that the current pluralistic situation in the world is a significant factor in the contemporary religious situation. This is so in spite of the fact that pluralism—defined as the condition in which diverse religions make competing and partly incompatible truth claims—is not something radically new. What is perhaps new is the degree to which adherents of one religion are today, as a result of the revolution in communications, almost forced to become acquainted with the tenets and spirituality of other religions. This makes it far more difficult to continue to hold derogatory stereotypes of religions other than one's own. I have no difficulty in evaluating this development positively. It was never God's will that we bear false witness against religions to which we do not belong.

But I fail to see why this consideration has an impact particularly and mainly on the Christology of Christian faith. Even without the turn that

Christian faith took at Nicaea and Chalcedon, there is a certain absolutism that Christianity derives from its Jewish origins. Suppose the dominant form of Christianity that developed lacked the trinitarian and incarnational dimension that it in fact did assume. Suppose Jesus were interpreted as a great teacher who renewed Judaism and opened the door for Gentiles to enter into the covenant with Abraham by adherence to the Noachide Laws (the basic moral law the rabbis derived from Gen. 9:1–17, which they interpreted as a covenant binding on all human beings).[5] A certain absolutist odor would still adhere to the Jewish-Christian story because God's covenant with Abraham and his revelation of himself in the context of the history of Israel, culminating in his revelation of himself through Jesus the Jew, would imply a certain priority to revelation through Israel, even if other revelations through the history of other peoples were not completely excluded. The only way to eliminate all vestiges of absolutism would be to consider God's revelation through Israel as one of many, none of them possessing any priority. My point is that the real problem of Christology is not the problem of pluralism but the question of the relation of Christianity to its Jewish origins.

It is John Cobb who sees this most clearly, but he then somewhat confuses the issue by adding Christianity's relation to Buddhism as an issue that also needs exploration in the light of classical Christology. He is aware that Christianity's relation to Buddhism is not the same as its relation to Judaism. "Whereas Christianity came into being as a Jewish sect," he writes, "its relations with Buddhism, through most of their respective histories, have been distant." But is this the question? The issue is not the historical fact that Christianity emerged out of Judaism, not out of Buddhism, but the incompatibility of classical Christology with the basic message of the Hebrew Bible, which Christianity incorporated as quantitatively the largest portion of its own Scripture. The question of Christology is then primarily an issue in the Jewish-Christian dialogue and only far more remotely an issue in Christianity's dialogue with other religions, including Islam. Although, as I have already noted, trinitarian and incarnational Christology is at least as unacceptable to Islam as it is to Judaism, the Moslem critique of classical Christology must proceed on a rather abstract, philosophical level, whereas the Jewish critique is rooted in a Scripture held in common with Christianity, a Scripture that Christianity cannot ignore but must listen to faithfully.

III

As I was reading the papers in this volume, I tried to ascertain the religious pressures that led Christianity to its high Christology. Davis approvingly quotes Moule, who wrote that "the impact made by Jesus on his own and the next generation was such as precludes an estimate of him as no more than a man." Specifically, Jesus forgave sin, he addressed his father with the intimate designation *Abba,* he spoke with authority, and Jesus himself claimed to be divine and his earliest interpreters accepted that claim. Davis adds that "apart from Jesus Christ, I would claim, people can have only a hazy knowledge of God."

Here we have come to the crux of the separation between Judaism and Christianity. I cannot do very much to erase that separation, but I can contribute a little to narrowing the gap.

Although I am convinced that in Nicaea and Chalcedon the church took a fundamentally wrong turn, I also think that the turn did not materialize out of thin air. Raymond Brown argued that in at least three references in the New Testament (Heb. 1:8–9; John 1:1; 20:28) Jesus is called God. He added that there is no evidence that Jesus referred to himself as divine and "there is no reason to think that Jesus was called God in the earliest layers of New Testament tradition."[6] It is also clear to me that Jesus "spoke with authority." The prophets of Israel delivered a divine message they had been entrusted with. They had no personal authority apart from their message, whose authority derived from God. The rabbis, in turn, came on the scene when God no longer sent prophets who invoked the formula "Thus says the Lord. . . . " The rabbis transmit traditions they have received and engage in textual exegesis, but they do not claim personal authority except in the instances in which they enact rabbinic legislation in the spirit of "building a fence around the law." They do, however, always distinguish between such rabbinic enactments and scriptural obligations. Jesus, on the other hand, invoked the formula "But I say unto you," which immediately raises the question as to who Jesus is and by what authority he proclaimed his teaching. So there is good reason to conclude that Jesus does not easily fit into the category of prophet or rabbi. On the other hand, this does not imply that trinitarian and incarnational theology was the only way this problem could have been handled.

Jesus' intimacy with God, his obedience to the will of his Father, his faith and dependence on God, the power and authenticity of his prayer—these are the characteristics that reveal the Jewish Jesus. I am not prepared to discuss whether his intimacy with God was greater than that of Abraham, Moses, David, or the other great figures of the Hebrew Bible. I do not think that such comparisons are proper. Abraham and Moses conversed with God as easily as we converse with our neighbors. The whole biblical period is characterized by great intimacy between God and the Jewish people. By the time of Jesus the prophetic period was over, and this is reflected in the New Testament, where we do not find recorded an easy flow of two-way conversation between Jesus and God. Jesus prays but is met by a certain silence of God, the same silence all humans encounter in postprophetic times. But this does not necessarily involve the impairment of intimacy with God. Even as God remains silent, the intimacy on the human side seems to grow, deepened by the magnitude of human suffering and the silence of God. Did not Jesus reach the height of his intimacy with God when on the cross (Matt. 27:46) he prayed to his Father with the words of Psalm 22:2; "My God, my God, why hast thou forsaken me?" and received no answer?

Can the gap between Judaism and Christianity on the issue of Jesus' divinity be narrowed? I think it can. On the Jewish side, the tendency has been to move toward the other extreme, speaking of God more as a metaphysical absolute than the person who speaks to us in the Bible and in rabbinic literature. The depersonalization of God reaches its apotheosis in the philosophy of Maimonides and its negative theology, according to which one can only say what God is not and not what God is. In *The Body of Faith: Judaism as Corporeal Election*[7] I tried to return to a biblical and rabbinic understanding of God that was not embarrassed by a God with human traits such as suffering and being surprised. To the extent that classical Christology is an attempt to preserve the personality of God, I think it is on the right track, though it goes much too far in speaking of a being who is both fully divine and human.

On the Christian side, the moves must obviously be left up to Christians. This book demonstrates a number of the options that are open to a revisionist Christology. As I have already noted, most of the christological movement in this volume comes not primarily from an encounter with the Jewish roots of Christianity but with contemporary religious pluralism. Although I would be happier with a reconsideration of classical Christology motivated primarily by the incompatibility of classical Christology with the Hebrew Bible and Judaism, I must also admit that some of the revisionism motivated by the encounter with pluralism nevertheless influences Jewish-Christian relations, even if that was not its primary motive.

IV

The doctrines of the Trinity and incarnation are not peripheral aspects of classical Christianity; they are central to Christian identity as it has been understood over the centuries. Modifications—if undertaken at all—must be cautious and performed with delicacy. One possibility for a modest revisionism motivated by respect for the Jewish roots of Christianity rather than a general respect for pluralism is increased emphasis on the one God within a triune theology. Christian theology, after all, has always insisted that trinitarianism does not abolish Christian monotheism. Still, the

Christian literature about the triune nature of God vastly exceeds the literature on the oneness of God. To a degree, this is understandable because it was trinitarian teaching that was uniquely Christian and therefore naturally attracted the interest of Christian writers. But perhaps the time has come for Christians to balance the picture, to emphasize the oneness of God as much as God's triune nature.[8] Christians, like Jews, will reject a trinitarianism that speaks of three separate Gods. Nowhere in Christian literature have I found the possibility envisaged of conflict among the persons of the Trinity. But how separate can the Three Persons of the Trinity be if conflict among them is not possible, even in principle? It is in this direction that the monotheism of Christianity remains intact.

There is much in James Robinson's essay that a Jewish reader will agree with (I hope this does not damage his case beyond repair). "Jesus did not need to be deified," he writes, "to receive the high honor he deserves. Probably he would have preferred we deify the cause: the kingdom of *God* [Robinson's emphasis]. 'Why do you call me good? No one is good but God alone. You know the commandments!' (Mark 10:18–19)." Robinson adds: "Jesus' activity could have been adequately conceptualized in the thought world of that day as a person possessed by God. . . . " Different persons are possessed by different aspects of the Spirit of God, and they are possessed in different ways. Wisdom and Logos are aspects of the Divine Spirit, and no fundamental problem arises from the Jewish point of view as long as aspects of the Spirit of God, or for that matter the Spirit itself, are not hypostasized into persons of one substance with the Father. In some respects, as someone who has been called a Jewish Barthian, I am not altogether comfortable with the Bultmannian presuppositions behind some of Robinson's points. But I am in substantial agreement with his evaluation of high Christology.

No discussion of Christology and its impact on Jewish-Christian relations is complete without some treatment of the impact of Christology on Torah. In the context of his rejection of supersessionism, the doctrine that Christianity supersedes Judaism because Jews have lost their covenantal relationship with God, Cobb writes: "But Christians have been called, not to observe the Torah, but rather to live in the freedom of the Spirit—in Christ. Christianity cannot, therefore, offer a fully structured way of life similar to that of Judaism without betraying its election. It is called to transcendence of culture, mores, ethnicity, and even gender."

Behind this statement is the age-old problem of the Pentateuchal law for Christians. Why do Christians, for example, eat pork when the flesh of pigs is expressly prohibited in the Pentateuch (e.g., Lev. 11:7)? The standard answer is that Christ abolished the old law and substituted for it the law of freedom. This is the answer that lurks behind Cobb's remark, quoted in the preceding paragraph.

It is not, in my opinion, a satisfactory answer. Did Christ abolish all laws, including the one against murder and incest? Clearly not, but which laws did he abolish and which not? It is customary at this point to distinguish between the ritual and the moral law, the former of which Christ abolished while leaving the latter intact. But I do not find this answer satisfactory either. For one thing, it is not found in the New Testament. The distinction between ritual and moral laws is even more foreign to the Hebrew Bible, which knows only the commands of God. Although I cannot go into all the details here, the picture of Jesus as condoning a cavalier disregard of the Mosaic law is simply false.[9]

The distinction that needs to be made, therefore, is not between the law before Christ and after Christ, but the law for Jews and for Gentiles. I believe that the early church (as reflected in Acts 15) expected Jewish Christians to continue Torah observance and to add to it their faith in Jesus as the Messiah. Gentiles would only need to obey the Noachide laws while sharing their faith in Jesus with Jews who believed in him.

Finally, a word about feminism. I have omitted discussion of this topic, not because I do not consider it important but because I do not think it impinges directly on Christology in the context of the Jewish-Christian dialogue. If the church had taught that one of the Three Persons of the Trinity, the daughter of God, became incarnate in a woman who was fully divine and fully human, the difficulties this contention would have presented to Judaism would have been no different from those presented by teachings about the Son of God. I therefore see no advantage in conflating these two issues.

Until very recently, the idea that in a dialogue about Christology a Jewish voice was worth listening to would have seemed perverse to most Christians and to many Jews. I am thus particularly grateful to the contributors to this volume for soliciting a Jewish response.

Postscript:
Encountering Jesus
JOHN K. ROTH

> And she gave birth to her first-born son and wrapped
> him in swaddling cloths, and laid him in a manger,
> because there was no place for them in the
> inn.—Luke 2:7

This book begins, not with an introduction by its editor, but with the birth of a child. That recollection made me wonder during the Christmas season when I first studied the essays found in these pages. Specifically, I pondered how Luke's Gospel depicts a heavenly chorus accompanying Jesus' birth in a Bethlehem stable. Its voices proclaimed glory to God and on earth peace and goodwill.

My earliest encounters with Jesus—like those, I suppose, of many other Christians—are associated with what John Hick calls "the beautiful poetry of the Christmas story." That story still moves me deeply, although *beautiful* is not the only word needed to describe it. *Grim* has its place, too. Adding Matthew's account to Luke's, Jesus' birth brought dissonance that marred peace and goodwill. It consisted of screaming children and grieving parents.

They were the victims of Herod, a king who probably neither met Jesus nor knew his name. Yet Christian tradition linked the nativity to events that made him fear a newborn pretender to his throne. Herod had no Christology. The New Testament's Christmas narratives are parts of it, however, and Matthew suggests that this sorry king made his contribution—albeit inadvertently—by killing "all the male children in Bethlehem and in all that region who were two years old or under" (Matt. 2:16).

According to the New Testament, Jesus asked, "Who do men say that I am?" (Mark 8:27). The answers differed then and they do now. Nor was the New Testament off the mark when it ascribed to Jesus the following judgment: "Do not think that I have come to bring peace on earth; I have not come to bring peace, but a sword. For I have come to set a man against his father, and a daughter against her mother, and a daughter-in-law against her mother-in-law; and a man's foes will be those of his own household"

(Matt. 10:34–36). Jesus can and should be a cause for rejoicing, but for centuries he has also been an occasion for division, the division often adding to the "slaughter of the innocents" that Herod reputedly started in Bethlehem.

The five contributors to *Encountering Jesus* are well aware of the multiple entries on both sides of the ledger. None wants to lend comfort to the likes of Herod. Each knows that Christianity's finest hours have not been provided by debates about Christology, however necessary and inevitable those discussions have been. All seek to make Jesus' name a joyous sound, and yet, as Hick observes, they are "a fairly contentious lot!"

When scholars of distinguished caliber engage in rigorous analysis of the kind represented here, a certain degree of argumentativeness should be expected. Indeed the visible tension among the writers admirably demonstrates the conflict and intensity that frequently arise when two or more persons attempt to get serious about Christology. But some questions are crucial. Does this book offer more than its individual parts or even their sum? May it foster reconciliation beyond its differences? Fortunately, the answer can be an emphatic *yes*.

Encountering Jesus tries to help people understand "who Jesus is and what he means or ought to mean to us today." What is said in this book is important to me and for all Christians because that aim needs advancing. This postscript, therefore, strives for more than a digest of arguments for and against John Hick's inspiration Christology, Stephen T. Davis' maximalist Christology, Rebecca D. Pentz' feminist Christology, James M. Robinson's Wisdom Christology, and the creative transformation Christology of John B. Cobb, Jr. On that count, suffice it to say that all those theories have commendable qualities. Probably none alone, however, will speak completely for anyone, including perhaps even their respective authors, because each involves trade-offs—strengths and weaknesses unpossessed by the others.

The essays provide no retrospective that quiets differences and concentrates on fundamental themes that the five authors share. Such an attempt ought to be made, but not with the intention of reducing *Encountering Jesus* to a lowest common denominator. Christological differences have their place. They are best understood, however, less in terms of what is acceptable or unacceptable for everyone and more in terms of William James' wisdom from *The Varieties of Religious Experience* (Garden City, N.Y.: Image Books, 1978). "No two of us," reckoned James, "have identical difficulties, nor should we be expected to work out identical solutions. Each, from his peculiar angle of observation, takes in a certain sphere of fact and trouble, which each must deal with in a unique manner. . . . We must frankly recognize the fact that we live in partial systems, and that parts are not interchangeable in the spiritual life" (p. 470).

Those words were part of James' plea that the varieties of religious experience should avoid being at odds. Even if religious conflict is more intractable than James hoped, the five contributors to this book are not the adversaries they sometimes appear to be. Not only do Cobb, Davis, Hick, Pentz, and Robinson share much in common; in their best moments they stand close to James. When doing so they show that Christology can be a godsend, not a squabble. In those moments they do not simply agree to disagree or merely encourage everybody to "do their own thing." What emerges is not the elimination of differences but mutual understanding and affirmation.

If those results dwell too often between the lines, they deserve to be more explicit. Thus, to explore some of those possibilities, consider the ten themes that follow beginning with John Hick's observation that for those who call themselves Christians *"the figure of Jesus has profoundly affected us by meeting our own spiritual needs."* All five authors concur. They would also agree that this meeting of spiritual needs fits well with John Cobb's interpretation: we Christians "owe to Jesus our engrafting into Israel's history with God." Through that engrafting, Christians look forward to the world's redemption.

Details about the meaning of redemption vary in the Christologies found here, but each seems to hold that Christians find in Jesus an "amazing grace." Not identical to any other, this grace can save "a wretch like me." It can also inspire and empower women, children, and men to struggle anew against death-dealing powers, including those bred by the Christian religion itself. This communion of outlook, which exists in *Encountering Jesus*, can provide a sufficient answer for questions concerning his ultimate significance. The health of this sharing, moreover, should not be taken lightly. It is more vital than arguments about orthodoxy or the correctness of details about Christology from "above" or "below."

Debate swirls around the Christian Bible: what does the New Testament say? That issue is more complicated than it looks; thus, the answers it elicits are disputable. Rebecca Pentz, however, expresses well a fundamental point shared by the other four. *"We do not have direct access to the historical Jesus,"* she affirms; then she adds her hunch that *"we are not going to be able to find some uninterpreted fact about Jesus."*

If the New Testament was not dictated or inspired literally by God, if it is not even a historical transcript of events recorded by eyewitnesses, then those Christian writings present a humanly interpreted Jesus. Interpretation, moreover, is everywhere in our experience; and wherever interpretation is found, the possibility of error will not be far behind. The result for *Encountering Jesus* is that multiple ways of regarding Scripture are opened, but none should claim finality. Some are rightly called more modern; they may achieve academic respectability denied to others. What is modern today, however, will not be modern tomorrow; academic respectability waxes and wanes as well. Those facts, on the other hand, license no claim that the truth in the New Testament is a face-value matter. Enough uncertainty exists to warrant caution from everyone about the strength and exclusivity of their scriptural concepts. As Cobb wisely recalls, where Jesus is concerned "we do not live by concepts as much as by images."

People are moved to follow Jesus by hearing the story of his life and by seeing it embodied again in those who are his disciples. Although a historical transcript of Jesus' life is lacking, we do have the portrayals in the New Testament. Those images are potent. If their origins are disputable, the scriptural images of Jesus can nevertheless transmute the reading of story into the basis for conversion. The power of the New Testament texts, then, is not simply the preserve of biblical scholars. In part, that power lives in what John Cobb calls "lay piety." That same potency may also be what Cobb has in mind when he remarks wistfully that it would be natural for his writings to contain more direct reference to Scripture if his "weakness" as a biblical scholar did not hold him back. Nonetheless, at times these essays show the attraction of Christian Scripture at its best. Within their spectrum, ample room exists for interpretations of Jesus to do their desirably transforming work.

Stephen T. Davis extends this line of thought by observing that *"each generation of Christians reads the Scriptures and does theology anew in the light of the problems and opportunities it faces."* Each of the five illustrates this principle. For example, a defense of orthodoxy—Davis holds that the future of Christian truth is problematic without it—is as much an indication of the desire for christological relevance as is Cobb's revision of his earlier theories in the light of feminist challenges. At the same time, all the writers seem sensitive to James Robinson's warning to take care lest a time-bound image of Jesus be confused with the person himself.

Once more, the point is to recognize the legitimacy of plural christological interpretations. The point is necessary in a particular context, moreover, because the five contributors are more receptive to the pluralism of the world's religions than they are to the variety within their own Christian tradition. A deeper appreciation of Davis' principle and Robinson's caveat could make their attitudes toward each other as cordial as they seem to be toward other traditions.

"Any attempt to fix the meaning of Christ," says John Cobb, *"is doomed to arbitrariness and artificiality."* That insight provides another source of reconciliation. Granted, Cobb uses it to develop his expansive Christology

of creative transformation, which goes too far for Davis and perhaps even for John Hick. But all of the five find Cobb's principle persuasive because it affirms something about Jesus that all of them warrant, namely, Jesus keeps disclosing goodness, God, and the Real in ways not duplicated elsewhere. Emphasizing disclosure, not finality, the sharing of Cobb's precept relativizes every Christology in a healthy fashion. If not sufficient to expunge arbitrariness and artificiality from *Encountering Jesus*, it is a necessary condition for doing so.

The essayists defend themselves. Each nevertheless admits that incompleteness or error, or both, may tarnish his or her thought. No window dressing, these disclaimers should be taken seriously. One of James Robinson's comments shows why. Noting that much of the New Testament's language about Jesus is metaphorical, he remarks, *"There is in metaphorical language . . . more . . . than its literalistic statement and more than any and every translation into a concrete and specific and limited point."*

Where Jesus is concerned, *more* needs to be said. The writers realize this maxim, although not as well as they might. What more should be said about Jesus? If they pursued that question further, they might locate greater convergence in their Christologies. That prediction is uncertain, but it does share a sentiment—the other writers hold it, too—with Robinson's appeal to dialectical theology and with Cobb's crucial observation that true Christians are called "again and again to iconoclasm." Usually the more that needs saying is a corrective against narrowness, idolatry, dogmatism, and exclusiveness. The five stand united against those sins.

What an individual considers most important christologically has much to do, Robinson reminds us, with *"potentially competing authorities— Scripture, dogma, philosophy, and experience."* More than potentially, these authorities do compete in this book. But here, too, the important prospects for mutual support should not be underestimated. Given the candidates nominated—Cobb, Davis, Hick, Pentz, and Robinson—experience is the ultimate authority. Nonetheless, as Pentz suggests, the problem is that in Christology, experience "will not prove anything." Experiences of Jesus differ. This book makes that fact abundantly clear, but it also shows five thinkers who share precisely because their experiences place them in affirmative contact with Christian tradition, including what Robinson designates as Scripture and dogma, and with a philosophical way of thinking, which insistently probes fundamental questions. Although such a base does not guarantee agreement, from that foundation one can glimpse Jesus' ability to differentiate people in ways that divide less than they bring together.

One characteristic that joins the five contributors is that all are scholars.

That same reality sometimes separates them as Christians. John Cobb discusses his concern about this situation—the others share it, but more quietly. *"A serious problem in the theological community, at least in [the United States],"* he says, is *"that of our division into disciplines."* There is more to know than individuals can master by themselves. In addition, scholarly specialization will not go away. It will, if anything, increase. In such circumstances, a spirit of sharing inquiry is all the more important, especially in an area such as Christology, where the crucial questions cannot belong to a single scholarly discipline.

What can be learned from one another? That question should remain the key for all who would open the labyrinthine doors of Christology. When asking that question, we should remember that being a scholar is no prerequisite for being Jesus' disciple. To follow him may entail Christology, if only in the minimal sense that affirmations about Jesus are required, but the faith of those outside the academy contributes to encountering Jesus in ways that cannot be replaced by the erudition of Christians who earn their keep as philosophers, theologians, and biblical experts. Christians learn that Jesus taught people to love one another. When that love is practiced, people teach and learn from one another. Then what Cobb calls a creative transformation may intervene to move even scholars beyond polemics.

Scholarship exerts tremendous influence on Christology by increasing awareness that *Christianity is*, as John Hick sees it, *"one religion among others in a manifestly pluralistic world."* All five of the authors recognize that influence. Where they differ is in what to make of its findings. "Apart from Jesus Christ," claims Davis, "people can have only a hazy knowledge of God." This view seems to put him at odds with John Hick, who understands the different global religions as ways of encountering the Real, which is never fully disclosed in any human apprehension, individual or collective. Hick, in turn, is uncomfortable with what he takes to be the exclusiveness of Davis' position. Perhaps these two examples are finally at odds, but in a "manifestly pluralistic world" another option may exist. Is there not a way to think about "irreconcilable" positions that finds truth—and falsity—in all of them and then moves beyond to something more and better? Beyond *Encountering Jesus*, where would such a question lead the Christologies of Davis, Hick, and the other three? That is for the writers to determine, but a careful following of that path seems essential if Christians are to grasp who Jesus is and what he means or ought to mean to us today.

"God must want, on some level, all people to believe in Jesus." At first glance, neither John Cobb, John Hick, nor James Robinson would say what Steve Davis claims and Rebecca Pentz would support. If we leave them

there, the book ends split, three to two. Perhaps the five can never interpret Davis' statement in such a way that they will agree. But they might get together on at least an aspect of it, and perhaps that dimension is the most decisive after all.

The part they could most obviously affirm together is that Jesus offers something of profound worth, something that all persons can appreciate and that it would be well if they did. Pentz succinctly illustrates the "something" when she testifies that Jesus can move anyone toward self-esteem, excellence, and wholeness. Whether Jesus is the only one who can do so perfectly is a bone of contention that does more harm than good. The world needs mending. Thankful that Jesus provides his healing touch, Christians should hope that others can do so as well, for on earth not everyone who can be moved by Jesus will be. Yet their needs for self-esteem, excellence, and wholeness remain.

"We are," stresses Rebecca Pentz, *"part of an organic whole with God,"* a motif whose ancient Christian roots are in Paul's image that those who follow Jesus should be like the parts of a vigorous body—each doing its best under God's will. She also supplements Paul's metaphor by adding her conviction that contemporary Christian feminism "is an inbreaking of Jesus' kingdom here and now on earth." The responding men may not put their agreement in just those words. Nonetheless the four of them share her belief—it is the most striking note of consensus in the entire book—that Christian faith must be reformed, if not first deconstructed, by the wisdom of feminist principles. The organic whole we need cannot be truly wholesome without that movement, and unless *Encountering Jesus* succeeds in promoting such well-being, its Christologies will not be worth the trouble in which they were conceived.

"And suddenly," wrote Luke, describing what the nativity brought forth, "there was with the angel a multitude of the heavenly host praising God and saying, 'Glory to God in the highest and on earth peace, good will'" (Luke 2:13–14). The quintet responsible for this volume may never be a heavenly chorus. Nevertheless, to the extent that their Christologies are moved beyond the writers' limitations, they can help people to care well about the child left out of the inn. When that happens, Cobb, Davis, Hick, Pentz, and Robinson will be more than contributors to a book. They will be part of an organic wholesomeness in which the Christmas story is less grim and more beautiful, one in which goodwill empowers peace on earth and thereby inspires glory for the Creator.

Notes

CHAPTER 1—An Inspiration Christology for a Religiously Plural World
JOHN HICK

1. The Q material, believed to reflect the earliest Christian tradition, is highly apocalyptic. See Howard Clark Kee, *Jesus in History: An Approach to the Study of the Gospels*, 2nd ed. (New York: Harcourt Brace Jovanovich, 1977), ch. 3.
2. See Helmet Koester, *History and Literature of Early Christianity*, vol. 2 (Philadelphia: Fortress, 1982), p. 89.
3. See Norman Perrin, *The New Testament: An Introduction* (New York: Harcourt Brace Jovanovich, 1974), pp. 42–43.
4. John Downing, "Jesus and Martyrdom," *Journal of Theological Studies*, n.s., 14 (1963): 284.
5. *Zohar* 3:218a. Quoted by Daniel Chanan Matt, trans., *Zohar: The Book of Enlightenment* (New York: Paulist, 1983), p. 19. For a list of similar passages, see ibid., p. 196, n. 50.
6. See William James, *The Varieties of Religious Experience* (New York: New American Library, 1958), pp. 201–206.
7. Paramahansa Yogananda, *Autobiography of a Yogi*, 11th ed. (Los Angeles: Self-Realization Fellowship, 1971).
8. R. H. Charles, *The Apocrypha and Pseudepigrapha of the Old Testament in English*, 2 vols. (Oxford: Clarendon, 1913), 2:408–409.
9. Wolfhart Pannenberg, *Jesus—God and Man*, trans. Lewis L. Wilkins and Duane A. Priebe (Philadelphia: Westminster, 1968), p. 327.
10. Hans Küng, *On Being a Christian*, trans. Edward Quinn (Garden City: Doubleday, 1976), p. 289.
11. Oscar Cullmann, *The Christology of the New Testament*, rev. ed., trans. Shirley C. Guthrie and Charles A. M. Hall (Philadelphia: Westminster, 1963), pp. 271–72.
12. Ibid., pp. 272–73.
13. Pannenberg, *Jesus—God and Man*, p. 117.
14. T. R. V. Murti, *The Central Philosophy of Buddhism*, 2nd ed. (London: George Allen and Unwin, 1960), p. 40.
15. Emil Brunner, *The Scandal of Christianity: The Andrew C. Zenos Memorial Lectures* (Philadelphia: Westminster, 1951).
16. Frances M. Young, *From Nicaea to Chalcedon: A Guide to the Literature and Its Background* (Philadelphia: Fortress, 1983), p. 178.
17. D. M. Baillie, *God Was in Christ: An Essay on Incarnation and Atonement* (New York: Scribner's, 1948). This book was written when Baillie was a professor of systematic theology at the University of St. Andrews.
18. Quoted by John Baillie, in Donald M. Baillie, *The Theology of the Sacraments and Other Papers, with a Biographical Essay by John Baillie* (New York: Scribner's, 1957), p. 35n.
19. G. W. H. Lampe, *God as Spirit: The Brampton Lectures, 1976* (Oxford: Clarendon, 1977). This book was written when Lampe was Regius Professor of Divinity at Cambridge University.
20. Pannenberg, *Jesus—God and Man*, p. 116.
21. Ibid.
22. Lampe's thought is more complex than this quotation alone suggests. He did hold "that Christ is the centre and climax of the entire creative work of God throughout history" (*God as Spirit*, p. 104); but *Christ* does not mean the historical Jesus but "the complex of Jesus and his interpreters, a complex to which many minds have contributed" (p. 27)—in fact, virtually the Christian tradition as a whole.
23. John A. T. Robinson, *Honest to God* (Philadelphia: Westminster, 1963), p. 74.
24. Dennis Nineham, "Epilogue," in *The Myth of God Incarnate*, ed. John Hick (Philadelphia: Westminster, 1977), p. 188.
25. John Hick, *God Has Many Names* (Philadelphia: Westminster, 1982); Hick, *God and the Universe of Faiths: Essays in the Philosophy of Religion* (London: Macmillan, 1973); Hick, *Problems of Religious Pluralism* (New York: St. Martin's, 1985).

CHAPTER 2—Jesus Christ: Savior or Guru?
STEPHEN T. DAVIS

1. I do not claim that all contemporary minimal christologists accept all six of these points or even that any one minimal christologist accepts all of them exactly as stated. Naturally, each minimal Christology has its own themes and emphases and differs from the others in striking ways.

2. John Hick, "Is There a Doctrine of the Incarnation?" in *Incarnation and Myth: The Debate Continued*, ed. Michael Goulder (Grand Rapids: Eerdmans, 1979), p. 48.

3. Henry Bettenson, ed., *Documents of the Christian Church*, 2nd ed. (London: Oxford University, 1960), p. 73.

4. For details see Stephen T. Davis, *The Debate About the Bible: Inerrancy Versus Infallibility* (Philadelphia: Westminster, 1977).

5. Arthur Wainwright, *Beyond Biblical Criticism: Encountering Jesus in Scripture* (Atlanta: John Knox, 1982), pp. 22–33.

6. Martin Hengel, *The Son of God: The Origin of Christology and the History of Jewish-Hellenistic Religion* (Philadelphia: Fortress, 1976), pp. 2, 10. See also Martin Hengel, *Between Jesus and Paul: Studies in the Earliest History of Christianity* (Philadelphia: Fortress, 1983), p. 31.

7. Charles Moule, "Three Points of Conflict in the Christological Debate," in *Incarnation and Myth*, p. 137. See also C. F. D. Moule, *The Origin of Christology* (Cambridge: Cambridge University, 1977), pp. 2–7.

8. Charles Moule, "A Comment," in *Incarnation and Myth*, p. 149.

9. I will not cite as reasons the facts (so I consider them) that Jesus performed miracles, predicted the future, allowed people to worship him (Luke 5:8; John 20:28), and was raised from the dead. Though to me these are important indications, the other reasons I will cite are more compelling.

10. John A. T. Robinson, *Can We Trust the New Testament?* (Grand Rapids: Eerdmans, 1977), p. 104.

11. Don Cupitt, "Professor Stanton on Incarnational Language in the New Testament," in *Incarnation and Myth*, pp. 167–68; and Frances Young, "The Finality of Christ," in ibid., p. 179.

12. John Hick, "Jesus and the World Religions," in *The Myth of God Incarnate*, ed. John Hick (Philadelphia: Westminster, 1977), p. 178.

13. For an exploration of the concept of God that criticizes the doctrine of essential prediction, see Stephen T. Davis, *Logic and the Nature of God* (Grand Rapids: Eerdmans, 1983).

14. Thomas V. Morris, "Divinity, Humanity, and Death," *Religious Studies* 19(1983):457.

15. Claude Welch, ed. and trans., *God and Incarnation in Mid-nineteenth Century German Theology* (New York: Oxford University, 1965); and Frank Weston, *The One Christ: An Enquiry into the Manner of the Incarnation* (London: Longmans Green, 1907). Weston's unjustly forgotten book is in my opinion one of the best ever written on Christology.

16. See William Temple, *Christus Veritas* (London: Macmillan, 1924), pp. 143ff.; and D. M. Baillie, *God Was in Christ: An Essay on Incarnation and Atonement* (New York: Scribner's, 1948), pp. 94–98.

17. Hengel, *The Son of God*, pp. 87–88.

18. Lucien J. Richard, *A Kenotic Christology: In the Humanity of Jesus the Christ, the Compassion of Our God* (Washington, D. C.: University Press of America, 1982), p. 112.

19. Brian Hebblethwaite, "The Incarnation and Modern Theology," in *Incarnation and Myth*, p. 28.

20. Dietrich Bonhoeffer, *Christ the Center*, trans. John Bowden (New York: Harper & Row, 1966), p. 97.

21. Wolfhart Pannenberg, *Jesus—God and Man*, 2nd ed., trans. Lewis L. Wilkins and Duane A. Priebe (Philadelphia: Westminster, 1977), p. 311.

22. Baillie, *God Was in Christ*, p. 96.

23. Temple, *Christus Veritas*, p. 142.

24. Peter Geach, *Providence and Evil: The Stanton Lectures 1971–2* (Cambridge: Cambridge University, 1977), pp. 25–28.

25. John Hick, "A Response to Hebblethwaite," in *Incarnation and Myth*, p. 194.

26. My views on this subject are more fully developed in Stephen T. Davis, "Evangelicals and the Religions of the World," *The Reformed Journal* 31(June 1981):9–13.
27. The resurrection is not of course a rigorous proof of the incarnation—I suppose God could cause a mere human to be not just resuscitated but resurrected. But Christians have always taken the resurrection as a kind of vindication of Jesus, a sign rather than a proof of the truth of Christian claims about him.
28. My views on the resurrection are more fully developed in Stephen T. Davis, "Is It Possible to Know That Jesus Was Raised from the Dead?" *Faith and Philosophy* 1(1984):147–59; and Davis, "Was Jesus Raised Bodily?" *Christian Scholar's Review* 14(1984–85):140–52.
29. I would like to thank my friends Tom Morris and John Schneider for helpful comments on a draft of this essay.

CHAPTER 3—Can Jesus Save Women?
REBECCA D. PENTZ

1. Quoted in Elisabeth Schüssler Fiorenza, "Feminist Spirituality, Christian Identity, and Catholic Vision," in *Womanspirit Rising: A Feminist Reader in Religion*, ed. Carol P. Christ and Judith Plaskow (San Francisco: Harper & Row, 1979), p. 137.
2. Karl Barth, *Church Dogmatics*, ed. and trans. G. W. Bromiley and T. F. Torrance, vol. 4, pt. 1, *The Doctrine of Reconciliation* (Edinburgh: T. & T. Clark, 1956), p. 137.
3. Phyllis Trible, *God and the Rhetoric of Sexuality* (Philadelphia: Fortress, 1978); and Paul Jewett, *The Ordination of Women: An Essay on the Office of Christian Ministry* (Grand Rapids: Eerdmans, 1980), pp. 35–47.
4. Mary Daly, "After the Death of God the Father: Woman's Liberation and the Transformation of Christian Consciousness," in *Womanspirit Rising*, p. 57.
5. Patricia Wilson-Kastner, *Faith, Feminism, and the Christ* (Philadelphia: Fortress, 1983), p. 100.
6. Elisabeth Schüssler Fiorenza, *In Memory of Her: A Feminist Theological Reconstruction of Christian Origins* (New York: Crossroad, 1983), pp. 143–51.
7. It is interesting to me that in Luther's treatment of the Magnificat he ignored Mary's feeling of specialness. Certainly Luther was right that the beauty of Mary is that she always points to the great things that God has done for her, none of which she deserved. But Luther never discussed how being chosen to be the mother of God made Mary feel. It is this feeling, which Mary expressed in the Magnificat, that touched me.
8. Fiorenza, "Feminist Spirituality, Christian Identity, and Catholic Vision," in *Womanspirit Rising*, p. 138.
9. Mary Daly, *Beyond God the Father: Toward a Philosophy of Women's Liberation* (Boston: Beacon, 1973), p. 85.
10. See Carol Gilligan, *In a Different Voice: Psychological Theory and Women's Development* (Cambridge, MA: Harvard University, 1982); and Valerie Saiving, "The Human Situation: A Feminine View," in *Womanspirit Rising*, pp. 25–35.
11. Ibid., p. 37.
12. See Heb. 9:12; 9:26; 10:10–14; and Oscar Cullmann, *The Christology of the New Testament*, rev. ed., trans. Shirley C. Guthrie and Charles A. M. Hall (Philadelphia: Westminster, 1963), pp. 98–101.
13. Thomas Aquinas, *Summa Theologia*, part 3, question 1, article 2 and 3.
14. John Calvin, *Institutes of the Christian Religion*, book 2, ch. 12, sec. 4.
15. Barth, *Church Dogmatics* 4 (pt. 1):134.
16. Wolfhart Pannenberg, *Jesus—God and Man*, trans. Lewis L. Wilkins and Duane A. Priebe (Philadelphia: Westminster, 1968), p. 193.
17. Oscar Cullmann argued that in the early New Testament church, Jesus was thought of primarily as Lord and derivatively as Savior. Later theology seems to emphasize Savior, but certainly Jesus' Lordship is not denied. For a carefully developed argument that Jesus' Lordship does not exclude women, see Letty M. Russell, *The Future of Partnership* (Philadelphia: Westminster, 1979), pp. 62–67. For an argument that Jesus' kingship is inclusive, see Fiorenza, *In Memory of Her*, pp. 118–30.
18. Rosemary Radford Ruether, *Sexism and God-Talk: Toward a Feminist Theology* (Boston: Beacon, 1983), p. 116.

19. Rosemary Radford Ruether, *To Change the World: Christology and Cultural Criticism* (New York: Crossroad, 1981), p. 53.
20. Ruether, *Sexism and God-Talk*, p. 137.
21. Pannenberg, *Jesus—God and Man*, p. 228.
22. Fiorenza, *In Memory of Her*, ch. 4.
23. Both these passages are quoted in Eleanor McLaughlin, "'Christ My Mother': Feminine Naming and Metaphor in Medieval Spirituality," *Nashotah Review* 15 (1975):233, 235.
24. Julian of Norwich, *Revelations of Divine Love*, trans. M. L. del Mastro (Garden City: Doubleday, 1977), pp. 191–92.
25. Wilson-Kastner, *Faith, Feminism, and the Christ*, p. 104.
26. Julian of Norwich, *Revelations of Divine Love*, pp. 192–95.
27. It is this last aspect of Jesus' work as Savior that speaks most clearly to me of his divinity. Jesus was not just a man who lived two thousand years ago and embodied an ideal. He is our present, reigning Lord, who empowers us to fight for that ideal today, both within ourselves and within society.

CHAPTER 4—Very Goddess and Very Man: Jesus' Better Self
JAMES M. ROBINSON

1. In lieu of more detailed notes, I refer to articles I have written about specific dimensions of this essay: "Basic Shifts in German Theology," *Interpretation* 16 (1962):76–97 (on the Wisdom Christology of Q); "LOGOI SOPHON: On the Gattung of Q," in *Trajectories through Early Christianity*, ed. James M. Robinson and Helmut Koester (Philadelphia: Fortress, 1971), pp. 71–113 (on Q as a Wisdom book); "Die Hodajot-Formel in Gebet und Hymnus des Fruhcristentums," *Apophoreta: Festschrift fur Ernest Haenchen*, Beiheft 30 to *Zeitschrift fur die neutestamentliche Wissenschaft* (Berlin: Alfred Topelmann, 1964), pp. 194–235 (on the christological hymns embedded in the Jewish-Christian prayers); "On the *Gattung* of Mark (and John)," in *Jesus and Man's Hope*, ed. David G. Buttrick and John M. Bald (Pittsburgh: Pittsburgh Theological Seminary, 1970), pp. 99–129, especially pp. 118–26, reprinted in *The Problem of History in Mark and Other Marcan Essays* (Philadelphia: Fortress, 1982), pp. 11–39, especially pp. 31–39 (on the *mythologoumenon* of the mother bird's giving birth to the Savior, in the *Apocalypse of Adam* and Rev. 12); "Jesus as Sophos and Sophia: Wisdom Tradition and the Gospels," in *Aspects of Wisdom in Judaism and Early Christianity*, ed. Robert L. Wilken (Notre Dame, IN: University of Notre Dame, 1975), pp. 1–16 (on the Wisdom Christology of Q); "Jesus from Easter to Valentinus (or to the Apostles' Creed)," *Journal of Biblical Literature* 101 (1982):5–37 (on the luminous visualization of the resurrection).
2. I am indebted to Stephen Gero for referring me to Robert Murray, *Symbols of Church and Kingdom: A Study in Early Syriac Tradition* (London: Cambridge University, 1975), for details of this development. See especially "The Motherhood of the Church and of the Holy Spirit," pp. 142–50, and "The Holy Spirit as Mother," pp. 312–20.

A Jewish Postscript—MICHAEL WYSCHOGROD

1. Joseph Klausner, *Jesus of Nazareth: His Life, Times, and Teaching*, trans. Herbert Danby (New York: Macmillan, 1927).
2. David Flusser, *Jesus,* trans. Ronald Walls (New York: Herder & Herder, 1969).
3. Jacob Katz, *Exclusiveness and Tolerance* (London: Oxford University Press, 1961), pp. 35, 163.
4. Maimonides, *Teshovoth Ha'Rambam (Responsa* of Maimonides), 3 vols., ed. Jehoshua Blau (Jerusalem: n.p., 1958), Responsum 149, p. 284 (Hebrew).
5. See David Novak, *The Image of the Non-Jew in Judaism: An Historical and Constructive Study of the Noahide Laws* (New York: E. Mellen, 1983).
6. Raymond E. Brown, *Jesus: God and Man* (New York: Macmillan, 1967), p. 30.
7. Michael Wyschogrod, *The Body of Faith: Judaism as Corporeal Election* (New York: Seabury, 1983).
8. An attempt to balance the score has been made in *Das Reden vom einen Gott bei Juden und Christen,* ed. Clemens Thoma and Michael Wyschogrod (Bern: Peter Lang, 1984).
9. See Flusser, *Jesus,* pp. 44–64.